Enlightenment, Romanticism,
and the Blind
in France

Enlightenment, Romanticism, and the Blind in France

William R. Paulson

Princeton University Press
Princeton, New Jersey

Copyright © 1987 by Princeton University Press

Published by Princeton University Press, 41 William Street,
Princeton, New Jersey 08540
In the United Kingdom: Princeton Unviersity Press, Guildford, Surrey

All Rights Reserved

Library of Congress Cataloging in Publication Data will be
found on the last printed page of this book

Publication of this book has been aided by a grant
from the Paul Mellon Fund of Princeton University Press

This book has been composed in Linotron Galliard
Clothbound editions of Princeton University Press books
are printed on acid-free paper, and binding materials are
chosen for strength and durability. Paperbacks, although satisfactory
for personal collections, are not usually suitable for library rebinding

Printed in the United States of America by Princeton University Press
Princeton, New Jersey

To my mother and father

CONTENTS

PREFACE

This book owes its existence to Lionel Gossman, my adviser for the Princeton University dissertation on which it is based. He accepted my decision to deform his original idea for the work beyond recognition, and continued to assist me on my own course. From the earliest stages I was also guided by the rigorous and thought-provoking suggestions of Suzanne Nash, who served as the dissertation's second reader. My appreciation and indebtedness to these two people extend as well to the many who suggested works to consider and ways of considering them, but special thanks are in order to Mary Cattani, for her thorough and sympathetic readings, to David Ellison, for his suggestions and encouragement, to Jacques-Henri Périvier, for his help with the translations, and to Lise Queffélec, for her perceptive critique of my ideas in their earliest form.

My research was materially supported by a grant from the French government in 1979–1980 and by a Procter Fellowship from Princeton University in 1980–1981.

English translations of quotations are given in the Notes. A note number following a parenthetical page reference in the text indicates that the note contains only the translation; where a note number precedes such a reference, the note contains additional material. All translations are my own, with the following qualification: I have made some use, with modification, of anonymous nineteenth-century translations of Balzac and Hugo.

All words italicized in quotations were italicized in the original unless otherwise noted.

South Hadley, Massachusetts
July 1986

Enlightenment, Romanticism,
and the Blind
in France

INTRODUCTION:
UNSEEING IN THE EYE

Why did the blind—their perceptual faculties and their surgical cure—become the subject of intense cultural interest in eighteenth-century France? How did this philosophic and speculative attention given to blindness by Diderot and others contribute to a changed presentation of the blind in literature? What effect did these developments have on the beginnings of modern educational programs for the blind, and how did the teachers in these programs contribute in their turn to the cultural fascination with those who do not see? How is this collection of discourses and activities arising from the Enlightenment related to the role of blind visionaries in romantic literature, in the works of such writers as Balzac and Hugo?

Questions like these seem to define an inquiry into the status of blindness in French writings from the early eighteenth century to the mid-nineteenth century. Such a topic might lend itself to a traditional, literary-historical approach to the study of a theme. The supposition could be made that blindness is simply a given object, a given real (or symbolic) entity, which is treated, written about, and represented in differing ways, at different times, and in different places. A study so conceived could take its place in the library of positivistic scholarship alongside studies of blindness in the sixteenth and seventeenth centuries or of deaf-mutes in the eighteenth and nineteenth centuries.

This kind of approach has an element of validity, and indeed it is not absent from the present volume. Blindness exists: some people do not see, a fact that has both psychological and social consequences, and people who do see are capable of imagining the loss of sight. What was written in France about these matters in the eighteenth and nineteenth centuries is but a small segment of all that has been written about, say, human perceptual faculties. If blindness were simply a real phenomenon, independent of the way cultures write and speak of it, then the

3

choice of the French eighteenth and nineteenth centuries would be fairly arbitrary, corresponding at most to an empirical observation that there was a great deal of writing about blindness during that period in a number of different genres and contexts.

Blindness, however, is also a cultural category constituted by those who write and speak of it. It means very different things, and moreover it *is* very different things, at different times, different places, and in different kinds of writing. To remind ourselves of this, we need look no further than the different meanings we attach today to the terms "blind" and "legally blind." What the late Michel Foucault noted about the mad can be said of the blind: who is considered blind depends on the kinds of statements that can be made about blindness. In many of the eighteenth-century writings studied here, blindness implicitly means congenital and possibly curable lack of sight; in many nineteenth-century writings it means incurable *loss* of sight. Within these general discursive contexts, individual writers take up diverse aspects of the condition of not seeing, so that those who write about blindness are only to a limited extent referring to the same thing—in fact, they are constructing the thing to which they are referring, and constructing it in different ways.

In particular, in eighteenth-century England and France a radically new kind of discourse about blindness arose out of parallel developments in medicine and philosophy. The cure of congenital cataracts became possible in some cases, and such a cure appeared to offer the promise of an experimental verification of important premises of philosophic sensationalism. With this new kind of interest, something changed in the way the blind enter speculative and imaginative discourse; new possibilities for defining and conceptualizing blindness appeared alongside older myths and stories. For one thing, the blind became the objects of psychological speculation: the problem of how their minds are both like and unlike those of the seeing became a major feature of philosophical disquisitions and pedagogical treatises, and left its mark even on romantic fiction. The present work might best be titled, with an apology to Walter Benjamin, *The Blind in the Age of Their Medical Curability*. Of course, all cases of blindness were not curable or cured, just as all works of art are not reproducible or reproduced; the technical possibility matters more than its actual realization. For with widespread awareness of cures of blindness, the difference between those who do not see and those who do appears to be no longer absolute, irreversible, and incomprehensible. It has, to an extent, been mastered by science and brought under the control of human reason.

What we witness in the Enlightenment fascination with cures of blindness is thus a *desacralization* of the blind, the construction of a new kind of social and cultural status for blindness. Of course, to speak of desacralization we must make clear in what sense blindness was previously linked to the sacred, and this means taking a brief look at how blindness was constituted as a cultural category before the eighteenth century. We shall not attempt to reach back to a "cultural genesis" of blindness, to its "original" status as mythological theme or category of social exclusion. No direct apprehension of the origin of this topic is possible—and it would lie outside the scope of this study in any case—but we cannot ignore the fact that, in writing on blindness, the philosophers and doctors of the eighteenth century were beginning not on a *tabula rasa* but in a context already shaped by myth, religion, and the literature of ancient and modern times. We must make a few remarks about that context, not to uncover origins but to prepare for an understanding of that belated pseudo-beginning in which the philosophers of the Enlightenment believed themselves to be participating.

To say that blindness was linked to the sacred is not to imply that the blind were considered part of religion. It is rather to observe that the difference of the blind—their otherness—was assumed to be radical, was attributed to some transcendent cause or mystery beyond the reach of human knowledge or of social control. Greek literature presents blindness as a terrible calamity, often a punishment for transgression involving sexuality or the gods. At the end of *Oedipus Rex*, the chorus tells the self-blinded hero, "Thou wert better dead than living blind."[1] Oedipus explains that it was the sun-god Apollo who drove him to put out his eyes. Earlier in the tragedy, the confrontation between Oedipus and the blind soothsayer Tiresias had established blindness as a symbol of the divine workings of fate. Oedipus mocked Tiresias for his blindness, but the sightless prophet, an initiate in the mysteries of the gods, knew the truth that Oedipus, for all his human powers of perception and intellect, could not suspect. As for Tiresias, his blindness and the powers of divination that accompanied it were held to be divinely given. There are at least three versions of the cause of his sightlessness. In the best-known story, told by Hesiod and Ovid, the gift of prophecy comes in compensation for blindness. Hera blinded Tiresias for agreeing with Zeus (on the basis of the seven years he had spent as a woman) that women enjoy more pleasure in sex than men, whereupon Zeus, to make amends, granted him the ability to see the future. In another account, given by Apollodorus, Athena blinded him as punishment for having observed her in her bath, and then compensated him by sharpening his hearing so that he could foretell events. Apollodorus also reports a version in which Tiresias was already a prophet before being blinded by the gods, who thus punished him for revealing their secrets.[2]

A similar ambiguity can be found concerning the blind seer Phineus, visited by the Argonauts on their outward journey. In the *Argonautica*, the only remaining full narration of the Quest of the Golden Fleece, Apollonius of Rhodes states that Phineus suffered blinding by Zeus because he revealed all of the god's designs to men in his prophecies. Another version, mentioned by Apollodorus, has him blinded by the Argonauts as punishment for his blinding of his own sons, wrongfully accused by their stepmother of incestuous advances.[3] In the case of the poet Thamyris, the sexual and sacred motifs are conflated in a single narrative, given by Apollodorus: "Thamyris, who excelled in beauty and in minstrelsy, engaged in a musical contest with the Muses, the agreement being that, if he won, he should enjoy them all, but that if he should be vanquished he should be bereft of what they would. So the Muses got the better of him and bereft him both of his eyes and of his minstrelsy."[4] Demodocus, the blind minstrel of Book VIII of the *Odyssey*, was also said to have been blinded by the Muses, but in exchange for his poetic gifts.

6

The theme of blindness as punishment appears on a number of occasions, albeit in very different forms, in the Old Testament. In the Pentateuch, destruction of eyesight figures among the threatened punishments for disobedience of the Lord's commandments (Leviticus 26:16, Deuteronomy 28:65); similar images of chastisement by blinding can be found in Job (11:20), Proverbs (30:17), and Zephaniah (1:17). In the laws given to Moses, blindness excludes a man from the priesthood (Leviticus 21:18), and an animal from being offered in sacrifice (Leviticus 22:22). By making outcasts of the blind, disqualifying them from important religious functions, and considering them to be hated by the gods, societies defined their difference as something external, irremediable. In ancient Greece and Rome, an infant born blind would be abandoned to die rather than be integrated into society. Far from remedying the exclusion of the blind, compensatory faculties such as prophecy or poetic inspiration confirm their separation—their links to the gods rather than to the profane doings of men.

The relation of blindness to the sacred was deeply altered, but not ended, by Christianity. The restoration of sight to the blind appears in Isaiah among the metaphors of redemption: "Then the eyes of the blind shall be opened, and the ears of the deaf shall be unstopped" (Isaiah 35:5). This metaphoric expression of salvation became a central motif of the New Testament, and the gospels contain numerous references to Jesus' healing of the blind. In two almost identical accounts (Mark 10:46–52 and Luke 18:35–43), the blind man recognizes Jesus and, believing in his powers, asks him to restore his sight. After healing him, Jesus says, "Thy faith hath made thee whole" (or "hath saved thee"). In this sense the cure, in addition to being a miracle illustrating the power of Christ, reinforces the metaphoric equivalence between seeing and faith, between blindness and the refusal to believe. In the most extensive account of Jesus' healing of a blind man (John 9), Jesus denies that blindness is a malediction or a punishment for sin:

And his disciples asked him, saying, Master, who did sin, this man, or his parents, that he was born blind?

7

Jesus answered, Neither hath this man sinned, nor his parents: but that the works of God should be made manifest in him. (John 9:2–3)

Rather than a malediction or chastisement, blindness becomes a negative moment (comparable to the lost sheep or the prodigal son), necessary as a contrast and precondition to display the power of redemption and grace. After the Pharisees deny that Jesus has worked a miracle and show that they still consider blindness a punishment by telling the blind man that he was "altogether born in sin," Jesus explains that his coming reverses the norms of seeing and unseeing: "For judgment I am come into this world, that they which see not might see; and that they which see might be made blind" (John 9:39). Christianity places divinely given cure, a miraculous end to difference, in the place of divine compensation to the blind. In Greek mythology, the gods showed their justice or compassion by giving to those whom they punished; the Christian miracles correspond to the redemptive assumption, by the Savior, of all violence and exclusion.

Christianity brought changes in the social status of the blind as well as in the metaphors of blindness. Beginning in the third century, hospices were opened for the infirm, lame, and blind. Outside such institutions, the blind often became the objects of charity, the association of blindness with begging being strengthened by the Christian practice of giving alms. The most famous hospice devoted exclusively to the blind, the "Quinze-Vingts" founded by Saint Louis, opened its doors in 1260 in Paris, where it still subsists today. The statutes of the Quinze-Vingts from the mid-fourteenth century include provisions governing the begging expeditions blind residents were to make for the profit of the entire community.[5] Even when there was no institution such as the Quinze-Vingts, the blind beggars of the Middle Ages, like other groups of mendicants or social outcasts, often formed organized corporative societies. Though benefiting from the practice of almsgiving and far less shunned than lepers, these large groups of blind wanderers were often feared and distrusted because of their association with more disreputable outcasts and infiltration by imposters. The phenomenon made famous in modern times by Victor Hugo's "cour des miracles" contributed to an image, by no means universally accepted, of the blind person as crafty scoundrel. In a thirteenth-century farce, *Le Garçon et l'aveugle*, the blind man is a clever hypocrite who exploits his handicap by continuing to beg even though almsgiving has already made him a man of means. The boy who accompanies him, however, is even more cunning and takes advantage of the man's blindness, first to beat him and then to steal his money. As a comic pair, the professional blind beggar and his valet were to go on tricking each other in many other farces and in the Spanish picaresque novel *Lazarillo de Tormes*. In mystery plays of the fourteenth to sixteenth centuries, these farce routines were often conflated with the biblical story of the blind man healed by Jesus. Sometimes, because of the comic misdeeds of the blind man or his guide, he never meets Jesus and no miracle takes place. The traditional exclusion of the blind is reinforced by their portrayal as either helpless and ridiculous or wicked and greedy, and in either case as objects of scorn. The practice of Christian charity and the reference to miraculous cures were not, in the end, incompatible with a view of the blind as mysterious, unknowable, and potentially dangerous outcasts, utterly different from the seeing.[6]

With the Enlightenment, with surgical cures and philosophical speculation, the difference of the blind is no longer situated in a distant and untouchable beyond; it becomes natural, accessible to science and subject to rational remedies. The history of blindness becomes, to a considerable extent, a story of desacralization, its consequences, and the forces that oppose it. To attempt to synthesize the successive moments of this "modern history of blindness," we might begin by recalling a paragraph from Hegel's Preface to the *Phenomenology*:

> Formerly they had a heaven adorned with a vast wealth of thoughts and imagery. The meaning of all that is, hung on the thread of light by which it was linked to that heaven. Instead of dwelling in this world's presence, men looked

beyond it, following the thread to an other-worldly presence, so to speak. The eye of the Spirit had to be forcibly turned and held fast to the things of this world; and it has taken a long time before the lucidity which only heavenly things used to have could penetrate the dullness and confusion in which the sense of worldly things was enveloped, and so make attention to the here and now as such, attention to what has been called "experience," an interesting and valid enterprise. Now we seem to need just the opposite: sense is so fast rooted in earthly things that it requires just as much force to raise it. The Spirit shows itself so impoverished that, like a wanderer in the desert craving for a mouthful of water, it seems to crave for its refreshment only the bare feeling of the divine in general.[7]

Hegel first describes the passage from a world whose meaning lies beyond it in the sacred to one in which meaning is sought in things themselves, within the world itself. One of the key elements in this passage, philosophically, was a changed view of the origin of ideas. Locke and his successors set out to show that the mind's ideas are not innate, do not have divine or ideal origins, but rather arise from sensory experience, from the mind's contact with earthly reality. To prove that the mind's eye could abandon the immutable realm of innate ideas, what better witness could there be than "one born blind, and afterwards, when grown up, made to see"?[8] The famous "Molyneux problem," first published in Locke's work, attracted several generations of philosophers to the question of how a blind person newly cured would perceive the world. The blind person's lack of experience, of perceptions, afforded an opportunity to examine, whether speculatively or experimentally, the origin of ideas. Cured by the surgeon's knife and brought forcibly to the visible world, he would be a stranger in a familiar land, capable of perceiving with virgin eyes all that the inhabitants had failed to notice. Michel Foucault has noted the fundamental place of this experience in eighteenth-century thought:

When it has untied its old kinships, the eye is able to open at the unchanging, ever present level of things. . . . What

allows man to resume contact with childhood and to rediscover the permanent birth of truth is this bright, distant,
open naïvety of the gaze. Hence the two great mythical experiences on which the philosophy of the eighteenth century had wished to base its beginning: the foreign spectator in an unknown country, and the man born blind
restored to light.[9]

The blind man's arrival is a mythical as well as epistemological
event, for if he brings with him no understanding of the visible,
then philosophy has a new myth, that of its own totally experiential origin. It appears that only around the beginning of the
eighteenth century was an effective surgical technique developed for the removal of cataracts that had caused blindness. The
operation known to the surgeons of antiquity could only remove incipient cataracts—those that had not yet attached themselves within the eye so as to produce a total loss of vision. But
even if successful operations of the cataracts of the blind were
found to have been performed earlier, what is most significant
is that only in the eighteenth century did the existence of such
an operation take on cultural and intellectual importance as
more than a medical curiosity.

The philosophical interest in the newly cured blind was motivated by the belief that ideas come from sensation, that knowing is analogous to perceiving and specifically to seeing. The
analogy is ancient and has both epistemological and rhetorical
implications. The sense of sight, more than any other, has at
least in Western culture been associated with the presence of a
world exterior to the subject and with the subject's representation of that world. Words such as "idea" (from the Greek *eidos*,
sight), "theory" (from the Greek *theorein*, to observe), and "intuition" (from the Latin *intueri*, to look at) imply that the objects of thought are conceived of as analogous to the images
seen by the eyes, to the visual representation of a perceptual
presence. In Plato's *Republic*, Socrates takes sight to be the only
sense worthy of figuring true knowledge: as the objects of direct
sight are to projected shadows, the sun to the fire of the cave, so
will the intelligible realm be to the sensible, the Good to the sun

11

itself. "Well, does there seem to be any difference, then," asks Socrates, "between blind men and those men who are deprived of the knowledge of what each thing is?"[10] The first philosophers to speculate on the perceptions of a newly sighted person did not call into question the notion of idea as representation, of knowledge as resembling vision; they simply questioned the source and origin of ideas so formed. For these early eighteenth-century thinkers, language was taken to be a set of signs overlaying the universe of sensations and concepts, its articulation mimetically related to the order of the universe.[11] Reference thus stands in relation to linguistics as sensation does to epistemology. In his *Essai sur l'origine des connaissances humaines*, Condillac proposed that mental operations, whether or not they make explicit use of language, be considered equivalent to the manipulation of sign systems. On the one hand, this semiotic system is autonomous: "Nous ne sortons jamais de nous-mêmes; et ce n'est jamais que notre propre pensée que nous apercevons."[12] On the other hand, thought depends for its first ideas on perception, on a reference to something outside of and incommensurable with itself: "La perception, ou l'impression occasionnée dans l'âme par l'action des sens, est la première opération de l'entendement. L'idée en est telle qu'on ne peut l'acquérir par aucun discours."[13] Perception is the necessary link of thought to its outside, as reference would be for sign systems. Since sight occupies a dominant conceptual place among the senses, it follows that blindness can be treated as a loss of linguistic reference.

This problem of blindness and language lies at the heart of Diderot's *Lettre sur les aveugles*, in which the blind are characterized by their poverty of denomination: they cannot attach visual concepts to the words that signify them. Consequently, they must rely on abstraction and figures, on the systematic, self-referential properties of language, the production of meaning out of contextual and formal relations rather than by denomination or reference. Diderot's blind man from Puiseaux speaks of a mirror, but for him the word has no referent. He has learned to use it from its functional role in the speech of others, from contextual clues, from the fact that language is a coherent

12

formal system as well as a means of reference. Thus blindness poses the problem of an opposition or connection between two properties of language, two ways of understanding language: the externally referential (or representational) and the internally referential (or systematic, or formal), language as a set of signs overlaying the universe and as a self-centered system of hierarchical interrelations. In other words, the blind man, by doing without much of the perceptual reference that Condillac had considered indispensable to thought and language, calls into question what Foucault has called the *épistémè* of representation. From Locke to Condillac, blindness had functioned as a pure negativity, a perceptual absence; Diderot transforms the problem by examining the four-sensed world of specific blind individuals.

Philosophical and scientific interest in the blind, their language, and their cure produced two notable cultural developments in the late eighteenth century. In literature, and especially on the popular stage, a new blind figure appeared: the blind person cured or curable, no longer grotesque or comic or pathetic, but innocent and sensitive, the object not of horror but of sympathetic fascination for the seeing. In the place of the old myths of exclusion, malediction, and compensation, new myths of blindness appear, based on the supposed inexperience and innocence of the blind, on the emotional experience of seeing for the first time. But if "curing blindness" can be said to constitute a modern myth, it is the word "modern" that must be stressed, for this is no myth related directly to the sacred and its role in society, but a substitute myth produced by the Enlightenment to designate its own activity as destroyer of old myths. The Enlightenment, and demystificatory thought in general, is unaware that it effectively sacralizes its own principle of demystification. The oculist becomes a "priest" of this desacralization, as far as the blind are concerned, for his is the power to redeem them and implicitly to confound those who, seeing, would have left them in darkness.

In social welfare, interest in the blind and their capacities for understanding provided the impetus for the first systematic attempts to educate them. In general, the Enlightenment desa-

cralization of society implies the application of rational remedies to those differences and exclusions previously attributed to
something external, be it "the gods," "fortune," or a specific
myth. Once the philosophers had begun discussing the understanding of the blind—their means of thinking and communicating—the blind had been "naturalized." No longer radically
different, the blind could be compared to the seeing, and their
difference, if it could not be overcome altogether, could at least
become the object of efforts to remedy it. In 1784, Valentin
Haüy founded in Paris the first institution for the education of
the blind. Haüy, his successors, and many others were to publish treatises on the teaching and supervision of blind students.
These works are characterized both by psychological speculation about the blind and by an attempt to win for them the sympathy and interest of the reader. Thus, while claiming to attack
stereotypes and misinformation concerning their charges, the
educators, like the dramatic authors, contributed to a certain
modern mythologizing of the blind. In place of the ironic and
relativistic speculation of Diderot, for whom the difference of
blindness called into question the very notion of human nature,
they began to theorize a mysterious, inner, almost mystical
"blind nature," an innate essence that the educators of the blind
must combat and exploit, destroy and preserve.

In this sense we might venture to say that pedagogical literature provides a transition from the philosophical writings on
blindness of the eighteenth century to the presentation of the
blind in the romantic literature of the nineteenth century. But
the notion of "transition" hardly does justice to the discontinuity involved, and it must not be taken in the sense of influence—for reasons of chronology which will soon become apparent. The romantics rediscover, or at least revive, the ancient
topos of the blind poet or seer, a visionary whose sight, having
lost this world's presence, is directed entirely beyond to the spiritual. Yet the role of the blind visionary is not a safe or simple
one, for the strands of light leading to the divine are no longer
felt to be immediately present. The poetic energy of language,
instead of flowing from them, must now be mobilized to re-
trieve them. The notion of an essential spiritual tie must be

added to the gaze of experience, as the romantic poet or novelist attempts to remythify the world by borrowing from a transcendence now seeming to reside in language itself. The blind seer figures the possibility of radical success in this enterprise and thus stands as both admired ideal and terrifying alter ego, for his success implies isolation from that earthly experience which, disdained though it may be, now occupies the place of origin. In Balzac's *Facino Cane*, the young future narrator of *La Comédie humaine* gingerly explores his own identification with an old and broken blind man, treating him alternately as a realistic character, friend, even mentor, and as a fantastic, deranged apparition. To him, blindness is equivalent to madness, a loss of contact with ordinary reality, and his first desire is to enter the powerfully charged world of the old man's memories and fantasies. But at the last moment, realizing his peril, he steps back and dismisses the blind man from his life, reducing him to a bit of raw material for the novels he one day intends to write. Similarly, when Victor Hugo fantasized about going blind and resembling Homer and Milton, he did so not without great fear and ambivalence, knowing that he was not only a visionary poet but also a poet of visual description and an enlightened demystifier of traditional poetic language. In his late novel *L'Homme qui rit*, Hugo found a way of making blindness comforting rather than terrifying to the visionary hero; he gave that hero, Gwynplaine, the blind Dea as his beloved. She alone cannot see the hideous scars and deformations that the violence of history has literally inscribed into her lover's face, so that he, for a little while, can live in an idealized universe, comparable to his prophetic vision of a society reconciled to itself and transformed without violent revolution and counterrevolution.

The foregoing summary, with its echoes of a Hegelian journey of the spirit from the Middle Ages to Enlightenment to romantic religiosity, might suggest that we can produce a linear history of writings on blindness, or even that these writings could be integrated into a total history of ideas in their succession. Yet although it may be useful to remember that kind of totalizing narrative, we must now cross it out, or at least place many question marks in its margins. This very summary, unified though it may be, reveals enough of the discursive complexity of these writings to undermine any attempt to synthesize them in this fashion. For one thing, the chronology of writings on blindness can hardly be reduced to linear succession. Plays glorifying the cure of cataracts flourished in the 1820s, more than fifty years after the Chevalier de Cerfvol had denounced oculists as hypocrites, more than twenty years after the ancient topos of the blind seer had been evoked by Chateaubriand and Madame de Staël. Some of the most important treatises from educators postdated the work of these and other romantic writers by many years. And yet overlapping chronology is but the least of the discontinuities that disrupt a "Hegelian" synthesis. The development of a specialized body of works such as educational treatises cannot be taken as simply an extension or a consequence of the literature and philosophy of the same era. Works from different genres, in which blindness is discussed for diverse reasons and in virtue of divergent interests, cannot be said to succeed each other or parallel each other in an ultimately universal development of ideas. The *philosophes* were concerned at first with undermining the doctrine of innate ideas, not with understanding the blind; the reverse was true of the pedagogues. As for the romantic writers, we cannot assume that their choice of blindness as a topic, or their treatment of it, was determined by medical and epistemological developments of up to one hundred years earlier. And even within the work of one writer such as Diderot, blindness should perhaps not be considered as a single topic or category for analysis, since it appears in two distinct contexts or registers: the first referential, the perception of the blind; the second rhetorical, the figure of the blind man in the *philosophes'* struggle against religion and superstition.

The study of blindness, then, brings us face to face with some of the major and by now well-known problems that have undermined confidence in traditional histories of ideas. It may well be asked, then, if this study is in fact an "archaeology" in the sense proposed by Michel Foucault, perhaps an *Histoire de la cécité à l'âge néoclassique*. After all, Foucault's objections to the methods that have dominated the history of ideas concern their neglect of the specificity of discursive forms, their refusal to acknowledge discontinuities or shifts in the structuring of discourse, and their reduction of complex and overlapping temporalities to a continuous and uninterrupted succession. In *L'Archéologie du savoir*, his most general statement of a method, Foucault defined "archaeology" as the study of *discursive formations*, structures that govern the conditions of existence of statements, that determine why in a certain field some statements can be made and others cannot. Is the study of blindness really the study of a discursive formation? The fields that Foucault probed in his own "archaeologies"—clinical medicine, madness, general grammar, natural history, economics, sexuality— do not at first glance appear to be fundamentally different, as kinds of categories, from blindness.

A closer look, however, suggests that blindness may be quite different from the topics investigated by Foucault. In attempting to define the unities that constitute discursive formations, he proposed as a first hypothesis that "statements different in form, and dispersed in time, form a group if they refer to one and the same object."[14] He quickly concluded, however, that in fact discourse forms and constitutes its objects, and not inversely. The madmen of one era are not likely to be the madmen of the next, for the discourse that constitutes the category of madness has changed. "The unity of discourses on madness . . . . would be the interplay of modes that make possible the appearance of objects during a given period of time."[15] It can be argued that this shift from the "object" to the "formation of the object by discourse" was prepared by Foucualt's choice of domains, all of which belong to the prehistory of the human sciences. Foucault denied that his discursive formations are the same as disciplines, but this means only that the disciplines and discursive formations are not identically defined. There remains what one might call a "disciplinary function" inherent in the discursive formations. There is, for example, an institutional discourse within which it is possible to make statements about madness, whose stated aim is to know madness, even if this discourse exceeds the boundaries of what is called psychiatry to appear in jurisprudence or penology or elsewhere.[16]

Is this inquiry into blindness defined by an object or by a quasi-discipline? The answer to this question should help the reader situate the project of this book in its difference from an "archaeology" in Foucault's sense. For the period under discussion, at any rate, blindness is not something formed by a single coherent field of discourse whose aim was to know or define or investigate blindness. Only in the treatises from educators of the blind does a quasi-disciplinary discourse organized around blindness emerge, and those works form but a small, though central, part of our topic. The philosophical and literary treatment of blindness cannot be reduced to a single discursive formation.

The juxtaposition of philosophical treatises and literary works arises from a decision to use literal blindness as an organizing principle, to treat it as an object, and yet to recognize at the same time that it is a set of objects formed by a heterogeneous set of discourses. Foucault wrote that his discursive formations define "a limited space of communication" and enable us to say, for example, that Buffon and Linnaeus "were talking about 'the same thing'" whereas Diderot and Darwin were not.[17] In this sense, certain writers on blindness—Locke, Condillac, and Diderot, for example—"were talking about the same thing," but these three were only in a very limited sense "talking about the same thing" as, say, Balzac. And so the study of blindness cannot be the study of one discursive formation, but must be the study of interferences between several. It can be a study of how, with respect to a given real object in a given period, different instances of cognitive, rhetorical, and imaginative discourse contaminate and cross-fertilize one another, even as they produce a set of distinct textual objects. Interest in the cure of blindness led, in the eighteenth century, to the formation of new fields of discourse concerning the blind, their perceptions, their emotions. These new fields then intersected, in a space difficult to define except by approximate references both to the object and to this intersection, with other, older ways of writing about or conceptualizing the blind. Hence we must take up the

problem of interference between different discourses constituted around the same object, rather than try to establish the coherence of a particular "discursive formation."

To study these interferences, to compare the status of a topic
in different kinds of writing, these projects require, in contrast
to Foucault's guidelines for "archaeology," the *interpretation* of
texts. Balzac and Diderot, writing about the blind, are both
concerned with what we would now call the problem of referentiality in language. Whether we are reading about special sign
systems or supplemental development of other senses, or about
visionary powers of insight beyond perception, what remains at
issue are forms of knowledge that are not perceptual, functions
of language other than representation and reference. When Balzac equates literary language with a *seconde vue* that makes of the
novelist a visionary, when Hugo writes of the *occultation* of the
material world in the mind's eye of the poet, we can discern that
they are in a sense treating the same domain that Diderot and
the teachers of the blind were approaching in another way—
even though they are not "talking about the same thing" in Foucault's sense, since their statements belong to radically different
forms of discourse. But to make this rapprochement, to lend
these texts a common language, we must *interpret* them, in this
case interpret them in modern terms that neither of them possessed, in terms of referential and nonreferential functions of
language. Similarly, in order to compare the symbolic functioning of blindness in works as disparate as a preromantic pastoral
poem, a Scribe comedy, and a novel by Hugo, we shall need to
interpret them in terms of the language of psychoanalysis. As
these examples indicate, interpretation is unavoidable if we are
to bring radically different kinds of texts into play with one another and not simply articulate their differences.

The use of interpretation, more than anything else, separates
the present work from "archaeology." Foucault and many
others have protested, with much justification, against the view
that the historian's or critic's task is to bring forth what lies hidden behind texts, to give voice to what has been left unsaid or
excluded, to write the "history of the referent."[18] Yet however
warranted their criticisms of the glibness with which many his-

torians of ideas or literature have claimed to transcend the texts and reach the very ideas or intentions animating them may be, interpretation can still become one of the legitimate rhetorical and epistemological modes of a study that lays no claim to going beyond discourse.

In her masterful study of *Les Métaphores de l'organisme*, philosopher Judith Schlanger resumed the epistemological problem of discourse in this question: "Parce que le métaphorique est inévitable, faut-il se taire?"[19] Should the irradicable presence of rhetoric in all cognitive activity be taken as an incitement to remain silent or, as often happens, to take that metaphoricity itself as the only legitimate object of knowledge? Schlanger herself has insisted that not only discourse but all cognition is inescapably rhetorical, inextricably "contaminated" by the impurities of language, yet her epistemological answer to her rhetorical question remains in the negative. Even if all conceptual and imaginative thought is immersed in the figurality of language, there remains the task of using that language as a means rather than a limit to knowledge, the task of rearticulating texts, of attempting to translate what is written into what could have been written, or into unexpressed implications of what has been written, or into what must be written in order to compare with what has been written since, or elsewhere. Without the interpretation of certain Balzac texts as providing, implicitly, a theory of certain nonreferential functions of language, it would be impossible to compare Balzac to Diderot in this respect, to define their difference more subtly than by an acknowledgment of radical incommensurability.

This book is about blindness, or more precisely the cultural meanings of blindness, as well as about discourse. For there is an approach to the referent, even as there is no escaping from the rich and dangerous translucence of language, an approach in and through language, implying no illusions that the veil of words will be lifted to provide a transparent, unmediated view of the object. The approach to blindness cannot escape the blindness that is part of this, or any, approach; it must be, in the words of Wallace Stevens, "A seeing and unseeing in the eye."

20

· 1 ·

"SUPPOSE A MAN
BORN BLIND . . ."

In the second edition of his *Essay Concerning Human Understanding*, John Locke exposed a problem concerning a person born blind and restored to sight that was to attract the attention of every major figure of the French Enlightenment. The Swiss philosopher Jean-Bernard Mérian, writing for the Berlin Academy in 1770, summed up its importance in these terms:

> Ce problème tient, dans la Philosophie moderne, une place distinguée. Les Locke, les Leibnitz, les hommes les plus célèbres de notre siècle en ont fait l'objet de leurs recherches. Il a été le germe de découvertes importantes, qui ont produit des changemens considérables dans la science de l'Esprit humain, & surtout dans la Théorie des sensations.[1]

Locke's friend William Molyneux, author of a *Dioptrica Nova*, had proposed the problem in a letter, and Locke inserted it, with his own comments, into his discussion of perception. He claims that Molyneux's question relates directly to the problem of the role, in perception, of judgments of which we are unaware, and also shows it to be indirectly related to his overall argument against the existence of innate ideas.

Locke devotes the first book of the *Essay* to the refutation of arguments in favor of innate ideas, propositions such as "Whatever is, is" and "It is impossible for the same thing to be, and not to be," often taken as innate on the grounds that they are universally accepted. In the second book, entitled "Of Ideas," he sets out to show that everything in the understanding is derived from experience, that is, that there is no need for innate ideas. This book was to become the most influential part of the *Essay* in eighteenth-century France, where it would serve almost as a bible for thinkers opposed to the church, the universities, and Cartesian philosophy. Locke declared that all ideas came into

21

idea of a figure, entering the mind either by sight or by touch, resembles the material figure that gives rise to it, so that the blind man's incapacity is solely in naming or recognition.[8] In other words, there would be a resemblance between the ideas received through touch and sight, but the blind man would have no way of anticipating or even conceiving of it. However correct this may be if Molyneux's formulation is taken out of context, the history of the question suggests that he intended it as a thought experiment concerning Locke's argument. He appears to have invented the problem in response to this section of the *Essay*, and the considerable correspondence between the two men contains no hint of disagreement on their understanding of it.[9] If one assumes that a figure can be perceived by the eyes only with the aid of judgment, then the analogy expressed by the "so or so . . . so or so" of Molyneux's syntax can only be the acquired result of experience.

The blind man provides a way for philosopher and reader to conceive of a mind without experience, to verify that what is in the understanding is property acquired through experience, and to abolish for a moment the workings of the prejudices of understanding in their own minds. The conceptualization of a lack of experience, more than an illustration of his argument concerning perceptual judgments, is for Locke the real contribution of the Molyneux problem; in fact, he does not offer an original solution to it. "This I have set down, and leave with my Reader, as an occasion for him to consider, how much he may be beholding to experience, improvement, and acquired notions, where he thinks, he has not the least use of, or help from them."[10] To conceive of the role of experience is to understand better the workings of perception, but even more so it is to avoid the temptation of ascribing faculties to innate ideas.

The price paid for experience, Locke seems to argue, is a degree of confusion about the source of the mind's operations, and that confusion can be resolved only by recourse to an original state before experience. In the case of sight, judgment has made one kind of idea into the marks or signifiers of another kind; light and colors are interpreted as indicating three-dimensional figures. Thus the ideas properly of sight, whose role becomes merely that of signifying other ideas, are devalued to the point of passing unnoticed, "as a Man who reads or hears with attention and understanding, takes little notice of the Characters, or Sounds, but of the *Ideas*, that are excited in him by them."[11] Something has been lost, excluded; the spatial ideas acquired by the habitual use of judgment now cover up their visual origin as ideas of light and color. The philosopher must try to undo and reverse the operation of understanding, turn back the clock and inspect the beginning so as to authenticate the present state of affairs. The philosopher is already implicitly what Condillac will call him in the *Essai sur l'origine des connaissances humaines*, one who retraces the steps of understanding, who comes afterward, and yet who discovers what came first.[12] The mind's return to the state of origin is blocked by the substitution of a cause for an appearance; the mind is "blind" to the appearances before it, for causes seem to appear in their place. In effect, a censor has been created, "by use," and now certain sensations simply do not enter consciousness because of what has taken their place, the cause evoked by the unconscious judgments of the mind. The term "unconscious" is not out of place here, though certainly we could not speak of an unconscious in the Freudian sense, since for Locke the perceptions not admitted do not constitute a stockpile but are simply lost. To study these impressions, then, one has not to recover them from the past as from a reservoir, but merely to open the present paths of perception and understanding to them. A kind of experiment or exercise must be performed, and then under the right conditions the origin will once again exist anew.

The man *born* blind has never sensed or perceived visual appearances. His knowledge, unlike that of a person who has become "blind" to these appearances by long use of the understanding, has been directly and originally that of three-dimensional figures perceived by touch. Locke, as we have noted, assumes these three-dimensional figures to be the cause of two-dimensional images in light and color. In the case of the blind man, the philosopher and his friend ask, what could possibly exist of the judgment or process of substitution to which most people become "blind" through experience, ceasing to notice that they have substituted cause for appearance, figure for "mark of figure"? Summoned to bear witness before the bar of philosophy, the blind man is of interest to his hearers for his prior sensory lack, for his negativity, for the unused portion of his understanding where certain acquisitions have not yet been made. He also interests them only insofar as he can be cured, made suddenly like (and yet unlike) one of the seeing. Locke and Molyneux consider the absence of sight only as a means of producing a moment of first sight. The new sight of the blind person, unsullied by experience, helps the philosopher free his interlocutor or reader from common-sense prejudices by enabling the reader to imagine a more original state of his own mind.

In this role the blind man restored to sight becomes a paradigmatic figure in Berkeley's *Essay Towards a New Theory of Vision* (1709, French translation 1734). The heterogeneity of the perceptions of touch and sight, suggested by the remarks of Locke and Molyneux, is for Berkeley a fundamental thesis, and Molyneux's question is but one of many appeals to the construct of newly original sight. "In order to disentangle our minds from whatever prejudices we may entertain with respect to the subject at hand, nothing seems more apposite than the taking into our thoughts the case of one born blind, and afterwards, when grown up, made to see."[13] Whether the concept previously acquired by touch be distance, magnitude, spatial orientation, number, figure, or motion, the blind man will not recognize it in his new perceptions, for "he would not think the things that he perceived by sight to be at any distance from him, or without his mind."[14] The perceptions of sight and touch are simply incommensurable, and they can represent one another only if linked by the experience of their association: "It is a mistake to think that the same thing affects both sight and touch. If the same angle or square which is the object of touch be also the object of vision, what should hinder the blind man at first sight from knowing it?"[15]

Although Berkeley, like Locke and Molyneux, used the blind man primarily as a conceptual device in a philosophical discourse intended to incite the reader to take an inventory of his own mind, he did indicate an interest in an experimental verification, upon learning of its technical possibility. In the appendix to the second edition of the *New Theory of Vision* (1710), he mentions a cure of blindness and suggests questioning the patient "to decide how far some tenents laid down in several places of the foregoing essay are agreeable to truth."[16] The cure in question was an operation performed by a surgeon named Grant and reported in the *Tatler* of 1709, where it was hailed as a matter "of a yet higher consideration" than the history of princes, empires, and wars, as an experience "proper at once to exercise our humanity, please our imaginations, and improve our judgements."[17] Although the Molyneux problem is not explicitly mentioned, the preparations made for the operation suggest a philosophic interest in the first observations of the new seer: "Mr. Caswell [the local minister], being a Gentleman particularly curious, desired the whole company, in case the blindness should be cured, to keep secret, and let the Patient make his own observations, without the direction of any thing he had received by his other senses, or the advantage of discovering his friends by their voices."[18] Whereas Berkeley was to propose questioning a former blind person long after his cure, inviting him to recall his first impressions upon seeing and to compare them with his former understanding, Caswell and Grant sought to observe and overhear the first spontaneous expressions of their patient at the moment of origin of his visual experience, a prerational moment when presumably his judgments would directly reflect his perceptions.

But at the moment of first sight, philosophical investigation gives way to an exemplary display of wonder and sensibility. "When the Patient first received the dawn of light, there appeared such ecstasy in his action, that he seemed ready to swoon away in the surprise of joy and wonder."[19] For a moment, the narrator describes the patient's visual scrutiny of the surgeon standing before him—his hands and his instruments—and it appears that the inquiry into ideas can coexist with the sense of wonder. But the young man has been staring at the surgeon in "amazement," and in fact the origin of ideas has been occulted by the dazzling power of the visible, and the blindness of excess replaces the blindness of lack. Here sight is incommensurable with other senses because of a difference not of form but of energy. The blind man cannot believe that the language he has already heard is adequate, or powerful enough, to name his new experience: "Is all this about me, the thing I have heard so often of? is this the light? is this seeing? Were you always so happy, when you said, you were glad to see each other?"[20] In this mythical awakening, this enlightenment version of Plato's fiction of the cave, there is no place for philosophical interrogation. The recovery of sight provokes a shift from one kind of discourse to another, in that after a preamble suggesting a philosophical experiment, the narrative passes into a sentimental and melodramatic mode as soon as the young blind man begins to see. In this brief article, the cure of blindness already constitutes a point of intersection between the intellectual problems of sensory perception and the emotional or rhetorical implications of the awakening of sight. The patient suddenly becomes a character, the hero of an edifying little apologue on fidelity. He recognizes successively his mother and his fiancée, who, alas, is rather plain. When the young girl expresses her fear that through his eyes he may come to love another more beautiful than her, he replies that their love surpasses by far even the pleasures of vision, and that for her he would sacrifice his newly opened eyes. "I wished for them but to see you; pull them out, if they are to make me forget you."[21] Sight calls forth a dangerous sexuality that threatens their idyllic love but is held in check by the symbolic possibility of renewed blindness.

It is not surprising that Berkeley could draw no conclusions from this cure, but he took the far more famous and influential observations made by Cheselden in 1728 as a verification of his theories. "Thus, by fact and experiment," he wrote in *The Theory of Vision Vindicated and Explained* (1733), "those points of the theory which seem the most remote from common apprehension were not a little confirmed, many years after I had been led into the discovery of them by reasoning."[22] The physical experiment is properly philosophical in that it confirms, by reproducing an origin, what late reason had retraced by a thought experiment. Although Cheselden does not mention Molyneux,

Locke, or Berkeley in his article in the *Philosophical Transactions*, he testifies repeatedly to his patient's inability to perceive distance, form, or magnitude. "When he first saw, he was so far from making any Judgement about Distances, that he thought all Objects whatever touch'd his Eyes."[23] Evidently Cheselden considered this sort of observation the chief object of his article, the raison d'être of scientific interest in cures of blindness. "He knew not the Shape of any Thing, nor any one Thing from another, however different in Shape, or Magnitude." Only through the slow and deliberate process of comparing visual and tactile impressions did the patient learn to attach familiar names to the objects he saw, but in making these connections he experienced confusion as a result of apparent contradictions, both affective and spatial, between senses. "He was very much surpriz'd, that those Things which he had lik'd best, did not appear most agreeable to his Eyes." Having no notion of perspective, or of the inference from two-dimensional appearances to three-dimensional "causes," he at first judged paintings to represent flat surfaces, and then to be themselves solids, so that he "ask'd which was the lying Sense, Feeling, or Seeing?"[24] Such conundrums, which for Diderot would form a springboard to a general questioning of aesthetic judgment and illusion, are cited almost humorously by Cheselden as examples of errors made by the uninformed and as implicit confirmation of a negative answer to Molyneux's query on grounds similar to those put forward in Locke's *Essay*.

As for his young patient, Cheselden characterizes him as expecting "little Advantage from Seeing, worth undertaking an Operation for, except reading and writing," but his indifference gives way to ecstasy and, as in the *Tatler* account, to the inadequacy of language to the pleasures of his new sensations: "He said, every new Object was a new Delight, and the Pleasure was so great, that he wanted Ways to express it; but his Gratitude to his Operator he could not Conceal. . . ."[25] Unlike Grant, who was forgotten as soon as the patient reinvented the aura of the visible world, Cheselden becomes the hero of this dazzling rediscovery, his patient "never seeing him for some Time without Tears of Joy in his Eyes, and other Marks of Affection."[26] There

29

is, in fact, no discontinuity between Cheselden's portrayal of himself and the role that the oculist was later to take on as a minor stock character in sentimental plays and novels.

Voltaire reported Cheselden's experiment in his *Eléments de la philosophie de Newton* (1738), proclaimed it a striking confirmation of the theories of Locke and Berkeley, and contributed in no small way to the almost mythical status that such experiments were to assume in eighteenth-century France. In several instances he rewrote Cheselden's observations using language more vivid or more precisely pertinent to the Molyneux problem. Concerning the inability to distinguish figures, he replaces Cheselden's "he knew not the Shape of any Thing" by "Il ne pouvait distinguer d'abord ce qu'il avait jugé rond à l'aide de ses mains, d'avec ce qu'il avait jugé angulaire."[27] As for magnitude, Cheselden had written that "the Things he saw, he thought extreamly large; but upon seeing Things larger, those first seen he conceiv'd less," but Voltaire recounts that "un objet d'un pouce, mis devant son oeil, et qui lui cachait une maison, lui paraissait aussi grand que la maison."[28]

Of no less interest than these anecdotal changes is the way in which Voltaire's presentation of the problem, the blind patient, and the surgeon made the topic appear as a decisive episode in the great combat against prejudice and innate ideas. He presents the recourse to experimental verification as the immediately obvious sequel to the philosophers' speculations, so that the operation is seen as a long-awaited and singular event that should decide the question once and for all: "Mais où trouver l'aveugle dont dépendait la décision indubitable de cette question? Enfin en 1729, M. Cheselden. . . ."[29] The curable blind man exists as a fortuitous accident, an object lying on the road of progress, to be used and discarded. The humanitarian interest in restoring the sight of the blind, present at least implicitly in the *Tatler* and *Transactions* articles, is absent from Voltaire's account, in which the blind man vanishes from the scene as soon as he has testified before the philosophers. Voltaire emphasizes the polemical and ideological, rather than sentimental, implications of the patient's naïvete. Nothing is said of the boy's pleasure upon seeing, but his prior disinterest and apprehension are exaggerated, deplored, and recuperated by a moralistic digression:

> L'aveugle eut de la peine à y consentir. Il ne concevait pas trop que le sens de la vue pût beaucoup augmenter ses plaisirs. Sans l'envie qu'on lui inspira d'apprendre à lire et à écrire, il n'eût point désiré de voir. Il vérifiait par cette indifférence qu'il est impossible d'être malheureux par la privation des biens dont on n'a pas d'idée: vérité bien importante.[30]

The patient appears to be passive and even stubborn, almost an obstacle to science; his very desire for literacy had to be instilled by others. Opposing him, Cheselden is arrayed as a champion of enlightenment, "un de ces fameux chirurgiens qui joignent l'adresse de la main aux plus grandes lumières de l'esprit."[31]

With its inclusion in Voltaire's widely read guide to Newtonian science, the Cheselden experiment became available in France as a commonplace of sensationalist epistemology. Rousseau mentioned it in the third of his *Lettres morales*, Montesquieu and Sade in unpublished fragments, and Buffon in the *Histoire naturelle de l'homme*.[32] Scientists and physicians such as Réaumur, Hilmer, Janin, and Daviel attempted similar or identical experiments. But not every writer accepted Cheselden's results, or even agreed that his experiment could be duplicated; La Mettrie and Condillac, the first *philosophes* after Voltaire to comment on it in published works, challenged both the conclusions and the methods of the English philosophers and surgeon.

In his *Traité de l'âme* (1745), La Mettrie places a series of stories intended to demonstrate that all ideas come from the senses, and among them is that of Cheselden's blind boy. He denies that the problem has been correctly solved and argues that the perception of light and color already implies the perception of extension, even if errors are made before the subject comes to understand perspective. In this his position resembles that of Locke. The blind acquire ideas of figures and distances by touch, he writes, and therefore do not need to have any innate spatial ideas or judgments prior to first sensations: ". . . ces

31

jugemens lui eussent été inutiles pour distinguer à la vue le globe d'un cube: il n'y avoit qu'à lui donner le tems d'ouvrir les yeux, & de regarder le tableau composé de l'univers."[33] Since La Mettrie assumes that ideas represent objects in the material world and are thus independent of the senses from which they arise, his affirmative answer to Molyneux's question remains perfectly compatible with his denial of innate ideas. "Or un globe attentivement considéré par le toucher, clairement imaginé et conçu, n'a qu'à se montrer aux yeux ouverts; il sera conforme à l'image ou à l'idée gravée dans le cerveau."[34]

In addition to these conclusions, which are diametrically opposed to those of Berkeley, La Mettrie offers a critical appraisal of the experimentation and of the epistemological status of the blind subject. The blind, he writes, have a finely developed sense of touch and can thus acquire "facilement par le toucher les idées des figures, des distances, &c."[35] The nature of blindness and the blind does not simply enable the experiment to take place; it also enters into the result, since the knowledge possessed by the subject is of positive importance, as it would be for an anatomist (in La Mettrie's example), who knows the organs of the body well by sight and thus could distinguish them by touch. If, then, Cheselden's patient was unable to distinguish the solid figures, it must be attributed to physiological trauma or to a prejudicial admiration for Locke's opinion concerning the Molyneux problem: "J'ose mettre en fait de deux choses l'une; ou on n'a pas donné le tems à l'organe dioptrique ébranlé, de se remettre dans son assiette naturelle; ou à force de tourmenter le nouveau voyant, on lui a fait dire ce qu'on étoit bien aise qu'il dît."[36]

The same alternative is propounded by Condillac in the section of the *Essai sur l'origine des connaissances humaines* (1746) devoted to the Molyneux problem and Cheselden's experiment. Like La Mettrie, and in opposition to Berkeley, Condillac assumes that the idea of extension or form is not unique to or dependent on any single sense, that "de quelque sens que l'étendue vienne à notre connaissance, elle ne peut être représentée de deux manières différentes. . . . Cet aveugle-né distinguera donc à la vue le globe du cube, puisqu'il y reconnaîtra les mêmes idées qu'il s'en étoit faites par le toucher."[37] But at the center of Condillac's argument is his rejection of Locke's theory that only by an unconscious judgment does the subject identify solid figures as the objects of his sight. Not only figure, he states, but also distance and position can be perceived by sight alone, for "les lumières et les couleurs ne retracent-elles pas nécessairement différentes distances, différentes grandeurs, différentes situations?"[38] He points out that Locke and Molyneux implicitly assume that the eyes can perceive extension when they demand that the globe and cube be of equal size, a condition that Condillac finds unnecessary and self-contradictory. He flatly denies the reality of judgments inaccessible to consciousness, and he finally states that for him the perception of form and extension by sight is simply a matter of "connoissance évidente," since the sensations of sight more perfectly than any other announce "l'ordre, la beauté, et la grandeur de l'univers."[39] He admits that the newly cured blind person will need time and experience to be able to reflect on his new perceptions, but he denies that this reflection would require unconscious judgments or the sense of touch.

However, writes Condillac, were a skeptical philosopher to ask the newly sighted person to justify the visual identification of globe and cube, to explain on what basis the visible objects can be supposed to be the same as the tactile ones, the formerly blind individual would be at a loss for words, and might well need the experience of simultaneously seeing and touching as a convincing proof. In other words, were the problem simply one of recognition of the same idea obtained from two senses (and Molyneux's statement of it certainly admits this interpretation), Condillac might well admit that its answer could be inconclusive or negative. But he hastens to point out that the problem did not ask for the subject to explain his discernment rationally, but simply to discern.

In his *Traité des sensations* of 1754, Condillac returned to the Molyneux problem and reversed his earlier judgment, though he remained critical of Locke's arguments concerning perception. In the *Traité*, Condillac introduces the famous model of an animated statue to represent a person with varying combinations of senses and thereby generalize the Molyneux problem to all possible correspondences between perceptions. When the statue first sees, it will sense light and colors, but will not realize that these sensations are in fact occasioned by objects external to it; this will be discovered only by judgments and the use of touch. Sight, concludes Condillac, only appears to give ideas of form and extension because its perceptions are always accompanied by those of touch:

> C'est donc parce que les odeurs et les sons se transmettent sans se mêler avec les couleurs, qu'elle [the statue] démêle si bien ce qui appartient à l'ouïe et à l'odorat. Mais comme le sens de la vue et celui du toucher agissent en même temps . . . nous distinguons difficilement ce qui appartient à chacun de ces sens.[40]

Condillac insists on the distinction between seeing and looking, *voir* and *regarder*: the statue will see immediately, but will have to learn to look in order to know what it sees.[41] He still denies, however, as he had in the *Essai*, the existence of the unconscious judgments propounded by Locke. We do not first see objects as flat, and then as solid, he argues, but rather the experience of touch is required if we are to realize that we are seeing objects at all. Concerning Molyneux's question itself, he develops his negative answer by resuming Voltaire's account of the Cheselden case in detail, and he finally proposes that in some future experiment the newly sighted subject should be placed in a glass box to determine whether he could ascertain the form and extension of objects beyond it, or whether, according to Condillac's own hypothesis, he would identify what he saw with the box itself, which would form the limit of his touch.

An opposing view of the problem surfaced in 1765 with the posthumous publication of Leibnitz's *Nouveaux essais sur l'entendement humain*. This detailed refutation of Locke's *Essay* had been written in 1703, but Leibnitz declined to publish it after the English author's death the following year. Leibnitz accepts without reservation Locke's opinion that there are perceptual judgments of which we are not aware, since his own system relies extensively on the notion of minute, unnoticed perceptions. But if an idea, such as that of form or extension, comes from more than one sense, Leibnitz says that it is "plutôt du sens commun, c'est-à-dire l'esprit même."[42] He thus answers the question in the affirmative, but with the proviso that the blind person be told that the visible forms are the objects he had touched before. Given this assurance, the new seer will be able to distinguish between the figures by virtue of their geometrical properties, which are independent of sensation. "Et il faut que ces deux géométries, celle de l'aveugle et celle du paralytique, se rencontrent et s'accordent, et même reviennent aux mêmes idées, quoiqu'il n'y ait point d'images communes."[43] If the subject were not informed that the objects of sight were also the objects of touch, however, Leibnitz would concur with Berkeley in stating that he would not realize that they could represent one another. Thus, though Leibnitz contends that the geometrical idea common to sight and touch is real (indeed, innate) and not merely a nominal category as Berkeley would have it, he does not claim that this real commonality of the senses would be immediately evident. The identity, for Leibnitz, is not that of the tactile and visual appearances of the solids, but that of the geometrical ideas produced independently, by abstraction, from either one.

Leibnitz's solution was included by Jean-Bernard Mérian in his summary and analysis of the Molyneux debate, presented in a series of eight papers before the Berlin Academy between 1770 and 1780. Mérian's stated aim was to provide an inventory of solutions to the problem and to display analytically the presuppositions underlying them: "Je voudrois tracer un tableau qui représentât ces matières subtiles et abstraites sous toutes leurs faces, & avec toute la clarté dont elles sont susceptibles."[44] To this end he proposes a number of alternative hypotheses that permit the classification of the solutions: for example, whether or not solid figures are the immediate objects of sight, whether or not the eye can perceive form and extension without experience, whether (and this remained the crucial question) the ideas derived from different senses are related by resemblance or by conventional affiliation. Resemblance would imply the existence of real general concepts of figure and extension, of which the senses perceive particular manifestations; conventional identification would imply that different perceptions are linked only by nominal categories constructed by experience.

Of greater interest than his summary are Mérian's own arguments in favor of Berkeley's solution, and his concluding proposal for a monumental experiment that would resolve the question once and for all. In defense of Berkeley's view that the objects of sight and the objects of touch are not the same and can be linked only by experience, Mérian proposes to explain the nature of their connection by a twofold analogy to language:

> Cette liaison est purement symbolique. Elle est la même qu'entre les mots et les choses, ou entre les mots écrits, & les sons articulés. Les objets visibles & tangibles ne se ressemblent pas davantage que les sons ne ressemblent aux pensées, ou les mots écrits aux sons. Mais la liaison une fois établie, la présence des uns réveille aussitôt la présence des autres.[45]

Sight and touch, in this nominalist position, are thus said to be conventional signs of one another. The relation is reciprocal, writes Mérian, since whichever sensation strikes us first takes on the role of signifier with respect to the second, which becomes the signified. And yet there is a "natural" direction to that priority, since sight is the sense of warning, of alerting: "Il nous importe donc bien davantage d'être avertis par la Vue de l'effet que feront sur nous les objets tangibles, que de l'être par le Tact de l'effet que feront sur nous les objets visibles."[46] This is the first instance of an argument concerning the Molyneux problem based on the functional specificity of the different senses, their respective role in contributing to the defense and survival of the individual, but Mérian does not develop it in this direction. He falls back instead on his analogies with the signs of language and writing, and hence on the greater importance of the signified as compared to the signifier. In this respect he restates one of Locke's arguments from the *Essay*. Sight is devalued in like proportion to signs and writing:

> Les sons articulés nous intéressent fort peu par eux-mêmes, ils ne nous intéressent qu'autant qu'ils nous retracent des

perceptions & des idées; & lorsque ces dernières sont présentes à notre âme, nous pouvons nous passer des premiers. Il est donc naturel qu'ils fassent l'office de signes à leur égard. Quant aux caractères écrits, il est encore naturel qu'à l'égard des sons ils soient plutôt signifians que signifiés; puisque dans son origine le langage de la parole a précédé celui de l'écriture.[47]

The valorization of touch as the sense giving direct access to the qualities of form and extension—and thus to the "meaning" of visual perceptions—thus parallels the concept of the sign as transparently, though arbitrarily, representative. Visual perceptions are to be understood as signs; the eye's gaze represents the world in the same manner as characters represent sounds, as sounds represent ideas. The newly sighted blind person, in effect, knows the "meaning" without knowing the language, indeed, without realizing that the perceptions from the eyes are the signs of anything.

The most extraordinary section of Mérian's papers is undoubtedly his proposal for a systematic experiment on a large number of individuals artificially deprived of sight. "Ce projet seroit de prendre les enfants au berceau, et de les élever dans de profondes ténèbres jusqu'à l'âge de raison."[48] Instead of waiting for the fortuitous arrival of a single blind subject, the *philosophes* would be able to perform psychological experiments in the modern sense of the term, measuring the effects of differing degrees of deprivation and education: "En un mot, comme leur esprit seroit, pour ainsi dire, entre nos mains, que nous pourrions le pétrir comme une cire molle, et y développer les connoissances dans telle succession qui nous plairoit, on seroit à portée de prendre toutes les précautions, et de varier les expériences de toutes les façons imaginables."[49] Of course, he conceded, there would be moral objections. "Je réponds que mon projet s'adresse aux philosophes embrasés de l'amour de la Science, qui savent qu'on ne va au grand qu'en foulant aux pieds les préjugés populaires."[50] Moreover, he adds, orphans are the property of the state anyway, and the children of the urban poor would be better off in darkness than with their parents.

But beyond these arguments, which display all the violence of what Roger Shattuck has called the "forbidden experiment," one that would deprive a child of human nurturing to get at "human nature,"[51] Mérian claims that the artificial blindness he proposes will in fact make possible an excellent education. His arguments on this point are twofold, prefiguring, on the one hand, many of the psychological observations of the educators of the blind and echoing, on the other hand, the awakening joy attributed to the restoration of sight in the accounts of Grant's and Cheselden's patients. When the senses develop simultaneously, he writes, each is hampered by the distraction of the others; their successive, methodical development would thus produce minds of greater order and force, and would be partially realized in his "Séminaire d'aveugles artificiels." The sense of touch especially would become keener and more discriminating. But when at last the children were released from their blindness, they would be rewarded with a moment of illumination:

> De quel torrent de délices vont-ils être inondés, quels seront leurs transports, lorsqu'on les fera passer de la nuit au jour, des ténèbres à la lumière, lorsqu'un nouvel univers, un monde tout brillant, éclora pour eux comme du sein du Chaos? Y a-t-il rien de comparable à un pareil instant?[52]

When compared to the first experience of sight, the orderly world of touch reveals itself to have been no better than chaos. Whatever the philosophers may write about the importance of touch, they continue to identify the act of knowing metaphorically with the gaze of the eye. The blind person restored to sight possesses that gaze at its most spontaneous moment, but for the *philosophes* he possesses little or nothing else, and can hold their interest only at the moment when he ceases to be what he has been.

It is this kind of revelatory moment whose value is called into question by Diderot in his *Lettre sur les aveugles*. For him, the moment at which the blind first receive light could be of no reliable philosophical importance and would be better replaced by lessons from the blind to those who see.

· 2 ·

DIDEROT: PHILOSOPHY AND
THE WORLD OF THE BLIND

In the series of texts inspired by the Molyneux problem, the *Lettre sur les aveugles à l'usage de ceux qui voient* stands out by its fame and by its title. From Locke to Condillac, the blind enter philosophical works as examples or as abstract paradigmatic figures. With Diderot, in 1749, philosophy sets out to study them and their ways of knowing, ways that are often surprisingly like those of the seeing. Yet this resemblance can be disconcerting, as Diderot notes in reporting his conversation with a blind man whom he had visited in Puiseaux:

> Il discourt si bien et si juste de tant de choses qui lui sont absolument inconnues, que son commerce ôteroit beaucoup de force à cette induction que nous faisons tous sans savoir pourquoi, de ce qui se passe en nous, à ce qui se passe au dedans des autres.[1]

The problem with the blind man is his facility with discursive language, a facility which is deceptive in that it masks the figurative, subjective, and perhaps totally nonreferential character of that discourse. Discursive language, the common speech of different subjects, permits and indeed involuntarily produces the induction from the mental processes of one individual to those of another. Such speech appears to establish a knowledge that is essentially independent of the subject, or rather that posits a single, universal, always identical subject. The illusion of truth rests on the assumption of a general field of knowledge related to a general human nature; the induction of which Diderot writes is a necessary foundation for a universe in which man, with his five senses, is the measure of all things.

We have already noted that arguments based on an identity or at least strong analogy between subjects play a fundamental role in the discussions of the Molyneux problem. Locke and

Berkeley invoke the blind man as a device for mental clarification: our own knowledge of sensory processes having been built up from experience, it is necessary to call to mind the case of one who lacks such experience in order to be able to conceive of our own perceptions. I use the first-person plural deliberately, for in these texts the reader is simply invited, indeed expected, to notice in his own mind, to confirm by his own experience, the phenomena under discussion. The blind man's difference is invoked only to permit the reader's mind to perceive, as it were, a mirror of its former self, itself as it was before the accretions of conventions, judgments, and interpretive mechanisms that time and the interplay of the senses have put at its disposal.

Diderot dismantles the Molyneux problem in the final third of the *Lettre*, without really answering its question one way or the other. It will be my contention in this chapter that he dissolves much more, that the entire philosophic edifice that rests not so much on the outcome of the Molyneux problem as on the very possibility of asking its question is shaken to and perhaps beyond the limits of its cohesion. That question can have meaning only in an epistemology of representation, in which a discursive language extends over the entire field of knowledge, with this field accessible to a single, universal gaze. To deny the possibility of Molyneux's question is to deny that this gaze can be taken as the origin of ideas, or that such an origin can be conceived of as an act of direct perception accessible to consciousness through rational thought and experimentation. Diderot does not take visual perceptions to be a universal system of signs representing the tactile qualities of form and extension, but rather treats all the senses as constituting a sign system. Thus the blind, with their four senses instead of the usual five, pose the problem of a radically different language of the senses, disrupt what Foucault calls the "universal extension of the sign within the field of representation,"[2] and introduce discontinuities and unstable figures into discourse. The problem of signification, absent from Foucault's classical *épistémè*, is everywhere present in the *Lettre*. So also is the problem of the difference between Self and Other, a difference that prevents language from being transparent or universal, that conditions the use of all sign systems and hence the very ability to communicate.

Diderot's point of departure in the *Lettre* is an experiment of the type performed by Cheselden, the observation and interrogation of a blind person newly cured by surgery. But instead of a description of such an event, Diderot's opening paragraph is an account of not having seen it, of the enforced blindness of those "témoins éclairés" (1) who might best have been able to *see* what was taking place, the *philosophes*. Instead, the observers are a group chosen for unknown and suspect motives, presumably incapable of seeing the implications of the experiment; Diderot humorously metonymizes them into "quelques yeux sans conséquence." What matters in this beginning is not so much the examination of the blind patient as the very possibility of such an examination in the rhetorical context of blindness and enlightenment, of mystifying and philosophizing. Réaumur's refusal to have enlightened witnesses constitutes a betrayal of philosophy, a turn from sight, the rational sense whose gaze penetrates beyond received authority, to hearing, the sense by which the faithful are indoctrinated: "Les observations d'un homme aussi célèbre, ont moins besoin de spectateurs quand elles se font, que d'auditeurs quand elles sont faites" (1).[3] The academician would exploit passive or incompetent senses to offer an experience of pseudo-enlightenment; Diderot's *Lettre* thus begins with a denunciation of a new obscurantism that arises within Enlightenment science itself.

Yet the opening is very much more than a denunciation, and Diderot's implicit critique of Réaumur goes far beyond the simple issues of professional vanity or dogmatism. Whatever the famous man's machinations, the experiment itself remains a kind of visual *spectacle* for those who are present, because the moment of first sight, which Foucault calls the rediscovery of the childhood gaze, is also a magical apparition or raising of a curtain ("laisser tomber le voile"). The theatricality of Grant's and Cheselden's accounts is not lost on Diderot, whose reference to his attempts to obtain a place among the audience for the woman to whom he addresses the letter confirms the experiment's status as entertainment. The epigraph from Virgil, "Pos-

sunt *nec* posse videntur," not only asserts a positive capability of
the blind (excluded by the Molyneux problem) but also locates
error in the customarily privileged faculty of vision. Diderot
thus abandons "une expérience où je ne voyois guère à gagner
pour mon instruction ni pour la vôtre" (2)[4] out of both necessity and free choice. Later he will develop at length his intellectual rejection of such experiments in terms of the differences between subjects and the importance of sign systems. At this point
he proposes a substitute, the account of a philosophic discussion among friends: the *Lettre* will constitute the generic transformation of a *spectacle* into an *entretien*. But having thus presented his text as a substitute, a *pis-aller*, a work authorized by
an absent pretext, Diderot undercuts this very presentation by
calling the conversation his "original plan" to which he will now
return. Réaumur's experiment is thereby reduced, at least
within the fiction of the *Lettre*, to being itself a substitute, apparently requested by the addressee. The persuasive rhetoric of
the letter will therefore be aimed at a reader known to be attracted by the experiment and hence by the concepts on which
the experiment depends—and which Diderot intends to question. As a first step in undermining the authority of an experiment alleged to reveal the origin of ideas, he thus blurs the origin of his own text. Is it a substitute for a perceptual spectacle,
or was the spectacle to have been a substitute for a dialogue? In
renouncing the restoration of sight, he claims priority for the
unseeing, sightless perspective that he will try to make his own.
Rather than treating the experiment as a real event whose absence must be supplemented by a text, Diderot incorporates the
experiment's presuppositions into the initial position of his addressee, a position susceptible to rhetorical persuasion and un-
doing.

From the foregoing it is clear that the language of the *Lettre*
must be both denotative and connotative, that in it blindness
must take on both literal and figurative meanings. Despite the
critique of the purely discursive philosophy of Berkeley and
Condillac, philosophic discourse remains the ostensibly dominant mode of the letter, whose rhetorically charged opening
paragraph appears to be an exception rather than the rule. But

the possible figurative implications of the work become evident if we examine it in the context of other early writings of Diderot, notably the *Promenade du sceptique*, in which blindness is a central motif of the satiric allegory. A single sentence of the *Promenade* concerning the darkening of the sky customarily appears in editions of and commentaries on the *Lettre*, but the rhetorical significance of the allegory for the more philosophic text has been almost universally neglected.[5] The symbolic and allegorical use of blindness in the *Promenade* is in fact so extensive as to deserve attention here for its own sake, aside from its role in the reading of the *Lettre*, for in the *Promenade* blindness is articulated in all its specificity as a term of opposition within the rhetoric of enlightenment.

That rhetoric, with is characteristic metaphors of sight or illumination to signify knowledge, its equation of prejudice, irrationality, or ignorance with blindness, shadows, and darkness, was hardly invented by the *philosophes*. They adopted it and transformed it from Christian apologetics, where it had been an established topos since the New Testament.[6] To have faith in Christ was to see or to receive illumination; to doubt or deny him was to be blind. Diderot uses this tradition ironically in presenting the blindfolded believers who travel the "Allée des épines" in the *Promenade*. Referring to Christians and Jews, he writes: "Ceux de la nouvelle création se prétendent favorisés exclusivement à ceux de l'ancienne, qu'ils méprisent comme des aveugles."[7] But for Diderot, the pot is calling the kettle black, since the Christians themselves wear a blindfold signifying their refusal of the evidence of reason and the senses.

If the Christians are to the Jews as the skeptics are to the Christians, a disconcerting possibility arises: that secular enlightenment, which comes to denounce yesterday's enlighteners as a new set of blind men and to restore their sight, may take the form of a new religious illuminism, of a conversion. The "Discours préliminaire" refers to the obstinacy of certain people in their blindness, their stubborn resistance to reason, which torments them as a lantern would a nest of owls. One may reasonably infer a certain zeal in obtaining converts when, in the "Allée des marronniers," one of the *philosophes* cries to a blind man,

"Que j'aurais de plaisir de te tirer de ce labyrinthe où tu t'égares! Approche, que je te débarasse de ce bandeau" (*OC* 1:361).[8] Even more telling, we find those reasonable enough to let fall their blindfold referred to as "ces illuminés" (*OC* 1:351), a term particularly strong in its religious connotations.

The implications of this analogy are never fully worked out in the *Promenade*. There are references to the differences in character and behavior between the Christians, who are vengeful and violent, and the skeptics, who are calm and forgiving. Diderot would clearly like to appropriate the rhetorical power inherent in the metaphor of light without accepting all the logical consequences of its application to secular enlightenment. But in the paragraph mentioning "ces illuminés," a comparison that relates the religious analogy directly to the *Lettre sur les aveugles* is made. The new seers "se trouvent tout à coup dans le cas d'un aveugle né à qui l'on ouvrirait les paupières. Tous les objets de la nature se présentent à lui sous une forme bien différente des idées qu'il aurait reçues" (*OC* 1:351).[9] The narrator thus proclaims a resemblance between the struggle against superstition and the well-known experiments, such as that of Cheselden, to determine the origin of ideas. The comparison emphasizes the vehemence of Diderot's critique of dogmatism and prejudice, and the positive mythic character of the experiments themselves, but at the same time such a comparison casts the *scientific* validity of experimentation with the blind into doubt, for a moment of conversion, no more than the moment of wonderment described in Grant's case, is hardly propitious for dispassionate observation or judgment.

Georges May has called the reference to the *aveugle-né* a simple allegorical representation, contrasting it with the more complex metaphors and analogies of the *Lettre*, and certainly the rhetorical and figural strategies of the two texts diverge to a great extent.[10] But it would be wrong to read the *Lettre* as a purely philosophical text, far removed from the allegory of the *Promenade*, simply because of the quantitative importance in it of philosophical discourse. The real interest of the *Lettre* lies in its articulation of the rhetorical and speculative modes of writing on blindness.

It is customary to refer to the *Lettre* as consisting of three parts: first, the conversation with the blind man from Puiseaux; second, the presentation of Saunderson; third, the discussion of the Molyneux problem. To these must be added the first and last paragraphs, which are related to the Puiseaux man not at all and to the Molyneux controversy only marginally. The division into three parts is usually assumed to accentuate the importance of Saunderson, placed at the center of the *Lettre* as Diderot's spokesman. His powerful deathbed speech is taken as the heart of the letter, highlighted by contrast with the more prosaic Puiseaux and Molyneux sections, just as the climax of D'Alembert's dream is enclosed by the layers of *entretiens* surrounding it.

The importance of Saunderson and in particular of his speech cannot be denied, but there are other implications to the ordering of the text. Although the Molyneux problem is treated last, the opening paragraph makes it clear that the *Lettre* will act as a substitute for an experiment concerning this problem (or vice versa). Its narrative will be of a philosophic discussion concerning "la matière importante qu'elle [the experiment] a pour objet" (2). Diderot's digressive rambling in the text overlays a logical and specifically methodical organization. To introduce the Molyneux problem, he writes a sentence that would have introduced the conversation with the blind man of Puiseaux: "On cherche à restituer la vue à des aveugles nés; mais si l'on y regardoit de plus près, on trouveroit, je crois, qu'il y a bien autant à profiter pour la Philosophie, en questionnant un aveugle de bon sens"(46).[11] Diderot has of course done just this, and followed it by examining the life and work of an *aveugle de génie*. In so doing he has prepared the reader for the rejection of the Molyneux problem by providing examples in advance of the kind of inquiry with which he would replace it.

But the Puiseaux man and Saunderson have an even more specific role in Diderot's final resolution, or precisely dissolution, of the problem. Diderot writes that even if all the physiological and psychological problems that threaten the experiment's validity are resolved, the outcome will depend on the intelligence and even more on the acquired knowledge of the subject. He mentions four cases: first, "personnes grossières, sans éducation, sans connoissances," who will be incapable of judgment; second, those who will be able to compare their ideas without really explaining them; third, a metaphysician; fourth, a geometer (62–64). Clearly the second and fourth cases have been announced by the chief blind figures of the text, of whom the former could make inadvertently perceptive remarks about optics, the latter teach it in a university. Diderot names Saunderson explicitly in this section, and a further reference to the man from Puiseaux would hardly be necessary after the allusion to the "aveugle de bon sens." Saunderson's intellectual superiority is beyond question, but the other man's definition of a mirror is worthy of a "Descartes aveugle-né" (4). Remarkable as Saunderson's teaching of mathematics and optics may be, it too has a parallel in the man from Puiseaux, who teaches his son to read. Moreover, Diderot attributes to both men the statement that life holds little pleasure for them because of their blindness. Such similarities invite the reader to make further comparisons, to place the two in the series of diversely educated blind men who will determine the experiment's outcome.

Diderot's "solution" of the Molyneux problem goes beyond skepticism concerning the feasibility of the experiment and amounts to a denial of the problem's conditions. Supported by the examples he has provided, Diderot asserts that the observations of the newly cured subject will depend on the mental and linguistic sign systems by which, while still blind, he had understood his tactile perceptions. Hence, respectively: a lack of understanding, common-sense understanding, metaphysical understanding, and geometrical understanding. In no case does the moment of first sight have any special importance; it brings neither recognition of forms nor a failure to recognize. Only by comparing his new perceptions with his old ones will the subject be able to answer the question. The subject who cannot compare them will be unable to answer, and the others will answer according to their different conceptual means of making the comparison. The subject must do with himself what Diderot has already been doing with the blind man of good sense: "On en apprendroit comment les choses se passent en lui; on le compareroit avec la manière dont elles se passant en nous" (46–

47).[12] Thus, unless the subject has the knowledge of a Locke or a Saunderson the experiment will be of little benefit.

This position shatters the foundations of the Molyneux problem. In the first place, Diderot is denying that an origin of perception or of ideas could be rediscovered by experiment or by simple mental exercise. Far from being capable of stripping away accessory notions obscuring the origin of ideas, as Locke, Molyneux, and Berkeley thought, the problems and the experiment are shown to be themselves dependent on acquired concepts. In the context of these philosophers' work, and even of Condillac's, Diderot's answer is a nonanswer. More important, his solution, with its different classes of subjects, implies that there is not a single discursive mode of understanding or communication common to all individuals, that mental processes and the use of signs are far from universal. Instead, every individual has at his disposal those signs with which his senses and education have provided him. Language, rather than naming and articulating all the objects of the universe, depends for its meaning on how it is used by sender and receiver.

Language and sign systems are central to the *Lettre*, and not simply because of the overt remarks concerning figural language in the speech of the blind. When Diderot proposes the comparison of "comment les choses se passent" in the blind and in the seeing, he is referring to the different structuring of mental operations provided by different sets of perceptions. In the blind man from Puiseaux, this difference in internal language seems to disappear in the common tongue of external language, but Diderot recognizes the gap between knowledge and discourse, the figurative and sometimes deceptive character of what the blind man says so well. The problem of figures, and linguistic or semiotic questions in general, thus offer a suitable beginning for a detailed analysis of the *Lettre*.

The blind man of Puiseaux speaks of mirrors and of other things that he cannot know, yet he speaks correctly by adopting the conventions of language. Indeed, by using terms entirely according to convention rather than according to his own understanding, he manages never to violate these conventions by errors in context or referent: "S'il n'attache aucune idée aux termes qu'il emploie, il a du moins sur la plupart des autres hommes l'avantage de ne les prononcer jamais mal-à-propos" (4).[13] Likewise, in aesthetic judgments, the blind man's statement "cela est beau" is merely a reported or conventionally repeated phrase; however, writes Diderot, so are the declarations of "les trois quarts de ceux qui décident d'une Pièce de Théâtre" (3). The blind speaker merely pushes to the limit a deceptive possibility already present in language, namely, that its users may speak about that of which they know nothing, while a facile illusion of communication is maintained by the inductive assumption that everybody understands and speaks in the same way. The difference in the blind man's understanding becomes obvious only when he must *define* the mirror, "une machine . . . qui met les choses en relief, loin d'elles-mêmes" (4).[14] The definition is metaphorical, in that tactile qualities replace visual ones. To be more precise, the speaker transfers to the vocabulary of touch a relational notion (the distance between an object and its reflection) from what he has heard concerning mirrors. Although perfectly capable of speaking on the properties and uses of mirrors or eyes, he can define them only by a figure, by transferring them to a register he understands referentially.

What the blind man lacks is *denomination*, the ability to name visible objects, to put signs and referents together. Yet without that ability he is able to manipulate the signs as well as anyone else, creating an illusion of reference that is broken only when one remembers that he is blind. Much seemingly referential discourse, argues Diderot, may thus be only a matter of convention; we assume that a critic of a play is referring to the play if that is how we would use language, whereas he may simply be repeating some discourse about some play. There is universal context, no general agreement as to denomination, for it is necessary to take into account how different speakers define, understand, and use their terms.

Once Diderot has recognized the blind man's metaphorical speech for what it is, he can interpret and appreciate it. The definition of eyes by analogy with canes is in fact a didactic metaphor used extensively by Descartes in the *Dioptrique*. The language of four senses differs from that of five by its relative poverty of denomination, by its greater use of composite signs, analogies, and other figures, but this does not mean that it is inadequate, as the cane analogy demonstrates: "Il n'y a point de questions auxquelles sa comparaison n'eût pu satisfaire" (6).[15] Again Diderot moves from his observation of the blind man to problems of language in general, for in every speaker's vocabulary there are many words that do not refer to sensory objects. These must be learned in much the same way that the blind man learns the terms signifying visual concepts. When the Puiseaux blind man asks why his visitors are surprised only by his deeds and not by his faculty of speech, Diderot makes the problem a universal one. "C'est une chose assez surprenante que la facilité avec laquelle on apprend à parler" (11).[16] Abstract, nonsensory ideas can be attached to the terms that designate them only by "une suite de combinaisons fines et profondes des analogies que nous remarquons entre ces objets non sensibles, et les idées qu'ils excitent" (11–12).[17] Sensorial denomination provides some terms in the network of language; the others must be filled in by the use of language's properties as a system, through combination, comparison, and associations in discourse. In the case of the blind man, the spaces in the field of language to be filled in are far more numerous. Hence the effort of comparison and combination will be much greater but will remain essentially the same in kind. "Madame, il faut manquer d'un sens pour connoître les avantages des symboles destinés à ceux qui nous restent" (21);[18] by examining those who cannot see, Diderot explores aspects of language that are often simply taken for granted, and shows that speech depends more on individual competence and less on a universal system of reference. On the one hand, the blind are unique in their reliance on abstraction and figure, but on the other hand, their use of language is itself a metaphor for any use of language. Language involves as much blindness as sight.

Like the man from Puiseaux, Saunderson is said to excel in the use of figurative language. As befits his intellectual eminence, the discussion of figures is here more precise and less anecdotal; the mathematician's metaphors are less amusing than they are instructive. Saunderson spoke in a language of the blind, as though addressing students who could not see, and thus he achieved a remarkable clarity for those who could, who possess "un télescope de plus" (31). The means to this clarity is the "expression heureuse," which has a proper meaning for one sense and a metaphoric meaning for another, "d'où il résulte une double lumière pour celui à qui l'on parle; la lumière vraie et directe de l'expression, et la lumière réfléchie de la méta-phore"[19] (32). With the blind man of Puiseaux, metaphor was a necessary supplement to inadequate denomination; with Saunderson it becomes an illuminating surplus as well, the bursting forth of linguistic energy beyond the speaker's designs. Saunderson himself "ne s'entendait qu'à moitié" and spoke metaphorically out of necessity, but he was thus able to provide his hearers with a felicitous double perspective.

The two poles of this figural economy coincide perfectly in foreigners, to whom Diderot compares the blind geometer and who are "forcés de tout dire avec une très-petite quantité de termes, ce qui les contraint d'en placer quelques-uns très-heu-reusement" (32).[20] Thus too for the imaginative author, beside whose creative inventiveness any language is "pauvre de mots propres" and who must resort to extraordinary forms of expres-sion. But like the foreigner, the writer risks a certain awkward-ness. His "tours de phrases," like those of Marivaux, may seem precious or obscure to a native reader, so that only a foreigner, his own knowledge of the lexicon deficient, will truly appreciate them. In both of Diderot's comparisons, the foreigner occupies the privileged position: creator like Saunderson of "expressions heureuses," the foreigner is also the ideal receiver of such fig-ures. Like the blind man, the foreigner relies on a limited range of terms, artfully combined.

Yet there is a slight problem in the analogy with Saunderson, for nothing in Diderot's presentation of the great mathemati-cian has authorized a comparison with the halting speech of for-eigners or the daring constructions of an author such as Mari-vaux whose style is best suited to English readers. Such a comparison would neglect the distinction drawn by Diderot be-tween the mathematical and the poetical uses of language. In the *Réfutation d'Hélvétius*, poetry and geometry are said to imply "des qualités contradictoires":

> Quelle est la fonction du géomètre? De combiner des espaces, abstraction faite des qualités essentielles de la matière; point d'images; point de couleurs; grande contention de tête, nulle émotion de l'âme. Quelle est celle du poète, du moraliste, de l'homme éloquent? De peindre et d'émouvoir. (*OC* 11:529)[21]

Geometry, the domain par excellence of abstraction, is the field in which the society "de cinq personnes dont chacune n'aurait qu'un sens" of the *Lettre sur les sourds et muets* could carry on intelligent conversation (*OC* 2:525). Between the language of four and five senses, then, the translation of a theorem in geometry would pose no problems, but the translation of poetic or eloquent language would not be so easy. In his "Eloge de Térence," Diderot laments the reductiveness of most translations, which take into account only the abstractable elements of a text. "Si un pédant s'empare d'un raisonnement de Cicéron ou de Démosthène, et qu'il le réduise en un syllogisme qui ait sa majeure, sa mineure et sa conclusion, sera-t-il en droit de prétendre qu'il n'a fait que supprimer des mots, sans avoir altéré le fond?" (*OC* 5:538).[22] The *expression heureuse*, providing a passage from the language of four senses to that of five, is in effect a means of translation. What works for Saunderson does not work so well for the imaginative writer; the former's "felicitous expressions" create a "double light," while the latter's turns of phrase risk falling into obscurity or preciosity.

Diderot's distinctions between the mathematical and the aesthetic, the translatable and the untranslatable, may be said to explain why a mode of language adequate to geometry can be only partially sufficient in literature. For Diderot, literary language could not be the purely representational language of general grammar. He wrote that no semiotic or conventional system (for example, the system of technical conventions in painting) was rich enough in signs to represent all reality directly, and he thus admired the "expression heureuse," the "hiéroglyphe syllabique" of poetry, the *faire* beyond technique of the greatest painters. But he demanded that in aesthetic works the *illusion* of representation be as developed as possible, that the gaps between signs be reduced to a minimum, that the use of artifice to bridge them remain unobtrusive. Thus in the *Lettre* and elsewhere he considers the blind excluded from the most important dimensions of aesthetic experience, even though their felicitous understanding of scientific concepts may be structurally analogous to the workings of literary language. The blind man of Puiseaux can judge symmetries by abstract reasoning, but "la beauté pour un aveugle n'est qu'un mot, quand elle est séparée de l'utilité" (3).[23] According to Diderot the aesthetic pleasures of the blind are severely limited. Their ideas of beauty are "moins étendues, mais plus nettes que celles des Philosophes clairvoyans" (4).[24] In his early aesthetic writings, Diderot defined aesthetic pleasure as deriving from the perception of relations, especially when this perception is rapid and greatly extended.[25] The blind may make such perceptions by touch, but they are necessarily much slower and more limited than the gaze of the eye, so that their aesthetic notions differ from those of the seeing not in kind but in degree, in intensity. In his article "Beauté" for the *Encyclopédie*, Diderot wrote:

> Il me semble qu'un aveugle a des idées de rapport, d'ordre, de symétrie, et que ces notions sont entrées dans son entendement par le toucher, comme dans le nôtre par la vue, moins parfaites peut-être et moins exactes: mais cela prouve tout au plus que les aveugles sont moins affectés du *beau*, que nous autres clairvoyans. (*OC* 15:110)[26]

The blind are hardly the vehicle for Diderot's expression of his aesthetic ideas. In this domain he constantly marks their difference from the seeing, whereas from observations on the language of the blind he proceeded by analogy to reflections on language in general. The blind in the *Lettre* cannot be taken as univocal symbols or spokesmen for any single position either accepted or rejected by Diderot. Rather, what is common to the linguistics and aesthetics of the blind must be seen as one of the poles structuring Diderot's often paradoxical writings on these topics. To summarize: the sign systems of the blind are poor in signs and rich (by necessity) in the abstractions and combinations that make up the formal structure of a system. Moreover, they must resort to figures to communicate with the seeing, and these figures must be interpreted in a process akin to translation. To study the language of the blind in a world of the seeing is to study language in an imperfect communicative situation where context can never be taken for granted, in which the perceptions and knowledge of codes possessed by sender and receiver displace pure reference. Diderot seems very close to accepting this view of sign systems as valid for natural languages, but he moves away from it when discussing aesthetic systems. The nature of human communication may have a large component of blindness, but it is the function of works of beauty to minimize or even transcend that aspect of language and signs, to render an illusion of presence. Philosophy is a different matter: the denial of blindness here would only perpetuate the illusory discourse of representation, which everyone can produce conventionally and claim to understand by assuming that others accept the same conventions. The *Lettre* exemplifies this differentiation of the philosophic from the aesthetic. It transforms a theatrical spectacle or *discours académique* intended for a general audience into an epistolary *entretien* whose addressee is identified with a particular intellectual position.

Much of the letter is devoted to the influence of the number and characteristics of the senses on thought, understanding, and indeed on science and philosophy. Criticizing both Berkeley and Condillac, Diderot finds their theories of the senses especially inadequate. The former, in his view, simply denies the existence of a perceived external substance, while the latter simply affirms it. (Condillac's *Traité des sensations* was not to be published until 1754.) But both philosophers would take the senses to be a conduit, a clear passage (whether from spirit or matter) into consciousness. In one of the most far-reachingly modern sections of the letter, Diderot denies this notion of sensory immediacy and proposes that the reality of sensations is only a consequence of a system of differential perceptions. The blind man restored to sight, he writes, will not need the experience of tactile verification to recognize visually the form, extension, and even existence of objects, but he will require considerable experience with his eyes alone before reaching that stage. The linguistic analogy: words are attached to concepts not by reference outside the sign system, by denomination, but rather by the process of identifying their function within the system itself.

In denying that the blind man will see objects or images immediately after the operation, Diderot argues that the impression of a visual perception presence is formed only by experience, especially by the experience of difference in perception. He describes how the alternate appearance and disappearance of persons and objects gives babies the notion that things exist independently of perceptions:

> Les nourrices les aident à acquérir la notion de la durée des êtres absens, en les exerçant à un petit jeu qui consiste à se couvrir et à se montrer subitement le visage. Ils ont de cette manière, cent fois en un quart d'heure, l'expérience que ce qui cesse de paroître ne cesse pas d'exister: d'où il s'ensuit que c'est à l'expérience que nous devons la notion de l'existence continuée des objets. (53–54)[27]

Diderot thus claims that sensations form a system of signs no less arbitrary than those of language:

> Il faut donc convenir . . . que par conséquent on ne voit rien la première fois qu'on se sert des yeux . . . que c'est l'expérience seule qui nous apprend à comparer les sensations avec ce qui les occasionne; que les sensations n'ayant rien qui ressemble essentiellement aux objets, c'est à l'expérience à nous instruire sur des analogies qui semblent être de pure institution. (55–56)[28]

From these conjectures, Diderot concludes that touch could have a considerable role in establishing rapidly "la conformité de l'objet avec la représentation." Thus, to the extent that visual perceptions are nonmimetic signs, tactile perceptions can be brought into play as an outside reference. Yet Diderot considers such external reference, though expedient, to be inessential. Why? Because vision, despite the arbitrary acquired conventions on which it depends, has the capacity to be mimetically representative in and of itself:

> Le nier . . . ce seroit se dissimuler qu'il n'y a point de Peintre assez habile pour approcher de la beauté et de l'exactitude des miniatures qui se peignent dans le fond de nos yeux, qu'il n'y a rien de plus précis que la ressemblance de la représentation à l'objet représenté. (57)[29]

Apparently Diderot wants to have it both ways: perceptions resemble objects, perceptions are arbitrary signs of objects. Of course at a physiological level the paradox could be resolved by differentiating between the retinal image and the mental perception.[30] But the *Lettre* juxtaposes these opposing positions, the heterogeneity and the homogeneity of perceptions and objects. When the context is that of aesthetics, perceptions are said to resemble objects (the comparison between painting and the retinal image provides an example). In the far more numerous cases where the context is one of linguistic speculation, perceptions are taken as a system of arbitrary signs.

By examining forms of thought and knowledge in the blind, rather than simply considering them to be deprived of visual concepts but otherwise like the seeing, Diderot implies that the nature of the senses, considered both singly and collectively, has a shaping and transforming effect on what passes through them. In a Cartesian representation of the human being, a person born blind, deaf, and dumb would place the soul not in the pineal gland but at the fingertips (18). Moreover, such differences are not confined to notions concerning the body or the senses themselves:

> Je n'ai jamais douté que l'état de nos organes et de nos sens n'ait beaucoup d'influence sur notre métaphysique et sur notre morale, et que nos idées les plus purement intellectuelles, si je puis parler ainsi, ne tiennent de fort près à la conformation de notre corps. (12)[31]

This statement points both to Diderot's interest in the blind and to the importance of his work to the history of blindness, for unlike his philosophical predecessors he raises the possibility that blindness as a specific sensory handicap will have unique and to some extent physically determined mental consequences. For Diderot, blindness makes possible the transformation not only of ordinary perception and language but also of science and philosophy.

Blindness revokes the epistemological primacy of the visual and favors relational rather than representational thought; it also shifts the center of attention from the *status* of perceptions to the workings and interactions of the senses. When the blind man of Puiseaux is told about such optical instruments as telescopes and microscopes, he responds with a flurry of questions—logical to him but seemingly nonsensical to the seeing:

> Il nous demanda, par exemple, s'il n'y avoit que ceux qu'on appelle Naturalistes qui vissent avec le microscope, et si les Astronomes étoient les seuls qui vissent avec le télescope; si la machine qui grossit les objets était plus grosse que celle qui les rapetisse; si celle qui les rapproche étoit plus courte que celle qui les éloigne. (5)[32]

The questions on size may be regarded as simply "unfelicitous expressions" in which the metaphoric light is deceptive. The questions about the users of the instruments, however, imply that the competence of the subject is a factor in perceiving and knowing, and they recall optical images used by Diderot in earlier writings. In the *Pensées philosophiques*, discussing the type of mind suited to skepticism, he had remarked, "Chaque esprit a son télescope" (*OC* 1:285). In *Les Bijoux indiscrets*, the *insulaires* are a race whose bodies incorporate the instruments of their science or profession:

> Chacun avait apporté en naissant des signes de sa vocation; aussi en général on y était ce qu'on devait être. . . . Ceux que la nature avait destinés à la géométrie avaient les doigts allongés en compas; mon hôte était de ce nombre. Un sujet propre à l'astronomie avait les yeux en colimçon; à la géographie, la tête en globe; à la musique ou à l'acoustique, les oreilles en cornet; à l'arpentage, les jambes en jalons. . . .
> (*OC* 1:763)[33]

The description of this natural scientific paradise amounts to a hyperbolic and ironic example of what Foucault has called "la prose du monde," a discourse of the world as structured by ubiquitous natural signs of analogy, resemblance, and correspondence. The analogism here does not undercut the classical *épistémè* or even sensationalism; its polemical force is directed against the prejudices and rigidities of a society like the "Congo" (France), where "tel qui ne voit non plus qu'une taupe, passe sa vie à faire des observations"[34]—in other words, against an order that obstructs the working of representation (*OC* 1:763). The notion of the fitness of the observer, which in the *Bijoux* is an ironic critique of the institutions of opacity, becomes in the *Lettre* a critique of the epistemology of transparency.

In the metaphorics of the *Lettre*, optical instruments that extend, intensify, or invert vision are to the unaided eye as sight is to blindness. The seeing understand Saunderson's courses more easily than the blind, because "ils ont un télescope de plus" (31). As David Berry has observed, the prism is used in Diderot's writings as a metonymy for Newtonian science.[35] The special vision afforded by the optical device can also be identified with the special competence of the scientist or *philosophe* (Saunderson as privileged subject for the Cheselden experiment). Of course, the optical device may also be an instrument of mystification, as may be the appeal to an additional sense. A sighted visitor to a country of blind people "leur annonceroit tous les jours quelque nouveau mystère qui n'en seroit un que pour eux" (14–15).[36] Were his fifth sense a fabrication and were the blind to believe him, he would have performed an act of mystification. In the *Promenade du sceptique*, the believers of the "Allée des épines" consider the blindfold they wear to be an optical instrument of revelation, illumination, insight: "On prétend [que] . . . loin de priver de la vue, on aperçoit, à travers, une infinité de choses merveilleuses, qu'on ne voit point avec les yeux seuls" (*OC* 1:329). Optically, such a blindfold is a "verre à facettes" or a "lanterne sourde" (*OC* 1:329, 367).[37] It is a machine for miraculously multiplying presence; with it one sees several beings joined into one (the three persons of the trinity), or "la présence d'un objet dans plusieurs endroits à la fois," or a similar prolif-eration and condensation of temporal states ("à le voir sans cesse et à être toujours aussi émerveillé que si on le voyait pour la première fois") (*OC*, 1:329, 367).[38] Christian theology takes on the properties of an illusory optical deformation.

The visual and optical metaphorics of the *Lettre*, when ex-amined in the context of other early works, are thus polemically multivalent. On the one hand, departures from the norm of di-rect and transparent perception imply complicity with religious superstition; a lack of visual capability stands for the suppres-sion of reason (the religious blindfold), while the illusions that nurture such a suppression appear to be the objects of excessive, deluded vision. On the other hand, both blindness and scientific optical instruments call the ubiquitous but naïve philosophical premises common to materialism and idealism into question, and go beyond common-sense understanding derivable from ordinary perception.[39] The consequent reversal may be prop-erly called dialectical, in that direct, unmediated perception, having been set against the doctrine of authority, becomes the object of a new, antithetical critique. In the *Promenade du scep-tique* we see primarily the first stage, but in the *Lettre* the two stages coexist, with the second finally dominant. This coexist-ence of opposing interpretive series, which generates the mul-tivalent figures, corresponds to the letter's polemical ambiva-lence. A critique of religious prejudices in the name of enlightenment, it also denounces a facile epistemology held to be almost a commonplace on the side of reason. Whence the text's beginning: the discrediting of an allegedly scientific ex-periment, wedded to the denunciation of the opacity of author-itative discourse.

The twofold working of sensory difference, alternately a sign of inferior and superior understanding, appears in its clearest and most paradoxical form in the passages of the *Lettre* concerning religion. In the first part of the text, moral, metaphysical, and theological ideas are said to be among those influenced by the number and form of the senses. The arguments mentioned briefly here are developed in the narration of Saunderson's deathbed dialogue with Holmes, a section widely held to be the most important in the work. It is not surprising that commentators have had difficulty determining just what Diderot meant by these sections, with their apparent internal contradictions. For the most part they have assumed that his real voice is that of atheism, that the arguments in favor of religious faith are advanced only for reasons of prudence. As such, of course, they proved to be inadequate, since Diderot was to spend three months imprisoned at Vincennes as a result of the letter's publication.

Diderot points out that the blind do not have the same reasons for believing that the seeing have: "Ce grand raisonnement qu'on tire des merveilles de la nature, est bien foible pour les aveugles" (14).[40] The argument lost on the blind is, as Jacques Chouillet has noted, a platonic and esthetic one, the revelation of the good through the beautiful.[41] Now the blind, Diderot implies repeatedly, can regard as beautiful only what they already assume to be good, that is, useful. Lack of sight impairs the aesthetic faculty more than it does any other. When Saunderson rejects a belief based on "ce beau spectacle qui n'a jamais été fait pour moi" and demands that God be made palpable rather than visible, Holmes proposes that he consider the organization of his own body, but Saunderson simply replies, "Je vous le répète; tout cela n'est pas aussi beau pour moi que pour vous" (40).[42] Without denying the tactile perception of order, Saunderson refuses to accord it an aesthetic value. Thus the religion unsuitable for the blind is not the superstitious faith of the "Allée des épines" but deism, the *religion naturelle* founded on principles of harmony and order.

But alongside this fundamental argument against the religion of the senses and reason are others more appropriate to religions of blindfolds and superstition. A sighted outsider in a country of blind people would have to keep silent to avoid being treated as a madman, for what he would have to say about vision would be beyond the understanding of his listeners. "Il leur annonceroit tous les jours quelque nouveau mystère qui n'en seroit un que pour eux, et que les esprits forts se sauraient bon gré de ne pas croire" (14–15).[43] The seeing visitor resembles the believer inspired by a vision beyond perception, who has difficulty conveying his insight to those who have only the usual five senses. Diderot stresses this comparison in the seemingly pious sentence that follows: "Les Défenseurs de la religion ne pourroient-ils pas tirer un grand parti d'une incrédulité si opiniâtre, si juste même à certains égards, et cependant si peu fondée?" (15).[44] This argument places those who deny the truth of religion in the position of blind people who deny the existence of light. But such a denial is in a sense totally logical, and Diderot may be suggesting that atheism is equally logical for those equipped with five senses. Indeed, this idea was to be stated explicitly by the Marquis de Sade: "Dieu n'existe donc pas plus pour l'homme que les couleurs pour un aveugle de naissance, l'homme est donc aussi en droit d'affirmer qu'il n'y a pas de dieu, que l'aveugle l'est d'assurer qu'il n'y a point de couleurs."[45]

Though Sade's argument is implicit in the *Lettre*, Diderot does not develop it here. Instead he emphasizes the resemblance of a sighted person among the blind to a rational deist whose teachings are rejected and ridiculed by the blindfolded fanatics of the "Allée des épines." The comparison to a prophet among skeptics turns out to be the bait in an argumentative trap for the defenders of religion: "Si vous vous prêtez à cette supposition, elle vous rappellera sous des traits emprunté l'histoire et les persécutions de ceux qui ont eu le malheur de rencontrer la vérité dans les siècles de ténèbres, et l'imprudence de la déceler à leurs aveugles contemporains." (15).[46] Accepting the pious argument implies accepting the parallel with those who, like Galileo, have been persecuted by a blind religion. Diderot has used the double edge of his comparison to impale religion on a dilemma. On the one hand, it claims to be an additional and superior form of vision, occupying the place of a sixth sense; on the other hand, it is simply a refusal to use the eyes, a reduction to four senses. If the reader wants to accept the notion of a superior vision, she must concede the self-inflicted blindness. If on the contrary one assumes that a belief in God derives simply from beholding with five senses the ordered beauty of nature, a naturally blind informant points out that this faith is no less relative than any other. Like language, beauty, and truth, religion is shown to be not universal but rather dependent on the ideas and characteristics of those who practice it.

Saunderson's physical blindness, his lack of eyes, makes him reject the deism underlying Holmes's remarks on the beauty and organization of the universe. "Voyez-moi bien, M. Holmes, je n'ai point d'yeux. Qu'avions-nous fait à Dieu, vous et moi, l'un pour avoir cet organe, l'autre pour en être privé?" (43).[47] Although not presented until three pages after the minister had proposed "le mécanisme admirable de vos organes" as a sign of divine order, this moving declaration is Saunderson's response to that argument, a response far more satisfying than his earlier refutation of the esthetic argument ("cela n'est pas aussi beau pour moi"). Saunderson is himself a monster, an irregularity of nature, a burr in the universal clockwork. The problem of monsters was crucial in the first half of the eighteenth century, not only to natural history but also to philosophy. As a mechanistic theory of order replaced older theologies, the universality and perfection of such an order became more and more important, the existence of monsters more and more scandalous.[48] With the concept of God so nearly assimilated to a clocklike regulatory order, the disruption of natural law appeared to be an almost insurmountable obstacle to deistic faith.[49] Thus, in making Saunderson his "spokesman" and his blindness the basis of a key argument, Diderot was situating his work in the context of an already influential critique of mechanistic deism.

If men find the animal mechanism astonishing, its order divine, says Saunderson to his listeners, "c'est peut-être parce que vous êtes dans l'habitude de traiter de prodige tout ce qui vous paroît au-dessus de vos forces" (40).[50] He notes that people have been unable to conceive of how he performs geometry. They assume that it is beyond the capabilities of someone with four senses and so must be miraculous, whereas he finds nothing extraordinary about it. Saunderson effectively reduces the minister's argument (which had been Diderot's own in the eighteenth of the *Pensées philosophiques*)[51] to a Cartesian argument in which God is proved by the existence of a concept superior to human understanding. Saunderson, who understands optical phenomena that would seem to be beyond his grasp, finds no reason for this leap into metaphysics and considers it a sign of human pride:

> Un phénomène est-il, à notre avis, au-dessus de l'homme? nous disons aussi-tôt, c'est l'ouvrage d'un Dieu, notre vanité ne se contente pas de moins: ne pourrions-nous pas mettre dans nos discours un peu moins d'orgueil et un peu plus de philosophie?[52] (40)

Now earlier in the letter it appeared that the defenders of religion could use the analogy of a sighted visitor in a land of blind people to show that what is not apparent to five senses may yet be real and true. Saunderson needs no such visitor. By using a little more philosophy than most men, he understands what is beyond his senses without invoking a transcendent knowledge beyond sensation. Thus the analogy with men of five and four senses could at most imply that what is beyond five senses is simply the province of a sixth or a seventh, not that it requires postulating a supreme being. The position of the deist in the earlier discussion concerning the man from Puiseaux was that of the ordinary, rational user of five senses. In Saunderson's discourse, the deist's error is to take those five senses for a valid measure of the universe. The existence of the blind shows that "human nature" can no more validly be used as the measure of the universe than as the basis of a general psychology or a referential language. Deism, the religion claiming the greatest generality and the greatest immediacy to human understanding, becomes simply the discourse produced by a certain common set of perceptual faculties.

But the minister tries one last, best argument: Newton, Leibnitz, Clarke and others esteemed by Saunderson believed an intelligent being to be the creator of nature in all its order. Conceding the strength of this argument, Saunderson nonetheless protests "que le témoignage de Newton n'étoit pas aussi fort pour lui, que celui de la nature entière pour Newton" (41).[53] Newton may see, but Saunderson can only listen. For the blind, rational faith is reduced to an uncritical faith like that of the "Allée des épines," to an extreme act of trust in the speech of others. The example of Réaumur's lectures at the text's beginning had already identified hearing as the sense par excellence for the reception of dogma. Saunderson then undercuts the position of the five-sensed philosophers by evoking past states of an ever-changing universe whose present order is only transitory, thereby introducing his famous and powerful defense of transformist materialism.

The status of Saunderson's arguments in the *Lettre* and in the development of Diderot's thought has given rise to considerable disagreement, for although the blind man moves the minister and others present to tears with his doubts, he finally calls on the God of Clarke and Newton to ask for mercy, and the narrator argues that this profession of faith constitutes a potent argument against atheism. This reversal has often been taken to be a precautionary step on Diderot's part, a veil hastily thrown over the powerfully expressed atheism of Saunderson.[54] It has also been read as indicative of Diderot's continuing attachment to deism, or at least to order.[55] According to this reading, the clash would be an embryonic dialogue in which Diderot presents another position that interests him but that he himself cannot yet adopt. What is at issue in the present discussion, however, is not Diderot's opinion but the structure of the *Lettre* and especially the role of the blind man, the way in which the discourse of Saunderson is related to the overall enterprise of the text, and hence the relation between blindness and the writing of philosophy.

Diderot's arguments in favor of belief are in several points reminiscent of the earlier discussion of religion and the blind, and even of passages in the *Promenade du sceptique*. In those texts the defenders of religion were to take comfort in the disbelief of the blind when confronted with reports concerning sight; now they are to rejoice at the blind man's faith in what Newton and Clarke have concluded from using their eyes. The parallel is subversive even beyond its overt contradiction, for we are reminded also of the five-sensed deist of the *Promenade*, unable to convince the self-blinded *dévot*. Saunderson has not willfully renounced any of his senses, and his superiority over a blind atheist comes from his willingness to listen to the deists. "La *voix* de la nature se fait *entendre* suffisamment à lui [Saunderson], à travers les organes qui lui restent, et son témoignage n'en sera que plus fort contre ceux qui ferment *opiniâtrement* les oreilles *et* les yeux" (45; emphasis added).[56] The critique of *dévots* (who close their eyes) becomes the critique of atheists (who close their ears) insofar as both refuse to exercise their senses and reason. Even had he remained an atheist until the end, Saunderson would hardly have been subject to such a reproach; thus even in calling on God he confounds the dogmatists of both parties.

But to his rational and philosophic arguments concerning God and the universe, Saunderson adds his inspired deathbed evocation of a disordered and material world. The connection between blindness and an intuition of materialism is stressed throughout the *Lettre*, so that once again Sauderson's speech cannot be read correctly if taken as an isolated or even uniquely privileged section. In the first part of the text, arguing that metaphysical ideas are shaped by the form of the senses, Diderot had suggested that the dualistic separation of thought and matter would be unfamiliar to the blind: "Comme ils voient la matière d'une manière beaucoup plus abstraite que nous, ils sont moins éloignés de croire qu'elle pense" (14).[57] Tactile "sight," by not transmitting secondary qualities such as light and color, produces a more abstract, geometrical notion of matter. But, more significant, Diderot has already stated that a blind Descartes would locate the soul in the fingertips, that is, at the point of contact with matter, the point at which through the sense of touch the object and consciousness of the object appear to be united. Sight, on the contrary, separates the locus of consciousness from the matter perceived, thereby creating the opposition between the abstract and the concrete, and relegating matter to a concreteness experienced as cut off from and opposed to the thinking faculties of the mind.

Diderot returns to the problem of matter and thought near the end of the letter in his discussion of the Molyneux-Cheselden question and of the difficulty the blind would encounter in judging composite objects without experience. Once again the text is difficult and must be quoted at length:

Mais s'il est d'autant plus difficile à un aveugle-né, qui voit pour la première fois, de bien juger les objets, selon qu'ils ont un plus grand nombre de formes, qui l'empêcheroit de prendre un observateur tout habillé et immobile dans un fauteuil devant lui, pour un meuble ou pour une machine; et un arbre, dont l'air agiteroit les feuilles et les branches, pour un être se mouvant, animé et pensant? Madame, combien nos sens nous suggèrent de choses, et que nous aurions de peine, sans nos yeux, à supposer qu'un bloc de marbre ne pense ni ne sent! (66–67)[58]

We encounter here another reference to the superficial theatricality of this kind of experiment and to the incompetence of its witnesses, for when the blind man's eyes are opened, the first object before them is a pompous and inanimate spectator who seems to be nothing more than part of his armchair. In this passage it is not the absence of sight, but its first exercise, that reverses the customary notions of animate and inanimate beings. Sight makes possible a distinction based on movement, but this distinction proves to be erroneous. The block of marble of the last sentence must be compared not to the swaying tree but to the human fixture, since only by *looking* at them does one conclude that both are inanimate. Diderot thus draws an analogy between a commonly held assumption (that a block of marble doesn't think) and an obvious error containing a grain of truth (that a spectator is a machine or piece of furniture). Ostensibly, he denies that this kind of judgment can be based on direct perception, but he implies surreptitiously that sight is the chief source of errors in these matters and that perhaps the blind intuition of thinking matter is no less reliable.

From thinking and feeling matter it is but a short step to the self-animated, self-transforming matter of Saunderson's intuited universe. Denying the hypothesis of a permanent universal order because of the occurrence of "productions monstrueuses" like himself, the geometer prefers the invisible past to the visible present as the terrain of his dispute with the minister: "Vous n'avez point ici de témoins à m'opposer, et vos yeux ne vous sont d'aucune ressource" (41–42).[59] This turn away from observable phenomena is more than a rhetorical tactic suited to Saunderson; it is a comment on the changing aims and status of contemporary science. As François Jacob has noted in his "history of heredity," mechanistic natural history, in which the order and form of living things were assumed to be eternal, took as its object the *visible* structure of plants and animals: "Reduced to the knowledge of the visible structure of living beings and to the laws of mechanics, the seventeenth-century scientist was led to relegate real generation, which organizes living beings from matter, to the domain of prime causes; and these he refused to consider."[60] The shift in interest to the cataclysms producing changes in living forms, an interest that Diderot shares with Buffon and Maupertuis, is thus a shift way from a science of the purely visible: the blind Saunderson is an appropriate spokesman for this new science.[61]

Beginning with the "ancien et premier état sur lequel vous n'êtes pas moins aveugle que moi" (41),[62] he shifts gradually from the hypothetical to the prophetic mode, at first repeatedly introducing his statements as conditional ("si nous remontions . . . Cela supposé, si . . ."). Only after evoking his own concrete blindness and thereby winning the sympathy of his audience does he take "un ton un peu plus ferme" and ask the listeners, in a series of imperatives, to follow him to the intuitive world of his conjectures ("O Philosophes, transportez-vous donc avec moi . . ."). Finally, he abandons even the pretense of a fiction and refers directly to the world. From this visionary outburst, with its repeated exclamations, he passes directly into a final delirium "dont il ne sortit que pour s'écrier: '*O Dieu de Clarke et de Newton, prends pitié de moi!*' et mourir" (44).[63]

Saunderson's frenzied outburst culminating in delirium must be regarded as akin to madness, dream, even ecstasy, for he has become disengaged not only from sight but from the other senses as well, and in his final sentence he casts aside all spatial and temporal reference: "Le temps, la matière et l'espace ne sont peut-être qu'un point" (44). In *Le Rêve de D'Alembert*, Diderot was to identify the collapse of dimensionality with the inward collapse of the psychic apparatus in madness or meditation:

Bordeu: Par exemple, si l'origine du faisceau rappelle toutes les forces à lui, si le système entier se meut, pour ainsi dire à rebours, comme je crois qu'il arrive dans l'homme qui médite profondément, dans le fanatique qui voit les cieux ouverts, dans le sauvage qui chante au milieu des flammes, dans l'extase, dans l'aliénation volontaire ou involontaire.
Mlle de l'Espinasse: Hé bien?
Bordeu: Hé bien, l'animal se rend impassible, il n'existe qu'en un point. (*OC* 8:130–131)[64]

Thus the apology of atheism comes in the form of a mystical, ecstatic discourse, structured more like a prophecy or predication than a reasoned argument. As in D'Alembert's oneiric exclamations, as in the *adieux du vieillard* in the *Supplément au voyage de Bougainville*, a powerful and emotional statement is inserted into an otherwise dialogical, ironic, rhetorically situated text. Saunderson's speech can be understood only as it is situated and integrated in the *Lettre*, yet its force is such that for a time this containing structure is forgotten in the apostrophe to the reader. There is, on the one hand, no adequate refutation of Saunderson; on the other hand, there is nothing to assure us that he speaks for Diderot. But the transformation evoked in Saunderson's speech—that of an ordered, created, deistic universe into a universe of continuous creation—parallels other transformations set in motion by the text: from representation to signification, from universal to situated discourse, from identity to difference, from visual experiment to dialogue.

Saunderson's speech can be divided into rational arguments against the hypothesis of order, and a poetic evocation of chaos, just as religious discourse could be separated, for Diderot, into its deistic and superstitious components. Thus the prophetic vision of disorder can be read as the mirror image of the religious dogmas or order. The blind man functions as an antiprophet, his admittedly delerious visions annihilating the doctrines of the church—by implication equally delerious—in favor of the nearly total skepticism with which the letter ends.[65] What remains is at most the dialogue of order and disorder, of culture and nature, in which science, philosophy, and language have no claim to universality but can create intelligibility under the right circumstances.

In making Saunderson a prophet of materialism, Diderot is of course using the ancient myth of the blind seer, and he makes this explicit by referring to Tiresias among the famous blind men of antiquity:

> . . . quelques autres qui ont paru si fort élevés au-dessus du reste des hommes, avec un sens de moins; que les Poëtes auroient pu feindre sans exagération, que les Dieux jaloux les en privèrent, de peur d'avoir des égaux parmi les mortels. Car qu'étoit-ce que ce Tirésie qui avoit lu dans les secrets des dieux et qui possédoit le don de prédire l'avenir, qu'un Philosophe aveugle dont la Fable nous a conservé la mémoire? (39)[66]

Several concepts here are important to Diderot's rhetorical relationship with his blind men. The tradition of blindness as divine punishment for visionary insight is indeed said to be a poetic construction, but not an unreasonable one; the poets have only embellished a reality that Diderot's own text has substantiated. Like many critical thinkers of the eighteenth century, Diderot does not so much reject myth as he does correct it by replacing its fantastic components with rational, realistic ones. Prophecy can be a metaphor for more concrete supplements to blindness, such as the arithmetical tablets of Saunderson, whose abilities are regarded by some as magical. Diderot may be desacralizing Tiresias, but he is also appropriating him to the cause of the *philosophes*. This approach to the sacred parallels Diderot's critique of revealed religion, an unnecessary collection of lies from which he retains (at most) only the foundation, deism. Yet in appropriating the figure of Tiresias and the myth of divine punishment, he makes the *philosophe* into the rival of the gods, who in turn become little more than the enemies of the *philosophes*, the ones whom Voltaire portrayed so well. Diderot thus attempts to utilize the power of myth without making his text depend on it, indeed, even in the act of denying its mythical status. His stance with respect to Saunderson's discourse is the same, for he uses it to sweep away the claims of deism without endorsing its own truth.

The poetic topos of blindness reappears at the beginning of the discussion of the Molyneux problem, where Diderot rejects the testimony of an oculist's ignorant patient in favor of "les découvertes d'un Philosophe qui auroit bien médité son sujet dans l'obscurité; ou, pour vous parler le langage des Poëtes, qui se seroit crevé les yeux pour connoître plus aisément comment se fait la vision" (47).[67] The "language of poets" evokes Oedipus, whose self-blinding coincided with his attainment of insight concerning himself, but in Diderot's incipient version of the myth there is no father to kill or mother to marry, no sun-god Apollo to drive the hero to blind himself, only a *philosophe* meditating tranquilly in the darkness. Diderot is of course advocating a comparative method over the sensory empiricism implied by such experiments as Réaumur's, but he is also reintegrating, as he does in presenting the deathbed delirium of the "Philosophe aveugle" Saunderson, the tradition of philosophy as meditation bordering on madness, on the detachment of the psyche from the perceptions of the senses. "Philosopher c'est apprendre à mourir," wrote Montaigne following Cicero, both because contemplation draws the soul away from the body and because the philosopher does not fear to die. The *Lettre* makes a similar connection between blindness and death. "Je renonce sans peine," Saunderson tells his family, "à une vie qui n'a été pour moi qu'un long désir, et qu'une privation continuelle"[68] (46). To be blind is to be contemplative; to meditate is to put out one's eyes. In his *Eléments de physiologie*, Diderot writes: "Il fait nuit en plein midi dans les rues pour celui qui pense profondément, et nuit profonde" (*OC* 13:809).[69] But Diderot's explicit reference to the "language of poets" desacralizes the notion of philosophy as meditation by distinguishing between the mythic tradition and the philosophic method. Blindness as transcendent insight is replaced by blindness as groping approach to truth. In *De l'interprétation de la nature*, blindness serves to figure the superiority of a philosophic method:

Nous avons distingué deux sortes de philosophies, l'expérimentale et la rationnelle. L'une a les yeux bandés, marche toujours en tâtonnant, saisit tout ce qui lui tombe sous les mains, et rencontre à la fin des choses précieuses. L'autre recueille ces matières précieuses, et tâche de s'en former un flambeau; mais ce flambeau prétendu lui a, jusqu'à présent, moins servi que le tâtonnement de sa rivale, et cela devait être. (*OC* 2:728)[70]

The so-called torch leads to bold but unsubstantiated pronouncements, dogmatic in the manner of Réaumur's lectures. The metaphorical use of blindness has here come full circle from the *Promenade du sceptique*, for the torch has replaced the blindfold as the sign of dogmatism, and philosophy no longer risks becoming a secular equivalent of religious illumination.

The Molyneux problem had been a thought experiment, not an inquiry into blindness but a means of inciting the seeing to take stock of their own ideas. For most of the writers and philosophers who considered the problem in the eighteenth century, the difference between the blind and the seeing was not crucial, in that blindness was simply the absence of sight, and thus the potential for sight was unsullied by experience. Diderot's *Lettre sur les aveugles* differs strikingly from these writings by approaching the blind as individuals having a different representation of the world, different ideas, a different language. Thus blindness does not offer a direct solution to the problems of vision, and the seeing do not provide a model with which to imagine and understand the blind. Only once, in a letter to Voltaire defending the *Lettre* against the charge of atheism, does Diderot attempt to apply his own experience directly to understanding the blind. Explaining to Voltaire that Saunderson must be excused his disbelief in God, he writes: "C'est ordinairement pendant la nuit que s'élèvent les vapeurs qui obscurcissent en moi l'existence de dieu; le lever du soleil les dissipe toujours; mais les ténèbres durent pour un aveugle, et le soleil ne se lève que pour ceux qui voyent" (89).[71] It is curious that Diderot had mentioned Saunderson's ability to sense by his skin the presence of clouds covering the sun, a fact which confirms that this passage is less about the blind than about the seeing. Indeed, it is perhaps the only *explicit* example in Diderot's work of an approach to blindness that would be widespread in both the treatises and literary works of the early nineteenth century: writing speculatively or imaginatively about the blind by projecting onto them the experience of the seeing self.

For the blind, as Others, are both like and unlike this self, and if Diderot emphasizes difference over identity, this is not to proclaim his separation from the blind but to underscore the philosophical implications of difference in general. There is no way to determine how seriously Diderot took his stance against Saunderson's atheism, but the dependence of abstract (and specifically religious) concepts and language on individual forms of sensory experience is undoubtedly central to the *Lettre*. The experience of blindness may enable the seeing philosopher to understand the Other, the blind person, on the latter's own terms, but it also enters into the formation of a "perspective" both sighted and blind. The philosopher attempts to create an understanding out of the dialogue of day and night, of seeing and unseeing, just as the nursery game of disappearance and return teaches the child of the existence of objects. The letter's title suggested a simple reversal: the blind were to guide the seeing. But the text's complexity, its dizzying succession of double-edged arguments and figures, forces the reader to occupy alternately both positions, and thus to confront the experience of differences so pervasive as to discredit the kind of universalizing discourse concerning the mind and the senses that had made the Molyneux problem possible.

· 3 ·

CURING BLINDNESS:
A MODERN MYTH

The blind can be cured, the blind can communicate intelligently with the seeing; their experience can even help the seeing to understand themselves. These changed ideas about blindness, though arising from science and philosophy, were not limited to these domains in their consequences. Even the brief accounts of the cataract operations performed by Grant and Cheselden displayed a sentimental and personal side of the interest in cures of blindness. Simply stated, curability modifies the imaginary conception of the blind by the seeing, and alters their status in society. Not all the blind can actually be cured, of course, but the *possibility* of cure changes the very concept of blindness. If it is sometimes within the power of science to abolish the difference between the blind and the seeing, then that difference can no longer be attributed wholly to forces beyond social or intellectual control; science and society begin to attain mastery over blindness. The blind can henceforth be integrated into a social order claiming to be transparent to itself, instead of being excluded by the very obscurity of their unknown and unexplored difference. That difference, explored by the philosophers, had been reduced to little more than a means of validating the sensory experience and acquired ideas said to be the property of each individual. Thus, to imagine or conceive of blindness was to confirm the transparency of the visual world to the seeing subject. The new image of the blind, like the intellectual interest in them, centers on the moment of their "conversion" to sight, on the power of this moment to verify the sensory origin of ideas and emotions.

In the farces of the medieval stage, in the picaresque novel, the blind had been comic, grotesque, often roguish or villainous figures, capable of evoking laughter but also scorn and revulsion. Now they were to become the heroes and heroines of the romantic plot in popular plays derived from *commedia dell'arte* scenarios. Sentimental relations between the sexes are the major theme of literary works in which the cure of blindness plays a part, both because this was the major theme of the kind of popular literature in which these cures became a topic and because the "awakening" to sight offered a particularly propitious moment for emotional or erotic revelations. The article from the *Tatler*, translated in the *Encyclopédie* and republished many times,[1] showed that love, in the absence of sight, could be portrayed as more virtuous, more amenable to fidelity and sentimental attachment, than the visually inspired seductions of the seeing. Even more important, the cure of blindness could add special intensity to the first meeting of the eyes, a moment traditionally given special attention in the literary representation of love. The cure of blindness thus marks the passage from one kind of idyllic love relation to another.

In verse, in novel, but most especially on the popular stage, the years from 1760 to 1830 were to witness a profusion of blind young lovers and beloveds, sometimes curable by potions or other magical remedies, but generally requiring the services of an oculist to restore their sight. The eye surgeon was to prove an ambiguous figure in this literature, sometimes a virtuous hero of enlightened science, sometimes a vain old schemer, sometimes an out-and-out charlatan. These varied presentations of the oculist appear to be inseparable from the ambivalent nature of the social integration, the desacralizing assimilation, of which he was cast as the chief agent. If the blind are to be brought from what was hitherto assumed to be an unknown and unknowable place of exclusion and placed in the world of the seeing, a number of questions arise. What are the motives of those who would make the blind like the seeing? What kind of society will they be entering? Is this transformation being performed in their interest? The oculist wields considerable symbolic power, with all the attendant possibilities for abuse and misrepresentation. The old farce routines in which the seeing deceive the blind can still be acted out, only in more subtle variations. After a *tour d'horizon* of sentimental mythmaking surrounding the cure of blindness, we shall examine a remarkable but little-known work from 1771, *L'Aveugle qui refuse de voir*, in which the critique of an unscrupulous oculist becomes a critique of the role of the Enlightenment in society.

There is no oculist, however, in *Sélim et Sélima*, a poem by Claude-Joseph Dorat about a young blind man and his beloved, first published in 1769. In this pastoral idyll, adapted from Christoph Martin Wieland's *Selim und Selima* (1752), the heroine herself provides the cure in the form of a magic herb to which she is led by a spirit who appears to her in a dream. Dorat's poem lacks the prologue that presents its German model as a religious apologue. Men alone among God's creation, we read in the opening section of Wieland's poem, are unsatisfied with the senses given them to delight in God's works; Selim's restoration to sight gives the visual universe the force of a miracle and leads him to give thanks to God for what others either take for granted or fail to notice. In removing the prologue and leaving only Sélim's concluding exhortation to love the Creator, Dorat makes the poem at most an illustration of a natural religion no longer residing in transcendence or in the sacred, but derived from sensitivity to the world as experienced by the senses. This natural world, as presented by Dorat, is above all the domain of the visible, so that to be blind is to be deprived of nature's spectacle:

> Esprit, grâces, noblesse, âme sensible & pure,
> Sélim rassembloit tout, hors cet organe heureux,
> Qui voit, parcourt, embrasse & la Terre & les Cieux,
> Et sans qui l'homme, hélas! est mort à la Nature.[2]

Yet Sélim expresses no regret, no complaints, consoled as he is by Sélima; the connections between blindness, sexuality, and the romantic couple, more than the awakening to the spectacle of nature, form the center of this work.

For Sélima, the blind Sélim is a providential gift, since he has all the virtues, attractions, and charms that she could desire, except sight, the absence of which deprives him of certain pleasures but deprives her of nothing. And so in her happiness and gratitude she asks him how he had come to love her, since love is an affair of the eyes:

Moi que tu n'as point vue, & qui ne sais qu'aimer,
Quel est donc mon secret pour t'avoir su charmer?[3]

Sélim answers that song and harmony had been since earliest infancy his greatest pleasures ("A peine je connus & je goûtai la
vie . . .") and that Sélima—whose name, by its resemblance,
suggests a sisterly relation—had thus been able to enchant and
captivate him both by the presence of her voice and by its absence, which he remedied in his fantasy:

Tu cessas, & je crus que j'allois cesser d'être.
Combien il m'échappa de pleurs & de soupirs!
Je cherchois cette voix qui m'avoit fait renaître;
J'avois, en la perdant, perdu tous mes plaisirs.
Je crus la retrouver, je crus encore l'entendre.
A mon illusion mon coeur abandonné
Chérissoit une erreur qui le rendoit plus tendre,
Et de ses mouvements il sembloit étonné.[4]

The mention of infancy, the allusion to rebirth, the importance
of fantasy, the family link suggested by the names—all these imply, in psychoanalytic terms, a relation to a love-object derived
without discontinuity from the primordial object relation to the
mother. The Freudian theory of object choice in love states that
although adult object choices may be attempts to recapture this
primordial relation, the two are sundered by discontinuities,
specifically by the liquidation of Oedipal sexuality under the
pressure of the castration complex. This split in object choice
can of course be denied in fantasy, and that indeed seems to be
the case in Dorat's poem, in which Sélim attaches Sélima's presence to the origins of his own sensations and consciousness.
The voice of Sélima is an extension of earliest wants and satis-
factions, a transition between fantasy and its realization. In
Wieland's original, it is in fantasy and dream that her voice,
hitherto only heard, becomes a bodily form, an object of love:

Bei Tag und Nacht umschwebte mich das Bild
Der Stimme, die mein Herz in seiner Schwärmerei
Mit einem Leib umgab. Im Träumen selbst
Besuchte mich die holde Sängerin,

Nahm meine Hand, zog sanft mich zu sich hin
Und sang das Lied; ich sass zu ihren Füssen
Und horchte still entzückt, bis Traum und Bild
Verschwand.[5]

I am not claiming to treat Wieland's or Dorat's poems as individual works that have a poetic coherence of their own. In shifting from one to the other I am reading them as one may read
two versions of a fairy tale, as partial textualizations of a mythic
construct not all of whose elements are incorporated in any one
version. For Sélim, blindness has created the form of his love for
Sélima. Because of it, he has loved her differently from anyone
else, and differently from the way he would have loved her had
he been able to see. With his eyes, he would have loved her for
her beauty, which the shepherds admire in classical, rhetorical
descriptions that for Sélim produce no meaning. As it is, he has
loved her without visual appropriation, without making her a
precise, sensory object that would have forced a disjunction between fantasy and reality, without risk of blindness as punishment for the erotic use of the eye. Since Sélim is already blind,
there is no Oedipus complex, no symbolic castration to
undergo—whence the nondisruptive transition between infantile fantasy and adolescent love described in his auditory seduction by Sélima.

If we now shift to Sélima's perspective, the way she cures her
lover suggests strongly that his blindness has been in some sense
the fulfillment of her wish—perhaps a wish to be loved for her
more spiritual attributes of song and voice rather than for her
physical beauty—since she seems able to cure him when she so
desires, immediately after he has told her how she had en-
chanted him:

Eh bien! dit-elle, Eh bien! mon Ami, prends courage,
L'espoir se glisse encor dans mon coeur amoureux;
Tu n'es pas loin peut-être, au moins je le présage,
D'obtenir, de goûter ce doux présent des Cieux.[6]

In attributing Sélim's blindness to Sélima's desires, I am undertaking an intersubjective reading modeled on Freud's interpre-

tation of "The Taboo of Virginity" in primitive societies. Freud proposed that ritual defloration was an evasive response to male anxiety, but that such anxiety could be accounted for only through the aggressiveness of the woman's desire (to appropriate the penis) and the inevitable disjunction between her own Oedipal object choice and the bridegroom. The taboo, with its accompanying ritual defloration by a priest or other father figure, would be a mechanism for acknowledging that disjunction and deflecting her aggression away from her husband.[7] Sélima, after expressing hopes for a cure, has a dream in which her *esprit tutélaire* appears to her, radiant with light and singing with the voice of a lyre, and explains that he has been her unseen but omnipresent companion since infancy:

Mes regards ont vu croître, & fleurir ta jeunesse,
Et dirigeant tes pas, quoiqu'absent de tes yeux,
Je t'ai, dès le berceau, prodigué ma tendresse.
Sur le sein de ta mère alors que tu jouois,
Oui, c'est moi, Sélima, moi, que tu caressois.[8]

For Sélima, who had already been compared to an angel by her lover, the Spirit seems to be a male counterpart to what she has been for Sélim: an original and invisible love-object providing an unbroken link between the pleasures of the mother's breast and the love-object of adulthood. The Spirit tells her that it was he who brought the two lovers together, as though authorizing her passage from an original (or transitional) love-object (himself) to a final one (Sélim). The religious idealization of Sélima and the Spirit suggests that the Christian symbolic equivalence of conversion, rebirth, and restoration of sight is at work in the poem, though in a somewhat secularized fashion, in that Sélim's cure gives him not Christian faith but a second birth and hence a second but original love-object. Or, one might say, original but curable blindness is the price paid to avoid the discontinuity induced by the castration complex and thus to elude the split, diphasic character of object choice. Sélim's blindness, and the dream figure who tells Sélima how to cure it, combine to produce an awakening into a libidinal paradise.

But in this paradise, once Sélim's eyes have been opened,

something has changed in his interaction with Sélima, who is no longer a voice and a pretext for fantasy, but an object of sight. Her charm had originally been as much in the moments of her absence as in those of her presence, for it was when the voice fell silent that fantasy enveloped it with bodily form. But when Sélim gazes on her eyes, he finds them at first unbearably dazzling, but then realizes that he cannot live without their presence:

> Je me sens éblouir... Ah! détourne leurs feux
> Arrête... que fais-tu?... J'ai perdu la lumière...
> Ne me les cache plus... Veux-tu donc mon trépas?...
> Que s'éteigne plutôt le Soleil qui m'éclaire!
> Mon âme est dans la nuit, quand je ne les vois pas.[9]

Blindness has thus served first to produce an amorous union characterized by childlike innocence and the absence of aggression, and then to heighten the erotic potential of the gaze once it can no longer be threatening to either partner. But the awakening to sight, however well prepared, does bring with it the demand for the presence of the beloved's eyes, felt to be as brilliant and as blinding as the sun. We have, in fact, a pastoral translation of the platonic fable of the cave: once the eyes have been brought into sunlight, once the sun has been acknowledged as a true point of origin, the former cave dweller is unwilling to return to the play of shadows and fantastic images from whence he came. Memories of the cave are banished from the new order ruled by the sun; in *Sélim et Sélima*, blindness or visual separation is now banished by the lovers, though it has been the determining factor in their history, in their coming into being as a couple.

In Fanny de Beauharnais's *L'Aveugle par amour* (1781) an oculist uses a substance made famous "par le petit Poème charmant de Sélim et Sélima" to cure the heroine's blindness. This undistinguished novel thus underlines the fact that the fictional appearance of ocular cures, though perhaps inspired by medical practice, can do without scientific verisimilitude. Moreover, *L'Aveugle par amour* demonstrates that the blindness cured in literary works need not be congenital, since its Eugénie has blinded herself (by means of a potion) upon learning from her fiancé that *he* had become blind. This revelation was false, a test of Eugénie's love invented by a wicked, older rival for the young man's affections. The lovers soon learn of the deception, and after the young man is dissuaded from in turn blinding himself, the two find themselves in a sentimental utopia similar to that of Sélim and Sélima, founded on the reduction of one partner's mental universe to the presence of the other. Eugénie exclaims:

Ô mon ami, quels plaisirs délicieux, quels divins ravisse-mens, quelle volupté pure! rien ne peut exister au-delà du bonheur que je goûte. Oui, oui, c'est dans ton âme qu'est mon univers; je le possède entier près de toi. Eh! crois-tu que j'envie au reste du genre humain la lumière dont tu ne te consoles point de me voir privée? Il est, il est, pour le coeur où tu règnes, une clarté plus douce, plus vive, plus durable.[10]

So great is her dependence on this idealization of her lover that when a half-volume's novelistic intrigues of more than usual ba-nality seem to have taken him from her, she refuses the aid of an oculist whom a suitably noble and virtuous benefactor has re-cruited. The treatment is finally applied while she is dying (of a broken heart, of course), and it succeeds only because the ben-efactor, omitting nothing in his quest for a happy ending, has fetched the fiancé as well:

O prodige! ô ravissement inattendu, & plus encore inex-primable!... Eugénie le nomme, elle l'aperçoit, leurs cris se répondent; ils se précipitent dans les bras l'un de l'autre; leurs baisers, leurs larmes, leurs coeurs enivrés s'unissent. ... Jamais, jamais, Amour, tu n'eus tant d'Ardeur . . . .[11]

The lovers are not the only beneficiaries of this secular miracle; their benefactor pays the oculist so well that he is rich to the end of his days. His essential role in this and other similar literary exploitations of blindness stems from the use of both unseeing eyes *and* eyes that see for the first time as devices to strengthen the sentimental exclusivity of the couple.

As the cure of blindness gave rise to a new and increasingly specific literary portrayal of the blind, the actual presence of a cure in that portrayal grew progressively less important. In two novels by Isabelle de Montolieu, *Sophie ou l'aveugle* (1812) and *Le Jeune Aveugle* (1819), we find identically idealized presentations of blind young girls, characterized by their innocence, goodness, sensitivity, intelligence, beauty, and so on, but in the former work the heroine marries, and in the latter an oculist cures her. These parallel destinies suggest implicitly the virginity symbolism of blindness that appears explicitly in the theater. Madame de Montolieu gives her Sophie two young admirers, one of whom marries her, while the other consoles himself with a bride possessed of particularly beautiful and sharp-seeing eyes. This beautiful Eléonore, however, has an eye for other men and for ruinously expensive interior decoration. Blindness appears to be little more than a device for ridding the middle-class bridegroom of his nightmares of cuckoldry and household expense by reducing his wife to a state of total dependence. Sophie is even called on to dissuade Eléonore from taking a lover; she not only succeeds, but goes so far as to convert the would-be seducer to a more virtuous attitude. The absence of sight confers on Sophie a moral authority within the two couples reminiscent of that of Julie d'Etange in *La Nouvelle Héloise*: "Les yeux d'Eléonore sont toujours beaux, et ne voient plus que ce qu'il faut voir; ceux de Sophie sont toujours fermés, mais son coeur y supplée: il sent tout, devine tout, et elle est vraiment notre ange tutélaire, le lien de notre heureuse société."[12] In *La Jeune Aveugle*, the cure does not do away with this special beauty, both physical and moral, of the blind girl, for even after the operation, "L'expression de sa physionomie et tous ses mouvemens avaient quelque chose de singulier et d'intéressant."[13] Thus although the derivative character of these novels with respect to the eighteenth-century fascination with the cure of blindness is evident, they are less concerned with the *moment* of first sight than with a stereotypical presentation of the blind derived from the fascination with that moment.

The restoration of sight as a spectacular moment was to enjoy its greatest literary fortune in the theater. Many of the plays involved are comedies, vaudevilles, and farces in which we find not only blind adolescents and their lovers and oculists, but also old, roguish, or duped blind men, descendants of the blind figures of medieval farce. Curable or not, the blind characters lend themselves to a kind of visual dramatic irony: scenes of deception and false recognition are played in full view of the audience, a device so obvious that it can be reversed, as in *L'Aveugle supposé* (1803), where a man in a shuttered room is persuaded that he has lost his sight.[14] The ability of the blind to supplant vision by skillful use of their other senses, discussed in almost every treatise about them from Diderot to the mid-nineteenth century and a frequent topic of digressions in fiction, is all but absent from these plays, which rely on the popular (and theatrically easy to exploit) notion of the blind as nearly incapacitated beings. The dramatic potential of cure far outweighs that of education or adaptation.

Cassandre oculiste ou l'oculiste dupe de son art, a one-act comedy and vaudeville staged in 1780, presents a surgical cure before a group of spectators (including Cassandre's fiancée Colombine) gathered in the doctor's office. The patient and the doctor's student, Isabelle and Léandre, are the play's romantic couple. Léandre comments on the worldly vogue of such scientific spectacles:

> Oui, dans ces circonstances,
>   Ne doutez pas
> Qu'ici vos connoissances
>   Portent leurs pas;
> Les femmes, les femmes sur-tout,
> Qui depuis un temps, pour briller en tout
>   Ont aux expériences
>   Su prendre goût.[15]

The oculist, after agreeing that Colombine and the rest of his audience are tedious bluestockings, confides to them his intention to marry Isabelle after curing her:

> Vous croyez qu'à son sujet
>   La gloire m'enflamme.

81

Mais sachez que mon projet
Est de mériter la main de cet objet.[16]

The surgical cure as equivalent to the patient's hand in marriage—in this belated *commedia* scenario we encounter an even clearer link in the chain of associations between blindness and virginity that will constitute a uniquely modern myth. But speaking to Isabelle, Cassandre associates this myth with an ancient one:

Tu me verras, je te jure,
Aussi-bien que je te voi.
A mon âme transportée,
Permets la citation,
Tu seras la Galathée
D'un nouveau Pygmalion.[17]

The cured patient would be awakened, reborn, to the sight of her healer and would-be lover, having seen or known no one before him. Just as the person born blind was supposed to present at least partially an epistemological *tabula rasa*, so the blind woman is assumed to offer a sexual and emotional *tabula rasa* equivalent to virginity, a condition deemed particularly important when the man who intends to win her is so old that no sighted young woman would want him.

The hymenal symbolism of the eye is not specifically modern and is expressed in words such as Greek *korē*, Latin *pupilla*, and Spanish *niña*, which signify both "young maiden" and "pupil of the eye."[18] Hagiography also provides examples of self-blinding as a sacrifice for virginity or a reaffirmation of chastity vows.[19] What arrives with the surgical cure of cataracts is a literal ocular equivalent of defloration. Since the concept of virginity includes the possibility of its loss, its symbolic equivalent must, to be fully adequate, present an analogous possibility—here, the cutting away of the clouded membrane by the surgeon's scalpel. In this comedy, however, Cassandre is unsuccessful, because he attempts to make the symbol function literally, only to discover that ocular virginity does not equal a total absence of ideas: Isabelle's fantasy image corresponds, predictably enough, not to the old doctor but to Léandre, who in a comic scene has already obtained kisses from her by imitating Cassandre's voice.

In other plays a cure of blindness is the price of a marriage for the oculist, but the bride is not herself the patient. Thus in *Cassandre aveugle* (1803) a servant claims to have become an oculist so as to cure his old master and obtain the object of his social and sexual desires: "Et moi je me suis fait oculiste, je lui ai promis de le guérir . . . et lui, en récompense, m'a promis la main de sa fille."[20] And in *Les Deux Aveugles* (1823), the unwilling fiancée of an old eye doctor demands the cure of the young man she loves as a condition of her marriage. After the operation, the doctor, suitably touched by the young couple, steps aside.[21]

The connection between blindness, virginity, and surgical cure is fully articulated in *Valérie* by Scribe and Mélesville (1822), doubtless the best known of these plays inspired by the cure of blindness. The heroine, blind since early childhood, had saved the life of a young man who, devoting himself to her out of love and gratitude, sets out from their native Germany for Paris to learn eye surgery from one of its most famous practitioners, only to be frustrated in his efforts:

> Mais bien différent de ces savans généreux qui croiraient trahir la cause de l'humanité en cachant une découverte utile, mon maître spéculait sur ses talens.... Il ne voyait que la fortune, les trésors; et avare de la science qui les lui procurait, il aurait cru s'appauvrir en la partageant avec moi...! Eh bien! cette science... je la lui dérobai![22]

Furtively reading the great man's papers and spying on his operations, the young Ernest de Halzbourg learns the technique of what is described as almost an occult science ("malgré lui je surprenais ses secrets") and returns to Germany to discover that he has inherited a fortune and could hire any surgeon in Europe. Now enters the connection between blindness and virginity, eye surgery and defloration. Ernest confides to a family friend: "Mais j'avais l'orgueil de croire en moi!... Et vous le dirai-je, madame, j'aurais été jaloux que celle que j'aime reçût d'une autre main que la mienne un pareil bienfait.... Il me semblait que ce prix m'était dû!"[23] This passage speaks for itself. It is significant, however (for here we again encounter elements of Freud's theory of the virginity taboo), that Ernest wants Valérie to believe that the operation will be performed by a friend of his—this because Ernest is anxious about his own ability to perform successfully in a moment of such great emotion. He believes that under these circumstances Valérie would be too fearful to undergo the surgery. She has, however, been eavesdropping on Ernest's conversation with her guardian, and she consents to the operation only after realizing that he will perform it, although she lets him continue the fiction about his friend. The circle of deception, or of anxiety-relieving fiction, is now complete: Valérie lets him think that he is letting her think that the operation is being performed by a friend—all this to protect them both from the anxiety he thinks she will feel if it is he, that she knows she would feel if it were not he, and that she realizes he would feel if he knew that she knew that it is he.

At the decisive moment of the operation, Ernest seems to be reduced to trembling impotence:

> *Ernest*: Arrivé à ce moment que j'ai tant désiré, je ne me reconnais plus...! toute ma résolution m'abandonne... je tremble....[24]

He overcomes this near-fiasco and applies the scalpel, only to be terrified of what ensues:

> *Ernest*: Un instant... je me suis flatté du succès.
> *Henri*: Eh bien...?
> *Ernest*: Qu cri qu'elle a jeté... j'ai fui épouvanté.[25]

What scribe shows us, then, is a young oculist-lover vacillating between the taboo and the overvaluation of virginity. Desiring to perform the operation himself as a means of assuring possession, Ernest worries about the reaction of his bride and patient and decides that it would be better to have her believe that the surgeon is someone else. Her reaction amounts to a denial of the sort of female aggression supposedly deflected by the taboo, though also an acknowledgment of how the fear of such aggression might be a factor in male impotence. The play thus reaffirms the dominant sexual custom of its public's culture: the overvaluation of virginity as a means of establishing, and with her own complicity, a wife's devotion to her husband, a husband's sexual possession of his wife.

Two imitations of *Valérie*, obviously designed to capitalize on the success of Scribe and Mélesville, also draw a connection between the surgical cure of blindness and the sexual appropriation of a virgin. *Valérien*, produced less than two months after *Valérie*, is a slightly disguised repetition of the earlier play in which the blind patient becomes the *brother* of the woman whom the oculist wants to marry, and because of whom he becomes an oculist (an apprenticeship that in this case takes six years). Like Valérie's Ernest, he combats anxiety with determination as he prepares to remove the cataracts: "Si mon courage ne m'abandonne pas, si ma main ne tremble point . . . je dois réussir."[26] In *M. Oculi, ou La Cataracte*, frankly labeled an "imitation burlesque de Valérie," the young gallant returns as an oculist only after growing old during an apprenticeship of fifteen years, and he firmly intends that he and no other should cure his future bride, Mademoiselle Cocotte. Monsieur Oculi de Bon Oeil encounters the same problem as "Cassandre oculiste"; the patient, upon seeing, first eyes a younger man, whom she says corresponds to her fantasies. The surgeon is no longer, as in *Valérie*, the male romantic lead, and though the patient resigns herself to marrying him, she warns that "ce ne sera que par reconnaissance, et je ne réponds pas des suites."[27] The excessive apprenticeship period and attendant transformation of the oculist into an old doctor of course satirizes the least believable aspect of *Valérie*, Ernest's unorthodox surgical education, but it also deflates the Scribe play's romantic treatment of marriage and virginity by condemning the husband to cuckoldry from the outset.

The theme of infidelity is in fact common in these plays with blind characters, and it serves as a counterpoint to the idealized and idyllic love that predominates in them. In *Cassandre oculiste*, the spectators warn the doctor that he should let the woman he wants to marry remain blind, since "Femme clairvoyante est souvent un fardeau." His reply unwittingly alludes to Léandre, who has just been kissing the patient:

> Morbleu! songez à quel point
> Une belle qui n'y voit point
> Peut se méprendre, quoique sage.[28]

This kind of humorous debate on the desirability of a blind spouse generally hinges on the traditional *commedia* juxtaposition of two ways of considering marriage—marriage as permanent love (the romantic theme), and marriage as institutionalized jealousy and cuckoldry (the comic theme)—with the main characters adopting the first assumption, their servants and confidants the second. In *L'Aveugle clairvoyant* (1082), Léonore cries out, "Epouser un aveugle! Ah! cette seule idée / Me fait frémir d'horreur,"[29] but Lisette has the practical answer: "Refuser un mari parce qu'il ne voit goutte! / Hélas! votre défunt ne voyait que trop clair, / Sur les moindres soupçons, toujours l'esprit en l'air."[30]

The dichotomy of idealized and low-comic presentations of blindness applies no less to the portrayal of the oculist, a portrayal that we have so far examined only in its sexual manifestations. The surgeon's role can be that of young lover, or old doctor and would-be husband; similarly, he can appear to be an almost saintly worker of good deeds, a vain and ambitious exploiter of patients, or even a charlatan. The real oculists, in their memoirs and treatises, did everything they could to encourage an exalted view of themselves. One of them, Jean-François Gleize, published alexandrines in his profession's honor:

> L'Oculiste possède un très-rare talent,
> Qui se fait en tous lieux désirer ardemment.
> Sa main fait un miracle éclatant sur la Vue,
> La faisant recouvrer lorsqu'on la croit perdue.
>
> . . . .
> Belle opération! inestimable cure,
> Qui rend soudain l'oeil clair, chasse la nuit obscure!
> O talent admirable! ô talent précieux,
> Qui donne au genre humain le jour sorti des cieux![31]

The oculist of *Les Aveugles de Franconville*, a one-act opera from 1802, cures without compensation a pair of poor, blind adolescent lovers in fulfillment of a promise he had made in prayer.[32] Similarly, in Madame de Montolieu's *La Jeune Aveugle*, the oculist refuses a large sum of money offered him by the girl's family.[33] More typical, however, is the fortune earned by the oculist of *L'Aveugle par amour*. The worldliness and self-interest of "Cassandre oculiste" are echoed in *Valérien*, in which a doctor explains how the cure of a single socially prominent person brought him more fame, clients, and wealth than years of healing the poor. And from the self-taught or amateur oculists of *Cassandre aveugle*, of *Valérie* and its imitations, it is but a short step to the fake oculists of *L'Aveugle supposé* and *Les Trois Aveugles* (1824). In this latter vaudeville, a local barber and tailor confronts three false blind men by threatening to operate on their eyes. When the first of them, Nicholas, who is terrified of being actually blinded by the scalpel-wielding Flanelle, suddenly "begins" to see, the charlatan ironically takes credit for the cure:

> *Flanelle*: Jeune homme, j'espère que vous n'oublierez jamais que c'est à moi que vous devez la vue, je vous ai opéré.
> *Nicolas*: Oui, vous êtes un fameux oculiste![34]

It is not surprising that, in view of the superficial vogue enjoyed by cures of blindness, the term *oculiste* underwent considerable discredit in the medical profession and came to denote a practitioner of cures of blindness and other eye remedies lacking in general medical training and competence. The physicians Guérin (1769) and Guillié (1820) deplored the fact that care of the eyes had been so often left to the oculists, whom the former calls "des empiriques dépourvus des connoissances nécessaires."[35]

Nowhere, however, does the figure of the oculist receive more criticism than in the Chevalier de Cerfvol's *L'Aveugle qui refuse de voir* (1771). The narrative consists primarily of two dialogues in which an ambitious oculist attempts to persuade a blind beggar to undergo a cataract operation, and the unwilling patient explains the reasons for his refusal. At issue here is not the doctor's medical competence, but his role as a representative of society. The blind man and the oculist, in their discussions, consider sight to be not a sensory or psychological matter but a means of participating in a certain kind of social and economic system. More than any other eighteenth-century text, this little work presents the integration of the blind into the world of the seeing as a sociopolitical act. The text functions allegorically as a critique not only of specific manifestations of reformist ideas but also of the enlightenment political project in its broadest sense.

Cerfvol directs some of his attacks at the physiocrats, that group of liberal economists who under Louis XV theorized that all wealth is fundamentally agricultural and advocated a free-market approach to the grain trade. Their reforms were to a degree tried out by the Choiseul ministry in the late 1760s and the Turgot ministry of 1774–1776, but were never really accepted by the monarchy. The physiocratic movement split the ranks of the *philosophes*, with Diderot and Madame d'Epinay (but not Grimm) opposing the free trade of grain. In *L'Aveugle qui refuse de voir*, physiocracy is designated both directly and by allusions to a contemporary civil disaster. On May 30, 1770, during the public festivities marking the dauphin's marriage to Marie-Antoinette, two enormous crowds of revelers attempted to pass in opposite directions on the same street. In the resulting stampede, hundreds of Parisians were trampled to death. The abbé Galiani, a foe of the physiocrats and the most famous conversationalist of his era, wrote of the catastrophe in *La Liberté des bagarres*, an almost sentence-by-sentence parody of the physiocrat Lemercier's *La Liberté du commerce des blés*.[36] Galiani wittily attacks the decontrol of grain prices by alluding to the consequences of the decontrol of large crowds. The oculist of *L'Aveugle qui refuse de voir* allies himself both with physiocracy and with the events of May 30. In attempting to persuade the blind man to swell the ranks of the seeing, he makes only a perfunctory reference to the beauties of nature before launching into a grandiose description of the pleasures of appearance in society, making particular reference to *royal ceremonies* and to *walking*:

> Je passe sous silence la pompe du Souverain & celle des principaux personnages de l'Etat. . . . Je ne parlerai que de ces plaisirs qui sont à portée de tous les ordres de citoyens. Il en est un dans le nombre que chaque particulier peut se procurer à son choix & sans bourse délier: c'est celui de la promenade. Je voudrais seulement que vous vissiez dans une heure décente ces boulevards, ces jardins consacrés à l'amusement public: vous ne pourriez plus vous résoudre à en être privé. C'est un tumulte, un tintamarre, une poussière....[37]

The oculist becomes the spokesman of a society glorifying in the rituals of self-representation and the illusion of social mobility, a spectacle where common people are invited to the sovereign's feasts, where a marquis passes for a farmer, and a merchant for a nobleman. When the blind man, in his rebuttal, denounces society's deceptions as a network of disorder, vice, and injustice, the oculist blithely alludes to reform and to the physiocrats' *bon prix*: "Vous me paraissez trop instruit, pour n'avoir pas connaissance des divers systêmes de Physiocratie que nous ont donné de laborieux Ecrivains, & suivant lesquels les moeurs & le bon ordre seront bientôt rétablis."[38] The reference is ironic, since physiocratic doctrines had to an extent become policy, without producing the expected immediate improvements. Moreover, the oculist has already been presented as a useful servant and flatterer of those in power. He has treated, without attacking the cause of the ailment, a lord whose vision had become inflamed by philosophy, cured an *abbé* by prohibiting strenuous reading and study, and improved a magistrate's eyesight without accusing the obscurity of the statute books. The oculist thus becomes a kind of *philosophe* turned worldly and hypocritical defender of the existing social order.

What is perhaps most curious about that order, as presented in this text, is the ease with which it is assimilated to sight and vision. Ostensibly a dialogue on the merits of seeing, *L'Aveugle qui refuse de voir* is in fact almost totally devoted to the advantages and disadvantages of being in society, as opposed to remaining in the solitary but uncomplicated place of the blind beggar. Epistemological or psychological speculation concerning blindness and sight is all but absent, and what psychological assertions can be found are immediately inserted into a social context. In neglecting the beauties of nature and stressing the worldly pleasure of the capital, the oculist suggests not simply that the blind are de facto social outcasts, but that society should be conceived of as first and foremost a spectacle, a scene of representations. The blind man accepts this view, or rather it is an assumption within which all parts of the text are written, for he argues that the deceptive appearances of society are so horrible as to be better left unseen, that sight would imply his entry into a system of needs, passions, and dependencies that he would do better to avoid.

Here the psychological and social implications of blindness converge. Sight, says the blind man, is the sense entailing diversion and dissipation:

> Concentrez en nous-mêmes, presque toute notre étude se borne à nous développer: votre attention, au contraire, divisée par tout ce qui vous environne, s'épuise ailleurs que sur vous; &, peut-être, la belle faculté de voir ne vous sert-elle qu'à vous corrompre par l'abus que vous en faites.[39]

This idea of intellectual concentration was to become a commonplace in early-nineteenth-century treatises and literary texts concerning blindness. Dufau and Balzac, among others, would identify it with the notion of a finite quantity of intellectual energy which must be saved or spent. Cerfvol, however, develops it not in terms of a general psychic economy but in terms of the subject's different position vis-à-vis the perceptions of the several senses. After denouncing the uncertainty and futility of the sciences of the seeing (in terms that sometimes echo Saunderson's speech in the *Lettre sur les aveugles*), the blind man explains that these difficulties are no concern of his:

> Comme Aveugle, je ne juge des choses que par les rapports qu'elles ont à moi. Je les appelle belles ou laides, bonnes ou

mauvaises, suivant la manière dont elles m'affectent. Le privilège de la vue généraliserait nécessairement mes juge-mens, en multipliant mes perceptions & mes sensations, & il me forcerait de prononcer sur une foule d'accidens qui ne me toucheraient point.[40]

Diderot's *Lettre* had suggested that beauty would be for the blind a matter of utility, but this was linked simply to the pre-eminence of sight in an aesthetic still dominated by representa-tion. Here senses other than sight are said to inform the subject of those things with which he has a functional relation, whereas sight is the sense that places before him things as objects, having no relation to him except their presence before his eyes in a largely useless and distracting tableau.

Thus sight, and indeed the objectified, nonfunctional uni-verse that it imposes, are said to be means of alienation, struc-tures that capture desire and lead it astray, multiplying needs, passions, and dependencies:

> Chaque objet qui frappera ma vue, deviendra pour moi une source inépuisable de chagrins; j'en désirerai la posses-sion, au moins, la connaissance: l'impossibilité de me satis-faire irritera mon amour propre, en l'humiliant, me rendra mon ignorance plus sensible, & me procurera, sans discon-tinuation, le regret d'avoir vu.[41]

The blind man assumes that the universe is not fully knowable, and he accepts this condition. He blames sight for the unwar-ranted attempt to make everything that exists the object of hu-man understanding. The spectacle of social masquerading and deception, which for the oculist produces a surplus of pleasure, the blind man thus describes as a web of crimes whose view can bring only needless and ineffectual frustration. "Loin donc de croire la félicité attachée à votre condition," he exclaims in his final outburst, "je présume au contraire que, pour vous qui voyez, la vie n'est qu'un tissu de jouissances, qui ne vous sont point propres & de regrets très-réels; de désirs qui se renouvel-lent sans cesse, & qui ne sont jamais satisfaits."[42] When the blind man prepares to receive the oculist at his home in the evening, he must buy a lamp, and he deplores this expenditure to which the seeing are constantly subjected and to which the oculist would obligate him as well. Enlightenment has its price.

The blind man decides not to pay that price and to remain in his place, that of the sage withdrawn from the passions of the world, but also that of the beggar outside the relations of economic exchange that govern society. It would appear at first that the blind man simply and indolently prefers his status of parasite to that of producer, but in fact he finds in the various social conditions proposed to him no real production, no one living peacefully from the fruits of his labor; all are parasites or their victims. The blind beggar's position can ultimately be distinguished by its marginality, even exteriority, its stability, and the simplicity of the relations that it entails. He lives apart from society, whose members maintain him in his difference, his distance from themselves, by the giving of alms. The choice proposed to him by the oculist can further be read as a choice between a certain kind of progress and a tradition, specifically between science and literature. For prior to the oculist, the blind man had another benefactor, a man of letters who composed for him a fine oration, filled with the devices of rhetoric, which he would recite while begging. The scientist now proposes to rid him of the condition that the man of letters had helped make agreeable. Rather than providing symbolic, discursive ratification of his otherness, as the rhetorician had done, the doctor would make him the same as everyone else by the rational application of a scientific discovery. The place afforded by rhetoric and eloquence had been a stable one, peripheral, singular, but assured, whereas the condition offered by surgery is a dizzying plunge into a society where differentiation appears to arise only from uncertainty, deception, and mutual exploitation. Indeed, so shocking are the inequalities masked by society's agreeable spectacles that the blind man accuses the seeing of using their eyes only to avoid reflecting on what they do not see.

Cerfvol, whom the *Dictionnaire des lettres françaises* dismisses as an author of trifling and superficial works,[43] thus uses the blind man and the oculist as an allegorical construct to write a critique of liberal society, an indictment of a culture dominated by exchange, both of money and social disguises. More important, however, the critique centers on the Enlightenment project of remedying all exclusions, imperfections, and injustices by means of rational understanding and action, the ambition of reducing all otherness to the comprehensible and controllable. The oculist is a figure of corrupt enlightenment. Wishing to cure the beggar so as to enhance his reputation, he remains indifferent to forms of misery from which he cannot benefit. He has been very successful in working on the sight and views of the rich and powerful, but the blind man warns him that in this case the treatment he proposes may have grave consequences: "Aveugle, je ne suis qu'un fardeau inutile de la Société; voulez-vous donc m'en rendre le fléau?"[44] The attempt to cure social exclusion by rational and scientific means would lead not to harmony, he implies, but to a new subjugation so lucidly perceived as to become intolerable. Whether obsequiously serving the figureheads of authority or sowing the seeds of revolution by forcing the splendors and miseries of society on those who have been denied them, the oculist appears to be capable of acting only out of vanity and self-interest, thereby confirming the blind man's insights into his society.

In refusing the "enlightened" project of integrating him into society, the blind beggar unmasks the violence and hypocrisy of this attempt to eliminate difference by scientific means. The valorization of blindness as difference, as something all its own, implied by this refusal, differs radically from the compensatory valorization of blindness in traditional myths involving prophetic or rhapsodic powers. It arises only in reaction against the modern attempt to put an end to blindness. There is no reference here to any sacredness of the blind, except indirectly insofar as the status of beggar depends on the concepts and practices of religion. The blind man opposing the oculist is not a sacred figure, but a figure of *resistance to desacralization*.

Almost nothing is known about Cerfvol, except that he apparently wrote pamphlets in favor of divorce, and it is irrelevant to speculate on whether he intended to call into question some of the most general characteristics of modernity and the Enlightenment, or whether he believed himself to be attacking only the excesses of hypocrites or doctrinaire physiocrats. In any case, he chose, in the cure of blindness, one of the fundamental images, scenarios, or experiences of the eighteenth century, and thereby gave his critique a mythic dimension, placing it on the level not of the sacred but of the peculiarly modern myths that enlightenment secretes of its own desacralizing activity. In poetry, fiction, and theater, the cure of blindness constitutes such a myth: the oculist's hand triumphs over the injustices of nature and provides an edenic experience of natural beauty and untainted love. There is, to be sure, a certain nostalgia for blindness as a state of innocent simplicity, but this does not prevent the ultimate triumph of science, sight, and social integration. In *L'Aveugle qui refuse de voir*, that triumph becomes a catastrophe to be avoided at all cost: a modern myth appears as nothing more than a modern mystification.

· 4 ·

A MODERN PROJECT:
EDUCATING THE BLIND

Diderot had distinguished two ways of approaching the Molyneux problem: the spectacular experiment and the dialogue with the blind. In the first case, blindness functions purely as an absence of perception; in the second, it is a factor determining certain relationships to signs and the world. If the dramatic moment of cure gave rise to a certain number of modern "mythic" notions about the blind, the interest in the mental faculties of those who do not see produced a more durable and concrete development: the establishment of institutions devoted to their education. With these institutions came a body of treatises on the psychology, cognitive aptitudes, teaching, and management of the blind, a literature that has never been the object of systematic historical study. Like surgery, education was supposed to reduce the gap between the blind and the seeing, to enable their integration into society, and to enable them to communicate more fully with their fellows and to participate in the transmission of culture. Sébastien Guillié, administrator of the Institution Royale des Jeunes Aveugles during the Restoration, wrote in 1817 that the blind child, like the savage, is a being so asocial that his education is no less than a mission of civilization:

> Le monde moral n'existe pas pour cet enfant de la nature; la plupart de nos idées sont pour lui sans réalité: il agit comme s'il était seul; il rapporte tout à lui. C'est de ce déplorable état qu'il faut tâcher de le retirer, en lui apprenant qu'il y a des rapports et des liens de communication entre lui et les autres hommes.[1]

The project of education is thus no less characteristic of an Enlightenment approach to a problem of natural injustice or exclusion than is the project of cure. But an important difference

95

arises: if the surgeon operates successfully, if the cataracts yield to the knife, then the patient has become one of the seeing, and his progress in integrating himself into their world is no further affair of the doctor's. For the educators, however, there is no such moment of completion. Their pupils remain blind, becoming at most somewhat more like the seeing, somewhat more able to function in a seeing society. Unlike the surgeons, the teachers must deal with the blind as the blind; their classrooms and schools are in fact micro-societies of the blind (in which, to be sure, a small number of sighted persons exercise a dominant role). The existence of special institutions for the teaching of the blind is justified not by virtue of their educability or resemblance to the seeing, but by virtue of the difficulty of teaching them, the irreducible character of their difference. The teacher, and to an even greater extent the administrator, while committed to the Enlightenment project of reducing differences, of ending exclusions by communication, has an institutional interest in affirming differences, in replacing one kind of social isolation, that of the blind beggar, with another, that of the blind pupil or ward. We might say that the teachers are concerned with *rationalizing* the difference that is blindness, with reference to the two meanings of this expression: the rendering accessible to reason of a hitherto indescribable difference, and the justification of its continued existence.

These considerations are not as abstract or theoretical as they might appear. In his book *The Making of Blind Men: A Study of Adult Socialization*, Robert Scott argues that behavior often considered typical of the blind is not inherent in their lack of sight but rather learned, particularly in agencies devoted to their education and care, in contact with the attitudes of the seeing.[2] And long before Scott published his work in 1969, integration into the schools had replaced separate institutions as the preferred strategy for the teaching of blind children. The French educators and administrators of the early nineteenth century, charged with maintaining and explaining their institutions, often resorted to postulating a mysterious and essential "nature of the blind." It is hardly to be wondered at if they then found "confirmation" of such a nature in the behavior of their pupils. Nor should we be surprised or indignant to find institutional administrators advancing this kind of argument to capture the attention and sympathy of their readers. From the last years of the *ancien régime* to the Restoration, the Paris institute for the education of the blind knew a fragile and struggling existence, its leaders appealing, sometimes desperately, to the public and the government for funds and facilities, never knowing if their needs would be remembered by the next regime. Their presentation of the blind *had* to be self-justificatory, *had* to appeal to the imagination. Having nothing so dramatic as a cure to offer, they attempted to make education itself into a theatrical spectacle. Thus, although we will be dealing in this chapter with a body of nonfiction texts, with a quasi-disciplinary institutional discourse, there is every reason to seek for connections between that discourse and the more strictly literary re-mythification of blindness and the blind.

Neither instruction nor hospices were new to the blind, but no systematic programs of education had been attempted prior to the founding of the Institution des Enfans Aveugles in Paris in 1784. Its material creation was the work of the Société Philanthropique, then enjoying great public favor and publishing almost daily press notices of donations received and new causes to support. In 1783 its members had announced a subscription to provide for the living expenses of twelve blind children of poor but honest working families in the capital. On February 20, 1784, the *Journal de Paris* published a letter from one Edmond Régnier, *mécanicien* to a leading member of the Société, the Duke of Chartres, praising the group's choice of action but suggesting that charity alone would not be enough: "C'est beaucoup sans doute de contribuer à leur subsistance; mais ne seroit-ce pas faire plus encore pour eux de fonder leur subsistance sur leur propre travail?"[3] After denouncing the idleness to which the Société's wards would otherwise be exposed, Régnier provides a long list of occupations suitable for the blind—largely manual trades but also (and here he cites the example of Saunderson) intellectual professions. The letter concludes with a summary of the social advantages of such a project:

Vous voyez, Messieurs, qu'il y a des occupations pour les Aveugles de tous les états; & que ces occupations, en rendant leur sort meilleur et plus heureux, fourniroit [*sic*] à la Société de nouvelles valeurs en mettant en activité des bras ordinairement inutiles, & des têtes parmi lesquelles il pourroit s'en trouver de bien organisées.[4]

Régnier did not invent the education of the blind. There is no evidence that he ever concerned himself with the matter after this letter, and his list of trades and activities hardly constitutes a program of instruction. What he wrote, however, resumed in advance the fundamental methods and aims of the Paris Institution: the learning of trades, with intellectual instruction where appropriate, improving the welfare of unfortunate individuals, and, more important, productive reintegration of these individuals into society.[5]

The Philanthropic Society's secretary thanked Régnier in a letter published on April 20, pledging, "Nous ne négligerons pas de profiter, autant qu'il nous est possible, des vues utiles que présente cette même lettre."[6] Four days later, the *Journal* published a letter on a related topic, an account of the education of Mademoiselle Paradis, a blind Austrian pianist then giving concerts in Paris. Like Saunderson, like Wessembourg, the blind German inventor of a system of reading with whom she had corresponded, Mademoiselle Paradis was one of a small number of blind persons who through their own ingenuity or that of friends had obtained an education. But with the exception of Diderot's *Lettre* and an occasional press report such as this one, the methods and discoveries connected with these isolated cases remained untransmitted; they had not been converted into systematic practice or organized knowledge. To systematize this information would be the task of Valentin Haüy, then Royal Interpreter, who during the summer of 1784 began to work with some of the Society's blind *pensionnaires* and who in the *Journal* of September 30 presented his work and its inspiration for the first time: "C'est à la lettre que vous écrivit M. de la Blancherie le 24 avril dernier, Messieurs, c'est à celle de M. Diderot, imprimée en 1749, que je suis redevable de l'idée d'un plan d'éducation à l'usage des Aveugles."[7] Haüy found the art of tactile reading common to the example of Mademoiselle Paradis, Saunderson, and the blind man of Puiseaux, and he decided to make it the basis of his first efforts with the Society's young wards.

Only with Haüy, who would come to be known as the father of the blind, does the education of the blind begin to have an organized history. By the end of the year 1784, Haüy had presented an academic paper on his new work, and in 1786 he published his *Essai sur l'éducation des aveugles*, the first treatise on the topic and the first in a long line of publications by persons responsible for or familiar with the Paris Institution. In this corpus we will find elements of the philosophical discussion of blindness so important in the eighteenth century, elements of romantic literary discourse concerning blindness, and pedagogical or social elements peculiar to these institutional writings. But before examining in detail what the educators had to say about the blind, I turn first to their presentation of their institutions and programs and to their observations on the problems and methods of the social recuperation that they deemed so necessary.

As its association with the Société Philanthropique indicates, the early movement toward education of the blind depended on widespread interest in them as appropriate objects of pity and compassion. Those responsible for educating the blind attempted from the outset to portray their charges as worthy of assistance—not so much on a moral plane as on an affective and social plane. Their writings would thus often attempt to induce the reader to identify with the blind, to create the imaginative substitution at the basis of pity. Beginning in 1786, Haüy was to give an account of his inspiration quite different from the one he had given in the *Journal de Paris*. This new version emphasized not intellectual influences but an immediate experience of compassion. Thirteen years before he actually began to work with the blind, Haüy wrote, he had witnessed a strangely moving sight at the entrance to a café:

> Huit à dix pauvres Aveugles, des lunettes sur le nez, postés le long d'un pupitre qui portait de la musique, y exécutoient une symphonie discordante, qui sembloit exciter la joie des Assistans. Un sentiment tout différent s'empara de notre âme; & nous conçûmes dès l'instant la possibilité de réaliser à la faveur de ces Infortunés, des moyens dont ils n'avoient qu'une jouissance apparente ridicule. L'Aveugle, nous dîmes-nous à nous-mêmes, ne connoît-il pas les objets à la diversité de leurs formes?[8]

What Haüy describes is a passage from farce to enlightened rationalism, but he makes this passage into an intensely personal moment of ravishment, of sympathetic understanding. In a later version of his narrative, he implies that it was actually an engraving of this spectacle that had so moved him, and that if such a revolting subject had been chosen by the artist,

> c'était pour que le tableau reproduit sous mes yeux, portant dans mon coeur une affliction profonde, échauffât mon génie. Oui, me dis-je alors à moi-même, saisi d'un noble enthousiasme, j'y substituerai la vérité à cette fable ridicule.[9]

It is irrelevant to speculate on the biographical truth of these three versions of the beginnings of Haüy's interest in the blind, but it is evident that he considered the last two more suited to his aim of promoting the Institution through his writings than a simple acknowledgment of his intellectual debt to Diderot or others.

The winning of public attention was crucial to Haüy's early efforts, and by all accounts he was quite successful. The Belgian writer and public official Alexandre Rodenbach wrote that in the 1780s philanthropy, especially that which had the blind as its object, had become almost a fad: "Il y eut une foule de souscriptions pour la nouvelle école, et par les effets magiques de la mode, les aveugles devinrent l'objet de toutes les conversations."[10] This curiosity had to be satisfied, and Haüy's students began presenting public exercises emphasizing musical performance, thus demonstrating the fulfillment of their teacher's original inspired plan. The oculist Gleize described himself as moved to tears by the innocence and sweetness of voice of the blind children;[11] the *Journal historique et littéraire* reported the presence of "un monde incroiable" at one of their concerts. Yet, in his *Essai*, Haüy expressed a certain ambivalence, even embarrassment, concerning the status of music in his work. Too closely linked to the stereotypes of the blind comic musician or gifted rhapsode to be an essential part of a rational program of education, music came to be an important activity because of the need to exploit the expectations of all concerned:

> En traçant le plan de l'Education des aveugles, nous n'avons d'abord regardé la musique que comme un accessoire propre à les délasser de leurs travaux. Mais les dispositions naturelles de la plupart des Aveugles pour cet Art; les ressources qu'il peut fournir à plusieurs d'entre eux pour leur subsistance; l'intérêt qu'il paroît inspirer aux personnes qui daignent assister à nos exercices; tout nous a forcé de sacrifier notre propre opinion à l'utilité générale.[12]

If the blind appeared to have a "natural disposition" for music, this was because music did not seem to require that the absence of vision be supplemented by some other resource, as did other activities. Their education, however, was to be aimed at providing them with new cognitive resources, with opening up new fields of endeavor—alongside which music would no longer have a special status. Haüy realized that this kind of transformation could not occur overnight, and he agreed to continue the emphasis on musical instruction as both public advertisement and "délassement honnête."

Despite the appeal of blind children raising their voices in touching or edifying song, Haüy and his successors were far more concerned with reading, writing, and manual labor, with demonstrating their young students' competence in manipulating the sign systems hitherto closed to them and their ability to replace charity by the fruits of their labor. The program of exercises performed for the royal family at Versailles in 1786 opens with all the children performing handiwork, which many of them continue throughout the performance. The others then greet the king with instrumental music, but the greatest part of the program consists of demonstrations of reading, writing, arithmetic, geography, and the composition of printing plates. A four-year-old seeing child reads *for the first time* under the tutelage of one of the blind students, and finally a song accompanies the royal family's departure.[13] From the very beginning, Haüy had placed extraordinary emphasis on teaching and printing as activities for the blind. The secretary of the Philanthropic Society announced on December 28, 1784, that Haüy's first blind student, Lesueur, was already taking over the teaching of others;[14] in 1786 Haüy's *Essai* was printed in relief characters by the *Enfans-aveugles*. In a parallel to their work as teachers of the seeing, the blind also printed the standard ink characters of what they call "livres en noir." Both activities showed them to be not simply the passive recipients of an education, but capable of communicating actively both among themselves and with the seeing. Haüy used teaching by the blind as an argument against the alleged futility of instructing them in reading.[15] To the objection that the blind would at best constitute an isolated community, he opposed the potential usefulness of their new activities to the seeing.

Until at least the Restoration, writings concerning the education of the blind remained dominated by the task of convincing benefactors and governments of the utility and interest of the enterprise. After its initial subsidy by the Société Philanthropique, the Institution received assistance from the monarchy, and during the Revolution had to take its case before the successive assemblies and governments as sources of private funds evaporated. Its name was changed to the "Institution Nationale des Jeunes Aveugles-Travailleurs," and then at the Restoration to the "Institution Royale des Jeunes Aveugles." In 1792 Haüy exclaimed in a speech to a revolutionary group, "Sous le règne du despotisme, la Bienfaisance les avoit accueillis. Que ne doivent-ils pas attendre sous les joies de l'Egalité!"[16] But the ensuing decade saw worsening conditions for Haüy and his students, and by 1801 he was protesting unsuccessfully the Consulate's decision to combine his institution and the Quinze-Vingts, the hospice for the elderly blind founded by Saint Louis.[17]

In 1796, faced with increasing indifference to his public exercises and a corresponding decline in funds, Haüy asked his friend Fabre d'Olivet to write a play especially for performance by the blind children.[18] The result was *Le Sage de l'Indostan*, *drame philosophique*, actually a dramatic prologue to yet another demonstration of the blind students' accomplishments. What makes *Le Sage* interesting is the philosophical and mythical context in which it places the work of Haüy's Institution. The play opens with the sage, who has been meditating on a sacred text, announcing that Nature's mysteries cannot be penetrated, that human intelligence must recognize its weakness and bow in obeisance to destiny. A worried and saddened father then arrives to consult the sage concerning his blind son. The sage admits that he cannot cure the child, and he admonishes the father, who has bitterly denounced Nature as unjust and treacherous. The father then pleads for some inner, compensatory faculty for his boy:

> Puisqu'il faut que mon fils renonce à la lumière,
> Du moins de la sagesse ouvrez-lui la carrière;
> Et qu'au fond de son coeur l'éclat de la Vertu
> Le dédommage, hélas! du jour qu'il a perdu.[19]

But the sage offers no divinely granted compensation. Instead he produces a magical spectacle in the service of reason: the spirits of Belisarius, Milton, Saunderson, and Homer appear successively to inspire the boy to courage and effort by their example. The presence of Saunderson beside the poets and figures of antiquity confirms that the topos of the gifted blind is undergoing a rational interpretation, capable of integrating science as well as the sacred.

The sage then announces the existence of a "Peuple éclairé, sage, vaillant, humain," the French, in whose midst a great teacher has dedicated himself to the blind.[20] A curtain rises to reveal the blind children of the Institution, singing, reading, teaching, printing, and working. The sage mentions that all the students make music during their moments of leisure, but it is the boy who concludes the play by showing that his priorities, as we would now say, are in the right place. To his father, he says:

> Mais le seul bonheur où j'aspire,
> En m'instruisant dans ce séjour,
> Hélas! c'est de pouvoir t'écrire
> Jusqu'où va pour toi mon amour.[21]

Thus the education of the blind, and most particularly their instruction in writing, takes the place of divinely granted compensatory faculties. The possibility of a magical cure is specifically put aside, with the suggestion that it would be almost an insult to nature. Fabre d'Olivet replaces the sudden revelation of light with the revelation of a society where the unseeing eyes of the blind are no longer an obstacle. In a sense, his play shows the educational project appropriating both the ancient myth of compensatory faculties and the modern myth of cure.

The Consulate and the Empire were particularly difficult periods for the Institution. Haüy was dismissed by the government in 1802, and conditions were poor and courses all too infrequent at the Quinze-Vingts until 1815. At the Restoration, Louis XVIII kept a promise made to Haüy at Mittau in 1806 and gave the school new and independent buildings, but Haüy himself, compromised by his minor role in the Revolution, was never reinstated. The new director, the ophthalmologist Guillié, embarked on an ambitious program of reform that was apparently designed to convince king and government that the pernicious influences of the Revolution were being purged. Among the signs of decadence found by Guillié were the excessive amount of time devoted to music and the intermingling of the sexes. "La confusion des sexes est aujourd'hui soigneusement interdite," he reported in 1819. "On ne favorise plus, comme autrefois, les mariages entre les aveugles et il n'est plus souffert dans l'Institution, de ménages, sources continuelles de discordes et de mésintelligences. Un gouvernement paternel et juste a donc remplacé le régime versatile et faible, qui, pendant si long-tems, a empêché le bien de s'effectuer."[22] The blind would henceforth be desexualized children subjected to a single paternal order, wishing for sight only so that they might glimpse their royal benefactor.[23] To achieve his ends, Guillié did not hesitate to expel forty-three students, "malheureux dépositaires de l'esprit d'insubordination et de licence qu'ils avaient puisé dans leur première demeure, et dont la tradition aurait été conservée par eux" (*G*, p. 24).[24] Indeed, Guillié's essay sometimes degenerates into little more than a sinister program for despotism with a liberal face:

> Comme nous, ils désirent ce qu'il est le plus difficile d'obtenir. Tous les aveugles ont un goût prononcé pour l'indépendance et la liberté. Rien cependant n'est plus contraire à leurs véritables intérêts que l'usage d'une chose dont ils ne pourraient qu'abuser. Alors, on le sent bien, l'art de ceux qui les entourent consiste moins à les satisfaire qu'à leur laisser croire qu'ils sont satisfaits. (*G*, p. 59)[25]

Rodenbach, who had been a student and friend of Haüy's, would later charge that the alleged impiety and other moral defects of the blind were an invention of those who, at the Restoration, wanted to obtain the replacement of the Institution's personnel.[26]

Given the rigidity of its administration, it is not surprising that the Paris Institution resisted innovation and eventually lost much of its initially favorable international reputation. Though within its walls Louis Braille perfected the system of writing that bears his name, the Institution resisted its adoption until after it had been accepted in many schools in Great Britain and the United States. When Samuel Howe, founder and director of the Boston school for the blind, published a report on his tour of leading European institutions, his French translator had to resort to censorship, declaring, "Ici l'auteur américain se livre à une série de récriminations contre l'Institution des Jeunes Aveugles de Paris, que nous ne reproduirons pas, parce qu'elles nous ont paru aussi inconvenantes que mal fondées."[27] What the American author had found was indeed disconcerting, and all the more so because it so well captures the tone of Guillié's writings:

There pervades that establishment a spirit of illiberality, of mysticism, amounting almost to charlatanism, that ill accords with the well known liberality of most French Institutions. There is a ridiculous attempt at mystery,—an effort at show and parade, which injures the establishment in the minds of men of sense.[28]

Howe goes on to remark that this attitude is widespread in European institutions dependent on governmental patronage. He also criticizes the Paris school for the inflexibility of its program, in which few students could master any single subject matter because all were required to take part in all activities without regard for their abilities.

In view of Howe's comments, it is not surprising that teachers of the blind and other French writers on the topic in the early nineteenth century viewed themselves as the keepers of a specialized if not occult field of knowledge. Their writings are characterized by the predominance of a relatively small number of problems or topics, and above all by a sense that the blind are a separate and particular class of beings whose special world it is the treatise-writer's task to make understandable to the reader. Given the economic importance that the appeal to compassion and sympathy had for these early promoters of education for the blind, it is no surprise that their reader is often called on to place himself, imaginatively, in the place of one who does not see. The Abbé Desmonceaux wrote quite lucidly of this phenomenon, which so many others who took up the topic were simply content to exploit: "Ils [the blind] trouvent à la vérité dans les uns une humanité compatissante, mais plus souvent dans les autres des refus cruels, parce que l'homme fuit naturellement ce qui lui représente ou lui rappelle les infirmités humaines: c'est pour lui, c'est pour son âme un mélange de compassion & de répugnance qui lui fait appréhender la possibilité du même sort."[29] The double movement of identification and distancing described by Desmonceaux had to be directed by the benefactors of the blind toward an acceptance of their charges, not a rejection. Rather than abandoning in horror those deprived of sight, the seeing had to be brought to admire the efforts by which misfortune and difference could be overcome, by which the blind could be made reassuringly more like the seeing.

The reader is thus made to imagine blindness from his own experience, a procedure that Guillié evokes at the beginning of his *Essai sur l'instruction des les aveugles*: "Comme nous ne nous servons habituellement que du moyen rapide, mais peu fidèle, de la vue, pour discerner les objets qui nous entourent, on croit que les aveugles ne doivent rien connaître de ce qui existe . . ." (*G*, p. 11).[30] Unlike Diderot, who would have immediately and ironically repudiated such a statement as a delusion of the seeing, Guillié implies that it would be true—unless, that is, the deficiencies of the blind are properly remedied by education. He often characterizes the blind either by their resemblance to the seeing ("Ne doivent-ils pas, comme nous, l'adorer en esprit et en vérité?") or by their difference ("La sensibilité n'a pas, pour eux, les charmes qui nous la font placer au rang des plus douces comme des plus aimables vertus") (*G*, pp. 57, 53).[31] A more striking example can be taken from a discussion of the dangers of solitude in *Des aveugles et de leur éducation* by the novelist and feminist Eugénie Niboyet:

> Nous l'avons tous plus ou moins éprouvé, quand tout est obscurité autour de nous, quand la nuit est profonde, il y a dans notre esprit des idées plus vives, plus colorées. . . . Souvent nous avons peur de nos pensées, car ellees vont, et trop vite et trop loin! la solitude nous effraie, nous appelons le jour. Nous repoussons avec fatigue cette profonde obscurité qui nous isole de tout, car nous sommes faibles, nous voulons voir!... ce que nous éprouvons ainsi quelquefois, l'aveugle l'éprouve toujours; aussi la crainte l'accompagne partout.[32]

This entire pasage is overtly structured by the alternate similarity and dissimilarity of the blind and the "nous" of author and reader. In no way can it be said to be a realistic or observational discourse about the blind; it creates relations of identity and difference between subject (author and reader) and object (the blind). Blindness becomes the perpetuation of darkness as experienced by the seeing. Once again, it is instruction that must save the blind person. Niboyet desires that "les bienfaits de l'éducation, en lui faisant mieux apprécier toutes choses, viennent le distraire de lui-même."[33] What must be restored is phenomenal reality, an outer world, so that the blind may become more like the seeing and be no longer left to the vertiginous inward spiral of isolation, which holds such terrors for the author.

Even Rodenbach, himself a successful blind student of Haüy's, did not hesitate to speak metaphorically of the blind as being "condamnés à une nuit éternelle."[34] The praise of sight and a corresponding lament over the catastrophe of blindness are routine features of these treatises. "La faculté de la Vue," we read in a collection of articles on blindness published by Auguste Schwenger in 1800, "est regardée avec raison comme supérieure à tous les autres sens. . . . C'est peut-être par cette raison que nous employons le mot *voir* dans un sens figuré, en donnant à toute vérité reconnue le caractère de l'évidence."[35] The treatises are replete with observations on the relative merits and characteristics of sight and the other senses, and with discussions of the special sign systems that must be put to use if the four senses of the blind are to be supplemented. The sense of touch receives the greatest attention. According to Guillié, touch is "la langue naturelle des aveugles" because it implies a gestural communication that imitates the form of objects (*G*, p. 14). Whence a repeatedly paradoxical configuration to the supplementary function of the senses: touch is said to be a more natural, more immediate sense than sight, but when called on to serve as a substitute for vision, its place is that of an unnatural, deferred and deferring sense. Mérian had considered visual perceptions the signifiers of tactile perceptions, but when touch is used to supplement sight (as in tactile reading), its perceptions no longer have the characteristics of a natural, mimetic form of representation, but are arbitrary signs (relief letters) of arbitrary signs (the sounds of speech).

Tactile reading was nonetheless from the beginning the centerpiece of all educational programs for the blind. Haüy wrote of his first efforts, "Déjà sous leur tact, devenu en quelque sorte une espèce de vision, les pensées prenoient un corps,"[36] and

Gleize, commenting on the new Institution, predicted that "leurs doigts savamment exercés leur apprendront tout ce que les clairvoyans apprennent par les yeux."[37] Despite the inevitability of arbitrary signs and of special reading techniques for the blind, the early educators acted as though it were necessary to use as natural and mimetic a system of writing and reading as possible and to reduce to a minimum all divergence between the instruction of the blind and that of the seeing. Thus the early relief letters had the same form as printed letters so that they could be read by the seeing (and, of course, so that a further level of conventional signs would not be needed). Haüy even rejected the arithmetical computation boards of Saunderson because "notre but étant de mettre sans cesse les Aveugles en relation avec les clairvoyans, nous avons cru devoir préférer la manière de ces derniers."[38] The early programs of education emphasized the teaching of writing to the blind, even writing in flat ink characters, as was evident in *Le Sage de l'Indostan*. In one system described by Rodenbach, a stylus was used to produce relief characters in thick paper, beneath which a sheet of carbon paper made a copy for the seeing.

When in 1830 a former artillery officer named Charles Barbier brought to the Paris Institution a system of relief characters using six raised dots, it was rejected by the administration on the grounds that its lack of resemblance to ordinary letters would somehow separate the blind from the seeing. Barbier had developed the system to enable messages to be read at night without the use of lights, which risked betraying a gun battery's position to the enemy, but he was convinced that it would be useful to the blind.[39] The Académie des Sciences and a blind student named Louis Braille agreed. The latter devoted the remainder of his life to the development and promotion of Barbier's system. Braille resumed his opponents' arguments as follows: "Mais, disait-on, ce ne sont là que des conventions, et les initiés seuls peuvent lire les pages écrites suivant ces deux méthodes [the respective versions of Barbier and Braille]."[40] Braille and eventually all teachers of the blind recognized that by adopting an arbitrary representation of the alphabet, by acknowledging a distinction from the seeing, the blind could obtain a system of characters far more suited to the sensory capabilities of their fingers. This acceptance of autonomy for the education of the blind was a major advance, not only in that it provided a better method of reading but also because it freed the blind and their teachers from the assumption that their education, even while taking place in separate institutions, must mimic that of the seeing.

The ability of the senses to supplement one another's absence is also a central topic of the numerous early nineteenth-century articles and chapters that purported to compare the blind to the deaf and dumb, and even to decide which of the two classes was the most unfortunate. Pierre-Armand Dufau, a successor to Guillié, implied that this question was a popular topic of speculation and thus a sought-after and inevitable feature of books about the blind or the deaf. In general, the discussion can be reduced to a simple contrast: the blind are most unfortunate when they are alone, but the deaf-mutes are more unfortunate in society. Rodenbach draws a somewhat different distinction based on social class: for persons of means, blindness is less disagreeable, but for the poor, deafness and mutism have the advantage of posing no obstacle to exercising a simple trade.[41] Dufau drew the lines somewhat differently: "Sous le rapport de la formation de la raison, du développement de l'intelligence, rien ne remplace le langage; mais pour les relations sociales, pour les nécessités de la vie positive, rien non plus ne saurait remplacer la vue."[42] As in *L'Aveugle qui refuse de voir*, sight appears to be the sense most crucial to an individual's insertion in a society. Each sense is assumed to have a domain in which it is the most natural, the most able to convey an immediate present, so that when they are extended to other domains they always seem to be mere replacements. However much sight may be exalted as the greatest of the senses, it becomes poor and indirect when used to supplement the absence of hearing, since writing is considered only a substitute for speech.

The exclusion said to be produced by the lack of some sense, and particularly of sight, was not limited to sensations and signs. Metaphorically, the blind were treated as if cut off from life itself. One of Haüy's poetically inclined students wrote of his teacher,

Les Arts et les Vertus lui prêtent leur flambeau,
Pour éclairer l'Aveugle au fond de son tombeau.[43]

The educators and administrators show themselves to be fully capable of integrating this ancient, traditional view of blindness as deathlike exclusion and torment into their scientific treatises. Guillié wrote that a blind person is "enseveli pour jamais dans les ténèbres" (G, p. 12). The surgeon Pierre-Nicolas Gerdy saw in blindness a moral humiliation: "A voir le visage assombri et monotone du malheureux aveugle, où ne brille pas plus la fièrté d'un noble regard que la vivacité de l'esprit et l'attachement de la reconnaissance, on dirait voir la face d'un réprouvé."[44]

These images of burial and condemnation imply isolation from a human community described as founded on the exchange of gazes, on the expressivity of the human eye and face. Bonald wrote in his major philosophical work that language is to so great an extent "une imitation, une représentation de l'expression que nous avons vue" that "la parole des aveugles est morte et inanimée."[45] Guillié considered the visual presence of the interlocutor to be the crucial difference between the vivacity of speech and the inanimation of writing: "Ils [the blind] sont continuellement, dans leurs relations avec les autres hommes, comme l'on est avec un individu qu'on ne connaît que par correspondance: on sait bien qu'il existe, mais on ne peut se figurer comment" (G, pp. 53–54).[46] Dufau argues, however, that the blind compensate by studying the voice, in which they hear "une foule de nuances délicates qui nous échappent . . . ils étudient la voix précisément comme nous étudions la physionomie, pour y découvrir les qualités du coeur" (D, p. 69).[47] While conceding that the blind cannot perceive facial expressions, Rodenbach found them to be particularly expressive, indeed, to present a kind of unwitting and innocent openness: "On peut lire sur la figure des aveugles les sentiments qu'ils éprouvent: ils s'y peignent d'autant mieux qu'ils ne cherchent pas à les cacher, et qu'ils ignorent l'effet de cette impression sur les clairvoyants."[48]

111

If the blind were thus seen as passive in the social intercourse of gazes, they were held to be no less so with respect to the erotic function of the eyes. We have already noted that the sexual undesirability of blind men was an element of the romantic theme in *commedia* plays with blind characters. The attractiveness of blind girls, on the other hand, was taken up in some detail by Dufau:

> Leur abord n'est pas dépourvu de cette grâce timide, charme principal de l'adolescence chez les femmes; leurs mouvements n'ont pas la raideur qu'on remarque en général chez ceux des jeunes gens. Dans le monde, rien ne distinguera quelquefois la jeune fille aveugle, dont l'oeil n'a pas subi une désagréable oblitération; au bal resplendissant et joyeux, elle pourra ne pas toujours rester silencieuse et inactive (*D*, p. 39).[49]

This passive desirability, present in such plays as *Cassandre oculiste* and *Valérie* and which we will encounter again in Hugo's *L'Homme qui rit*, is attributed by Dufau to the "natural" attention women pay to their appearance, their "désir de plaire." Blind men, conversely, could be characterized sexually by their immunity to the visual seductions of women. Niboyet writes:

> L'amour, par exemple, qui n'est le plus souvent, pour les clairvoyans, qu'une passion sensitive, a chez eux un caractère plus moral. Comme ils ne le prennent point par les yeux, ils sont soustraits aux séductions physiques. Que leur fait le jeu de prunelles d'une coquette, la grâce de son sourire, les minauderies de son allure? tous ces agens de la puissance des femmes leur sont indifférens et nulle ne leur paraît belle si elle ne commence par être bonne![50]

To the extent that the sexuality of the blind did not conform to the reassuring patterns described by Dufau and Niboyet (passivity for women, morality for men), it seems to have been a source of considerable worry to their caretakers, as Guillié's insistence on the segregation of the sexes indicates. August Zeune, director of a Berlin institution for the blind modeled on that of Paris and generally regarded as progressive, claimed that masturbation and nymphomania were common among the blind, and blamed those watching over them for insufficient vigilance.[51]

What was written about the sexuality of the blind thus conforms to a far more general conception of their solitude, a solitude that in moderation was said to produce a grave and serious temperament, the pride of their caretakers, but which in excess could lead to dangerous and potentially mad behavior, controllable only by the efforts of educators to replace the missing visible world. We have already noted Niboyet's treatment of this theme. The educators were unanimous in their belief that the absence of sight removed the greatest source of distractions to the mind and thereby created a potential intellectual advantage. "L'esprit libre de cette foule d'images dont les impressions se croisent sans cesse malgré nous dans notre cerveau," wrote Haüy, "tout le monde sait à quel degré les aveugles jouissent de ce doux calme si favorable à l'étude."[52] A similar argument had been made by the beggar of *L'Aveugle qui refuse de voir*, and the educators, interested in stressing the advantages of not seeing, were to speculate at length on its consequences.[53]

Preserved from the distractions of sight, the blind were said to be capable of concentrated and sustained attention, a faculty that Dufau attributed to spatio-temporal differences between sight and the other senses: "Ce n'est pas tant par la distraction qu'elle nous cause, que par la simultanéité des impressions dont elle est l'origine, que la vue nuit en nous à l'attention. . . . Les impressions de l'ouïe et du tact sont au contraire isolées par leur nature. L'âme les perçoit en quelque façon une à une" (*D*, p. 34).[54] The methodical or analytical mind, then, would follow the successive order of hearing and touch, not the spatial order of sight. According to Dufau, the blind judge less swiftly but more surely (*D*, p. 43). Dufau uses the distinction between simultaneity and succession to justify a radical opposition between synthesis and analysis in the thought processes of the blind: "Il suit naturellement de là que l'intelligence de l'aveugle-né, qui excelle dans l'analyse, reste à un degré inférieur sous le rapport de l'opération synthétique qui en est l'inverse" (*D*, p. 43).[55]

113

Thus the blind were assumed to be particularly gifted at logical, relational operations. "Ils peuvent, il est vrai," wrote Gerdy, "se livrer avec succès aux méditations les plus profondes, à la philosophie, aux mathématiques, et faire de véritables découvertes dans le champ de la métaphysique."[56] The spatial metaphors of arguments such as these are those of superficiality (identified with the simultaneity of vision) and depth (likened to the deliberate intellectual march of touch and hearing). Guillié credited the blind with "beaucoup de rectitude dans le jugement," and Dufau remarked: "Leur intelligence suivant toujours une marche lente et graduelle, ses acquisitions diverses doivent s'enchaîner plus facilement dans un ordre méthodique" (*G*, p. 47; *D*, p. 35).[57] Gerdy was far from alone in supposing that the blind have a special vocation for the abstract thought of philosophy and mathematics. Rodenbach wrote: "Ses idées ne s'offrent jamais à lui sous des formes matérielles, ses pensées sont toujours distinctes, et une image ne peut lui tenir lieu d'un raisonnement ou d'un sentiment."[58] For Guillié, "ils voient les choses d'une manière plus abstraite que nous";[59] both he and Dufau agree that the separation of concepts from sensory attributes, that is, abstraction, is in fact performed naturally for the blind. The praise of abstraction thus goes hand in hand with the idea that sight is the sense of error, of superficial and illusory judgment. "On sait à combien d'erreurs la vue nous expose," noted Guillié (*G*, p. 50).[60] In a passage reminiscent of *L'Aveugle qui refuse de voir*, Dufau wrote that the blind would be spared both the seductions of illusions and the pain of their loss, for "ils sentent les choses comme elles sont" (*D*, p. 31).[61]

The mental universe of the blind, their teachers thus believed, justified comparing them rationally to great thinkers and sages. Guillié evokes Milton and Homer, and Dufau concludes his chapter on moral character in the following terms:

> Enfin, je dirai qu'essentiellement réfléchis et positifs, ces êtres auxquels notre monde visible est étranger, paraissent destinés, s'ils ne sont en quelque sorte dénaturés par nous, à donner beaucoup plus à la raison, et à traverser plus sagement cette rapide carrière; semblables à ces hommes graves

que nous voyons quelquefois vivre au sein du tourbillon de
la société comme s'ils ne le voyaient pas, et rester toujours
étrangers aux passions délirantes qui s'agitent autour
d'eux! (*D*, p. 32)[62]

One phrase in Dufau's panegyric deserves particular attention:
"s'ils ne sont en quelque sorte dénaturés par nous." In his introduction, Dufau proposes to consider first "l'aveugle de la nature" as a prelude to understanding "l'aveugle de la civilisation."
Later he refers to "leur nature d'aveugle," capable of being ob-
scured but not effaced by contact with the seeing. The project
of education thus takes on a strange ambivalence. On the one
hand, the blind as deprived beings must be given substitutes for
sight, must be given a system of understanding compatible with
that of the seeing, but on the other hand, this education must
attempt to preserve some of the unique benefits assumed to be
associated with their difference. The teachers must help the
blind become more like the seeing, but they must also be sure
that they remain like the blind. Like Dufau, Guillié conceded
that the intellectual aptitude specific to the blind could only be
attenuated through contact with the seeing. "Cette grande faculté d'analyse et de décomposition, qu'on remarque dans les
aveugles-nés, est beaucoup plus intense pendant qu'ils sont en
état de nature; on s'aperçoit qu'elle faiblit lorsque, par les idées
communiquées, ils adoptent nos procédés et nos formes de raisonnement (*G*, p. 49).[63] In terms reminiscent of Diderot's
Lettre, he calls the *aveugle de nature* a man of four senses, unaware of a fifth, and proposes that an experience of deficiency
would arise only in the attempt to communicate with persons
using the system of five senses. But whereas for Diderot this
contrast called into question the notion of a human nature, for
Guillié it merely gave rise to an additional "nature," that of the
blind, and thereby contributed to the notion that the blind live
in a special world of mysterious concentration. Dufau found intellectual inferiority in blind students whose eyes transmit just
enough indistinct perceptions to create the impression of a
point of view. This condition produces distractions "et gâte,

pour ainsi dire, leur condition d'aveugles en ce qu'elle a de spécial" (*D*, p. 40).[64]

Another mitigating factor which, according to Dufau, causes the adulteration of the "blind nature" is the female sex. Blind women, he wrote, show less analytical intelligence than their male counterparts—a situation, he hastened to add, which is to be found among the seeing as well. In other words, the opposition "male-female" repeats and supports the opposition "blind-seeing": "les conceptions fortes, les travaux opiniâtres d'un côté, les grâces faciles de l'esprit, la vivacité de l'imagination de l'autre" (*D*, p. 38).[65] Method and imitation, depth and superficiality, abstraction and sensation—all the oppositions already made between the blind and the seeing can be referred to the most conventional discourse concerning secondary sexual characteristics. The argumentative recourse to a "blind nature" brings with it some of the cultural stereotypes of "male nature" or "female nature." Thus blind girls are said to be more like the seeing than blind boys: "Elles entrent plus facilement dans nos idées, dans nos conventions sociales; elles sont moins aveugles, si je peux m'exprimer de la sorte" (*D*, p. 38).[66] To the extent that blindness and masculinity are said to entail similar mental processes, these processes could be seen only as diffused in a blind woman, whose faculties would be the products of determinants working at cross purpose.

Along with analysis and abstraction, the intellectual faculty most generally attributed to the blind man was an enormous memory. Charlevoix had reported that in Japan there were academies of the blind whose task it was to preserve historical and literary tradition by memorization and recitation, a fact that found its way into many treatises on blindness. Already in 1784 Haüy referred to "cette mémoire prodigieuse qui, chez les aveugles, retient aussi sûrement les idées qu'elle les reçoit avec aisance."[67] Both Guillié and Dufau quote the dictum off Helvétius that "une grande mémoire est un phénomène d'ordre" and thereby link the memory of the blind to the methodical and analytical structures that are supposed to characterize their intelligence. They reject the conventional mnemonic technique of associating facts with unrelated images as unsuitable for the blind, Guillié declaring that their only mnemonic technique is that of their mind's internal ordering. He refers to the model, made famous by *L'Homme machine* and *Le Rêve de d'Alembert*, of a network of vibrating strings whose continuing resonances would preserve sensations, ideas, and the relations between them; the teaching of the blind thus becomes an exercise in producing multiple and harmonious resonances by means of transitions and analogies:

> Nous évitons soigneusement, soit en les instruisant, soit même en conversant avec eux, de les faire passer trop brusquement d'une idée à une autre, surtout quand ces idées sont disparates, et qu'elles doivent laisser entr'elles un trop grand nombre d'échelons inoccupés. Nous tâchons, au contraire, en procédant analytiquement, de rattacher à ce qui est déjà connu ce que nous voulons faire connaître, et pour user de la théorie ci-dessus développée, d'attaquer toujours une corde qui vibre avec une autre. (*G*, p. 42)[68]

Elsewhere, however, Guillié and Dufau abandon these eighteenth-century metaphors of orderly, associative structures in favor of an energetic economy of concentration and dispersion:

> Voyez en effet s'il n'y a pas de toute rigueur dans le récit d'un événement important, d'une bataille par exemple, une somme d'idées partielles beaucoup moins considérable pour un aveugle que pour un clairvoyant, et si, par conséquent, la trace n'en doit pas rester dans l'esprit plus nette et plus précise (*D*, pp. 46–47)[69]

In this metaphoric space of impression and engraving, a reduction in overall quantity (i.e., in surface area) can be converted into an increase in precision over a small space. Guillié states: "L'attention plus concentrée, fait que les objets qui ne laisseraient en nous que des impressions insensibles, se gravent très-fortement dans leur esprit" (*G*, p. 44).[70] The blind, receiving fewer perceptions, would be able to let those that do enter penetrate more deeply into the psyche, according to an economic relation that implicitly posits a finite reserve of capacity to receive impressions.

Dufau thus concludes that the mental activity of the blind emphasizes internal structure at the expense of wide-ranging interaction with the world and others. This intensity gives the blind man an internal life that makes him the object of almost occult fascination on the part of the seeing theorist:

> La nature des choses veut qu'il vive beaucoup plus en lui; qu'il demeure dans un état de concentration habituelle; que ses pensées, ses sentiments restent ordinairement voilés pour nous, et qu'enfin la vie tout intime de son âme soit une sorte de mystère à pénétrer.[71]

These words were first published in the *Revue de Paris* of 1831 alongside such literary works as Balzac's *Maître Cornélius*, Nodier's review of *Les Feuilles d'automne*, and poems by Musset and Lamartine. The blind could hardly have been made into more romantic figures by the men of letters than by their eloquent teacher. Instead of being a sensory difference, as it had been in so many philosophical writings and other treatises of the eighteenth century, blindness has become a mysterious inner life of the soul. The old myths of compensatory faculties have returned in the guise of an essentialist psychology.

Although Dufau did not imply that his students resembled Homer or Milton, there are in the treatises many suggestions that the blind have a distinctive and unconventional rapport with the signs of language, indeed, that their use of these signs may parallel that of the poet. Already Diderot had compared Saunderson's striking figures of speech to those of a nonnative speaker or of a stylistically audacious writer such as Marivaux. Guillié lamented that signs do not correspond to the same concepts for the blind and that a great many signs are lost to them altogether, but he found that they remedy their shortcomings by "une activité prodigieuse d'imagination" (*G*, pp. 13, 53–54). Like Diderot, Dufau found "des tours inaccoutumés, des figures qui surprennent" (*D*, p. 60). He considered most poetry actually written by persons born blind to be mediocre versification, but then suggested in a remarkable passage that some future blind genius might succeed in poetry by forging "une langue à lui, une langue dans laquelle il pourrait cesser d'être pâle

imitateur, et commencer à être écrivain original" (*D*, p. 63).[72]
Rather than imitating the five-sensed writer, he should become
the poet of four senses. Here is what such a blind poet, according to Dufau, would have accomplished:

> Il se serait fait, par intuition, de vives images de tout ce qui
> doit rester éternellement voilé pour lui, et dans les voix
> mystérieuses de son âme se révèlerait tout un monde in-
> time que se forge bien réellement son imagination au sein
> de cette solitude silencieuse, véritables ténèbres de l'ouïe,
> où il se complaît, surtout quand il est doué du sentiment
> poétique. (*D*, pp. 63–64)[73]

The blind poet would have created a language of his own, a language appropriate to a system of four senses, but he would still
be living in a world of light and images, which would be suggested to him in the speech of others. The genius of his poetry
would be to intuit and express through figures a reality beyond
the perceivable and nameable world of the senses. For him, the
material world would be a mysterious, animated universe, echoing and palpitating with the effects of an unknown force, of a
presence beyond what is present, of a dimension inaccessible to
the senses, perceivable and expressible only through the figures
of language. The blind poet's accomplishment would thus resemble that of a seeing poet capable of evoking the presence of
something mysterious and essential beyond the representable
world of the five senses.

Dufau, even more than the other early teachers of the blind,
appears to have revived the ancient myth of a compensatory faculty such as poetic inspiration. His attitude toward such myths
was ostensibly rationalistic in that he would substitute processes accessible to human understanding for fantastic or divinely granted powers. After advancing psychological arguments in favor of the "absolute superiority" of the intelligence
of the blind, he noted:

> L'idée d'une sorte de supériorité absolue, chez l'individu
> privé de la vue sous le rapport des fonctions de l'esprit,
> n'est pas nouvelle au surplus; je la retrouve chez les anciens,

qui attachaient souvent à la cécité un caractère mystérieux et sacré, et jusqu'au don de la divination. (*D*, p. 36)[74]

This is a typical Enlightenment treatment of myth. But like his colleagues, Dufau treated the difference that is blindness not as a contingent, empirical product of a particular sensory configuration, but as a set of essential characteristics, as a "blind nature." No less than the conceptions derived from imagining blindness as curable, the assumptions made by the teachers of the blind constitute a source of modern mythic notions. But the educators, concerned as they were both with utilizing the "essence" of blindness in the classroom and with exploiting or taming the fascination and horror with which the seeing imagine the condition of incurable blindness, came much closer than the philosophers, the surgeons, or the writers inspired by them to reviving old myths, myths whose origin and meaning were bound to a concept of blindness as radical difference and isolation.

· 5 ·

FROM CHATEAUBRIAND
TO BALZAC: LITERATURE AND
LOSS OF SIGHT

From the Molyneux problem to the theatrics of ocular cures to treatises on the teaching of sightless children, we have been examining writings in which blindness is linked, however indirectly, to modern philosophic or scientific achievements. Without the operations of Grant and Cheselden, without the writings of Locke and Diderot, the new representations of the blind found in popular literature and institutional pedagogy could not have been as they were; *Valérie* and *Le Sage de l'Indostan* would be inconceivable. One common trait, moreover, unites all the blind people presented in the writings we have considered: they were born blind. For the most part, they are young, and their blindness, like their inexperience and their innocence, marks them as bearers of an as yet unrealized intellectual or affective potential. The blind in this corpus of texts will one day see, or love, or use their fingers to read.

There are, of course, other ways of representing or evoking those who do not see. At the beginning of the nineteenth century, in particular, there is a resurgence of interest in the ancient topos of the blind poet or seer. There is no evidence that this interest was brought on by Enlightenment writings on cured or curable blindness; rather, the figure of the sightless bard took on meaning in a specifically literary context. Madame de Staël, in *De la littérature* (1800), placed blind poets at the origins of all European literature: "Il existe, ce me semble, deux littératures tout-à-fait distinctes, celle dont Homère est la première source, celle dont Ossian est l'origine."[1] Ossian, as portrayed in the poems of James Macpherson attributed to him, had lost his sight after his years as a warrior but prior to his career as a bard. First presented in France in the 1760s in fragmentary translations by Turgot and Diderot, the Ossian poems had been translated in full by Le Tourneur in 1779, but would be most widely diffused in the verse translations of Baour-Lormian, published in 1801.[2] Chasteaubriand, who was convinced that Macpherson was the true author of the presumed Ossian poems, nonetheless expressed his fascination for the image of blind bards as the fathers of poetry:

> J'avoue que cette idée de Mme de Staël me plaît fort. J'aime à me représenter les deux aveugles; l'un, sur la cime d'une montagne d'Ecosse, la tête chauve, la barbe humide, la harpe à la main, et dictant ses lois, du milieu des brouillards, à tout le peuple poétique de la Germanie: l'autre, assis sur le sommet du Pinde, environné des Muses qui tiennent sa lyre, élevant son front couronné sous le beau ciel de la Grèce, et gouvernant, avec un sceptre orné de laurier, la patrie du Tasse et de Racine.[3]

In accepting the myth of Ossian even while denying him the authorship of "his" poems, Chateaubriand makes it clear that he is not concerned with a literal, biographical connection between blindness and singing or writing; the sightless bard interests him by his figuration of age, originality, and authority.

The figure of a blind poet as founder of literature would again be set before the French reading public in 1819, with the posthumous publication of André Chénier's *Oeuvres complètes*. Among the major pieces of this influential collection is "L'Aveugle," an evocation of Homer, old, exiled, scorned, yet finally befriended and given refuge in an island city-state where poetry is honored. The young shepherds who find him take his blindness as a sign of divinity, but the old man disavows it:

> Ces rides, ces cheveux, cette nuit éternelle,
> Voyez; est-ce le front d'un habitant des cieux?
> Je ne suis qu'un mortel, un des plus malheureux![4]

The old poet's misfortunes have been brought on by his poverty and by the "riches, grossiers, avares, insolents" who have mocked his blindness:

Aveugle, vagabond, dit l'insolente troupe,
Chante, si ton esprit n'est point comme tes yeux,
Amuse notre ennui, tu rendras grâce aux Dieux.[5]

Misunderstood and abused by the public, the blind poet of antiquity is a social model, not a psychological one, for the modern writer. In Chénier's poem there is no attempt to link the
perceptions or psychic functioning of the blind man to his capacity for poetic creation, although the magnitude and power
of that creative capacity is one of the poem's major themes. Jean
Starobinski has called "L'Aveugle" a "nostalgic gaze towards a
world ideally and historically 'first'—towards, in short, a lost
poetry."[6] The figure of Homer thus symbolizes a return to the
origins of poetry, or rather a rejuvenation of poetry through
contact with its origins. Blindness, as the mark of the original
poet, can be either hailed or ridiculed; the poet can be recognized as a sacred figure or derided by those to whom such signs
of the sacred have become meaningless objects of scorn.

In the figure of the Ossianic or Homeric bard, blindness is
linked to a problem of origins, as in fact it had been in the philosophic writings of the eighteenth century, but the kind of origin in question is completely different from that which had
preoccupied the epistemologists and surgeons. In place of an individual, experimentally reproducible origin—be it of sight,
thought, or feeling—we now have a collective, historical origin,
lost and forever separated from the present by the passage of irreversible time.[7] To evoke the unencumbered gaze of the first
poets of antiquity is to evoke a gaze now extinguished by age,
by the very age of civilization. The blind bard, having lost his
original sight of the world, recreates that sight from within,
through language. Modern literature, in taking that blind bard
as its emblem, acknowledges that it too has been sundered from
its experiential origins, which are now to be sought only in an
inward turn to tradition. The references to Ossian and Homer
are the self-conscious products of a literature seeking to designate itself as literary, and they function only because they are
elements of that literature's own past. They do not imply that

123

poets should blindfold themselves or put out their eyes so as to write in the manner of antiquity, or that a student from the Institution des Jeunes Aveugles will soon come forth to give new life to poetry.

If this literary figuration of blindness were entirely a matter of tradition, wholly removed from all attempts at medical or epistemological or psychological representations of the blind, then we might say that it has nothing to do with the modern writings on blindness that begin with the Molyneux problem. Were that the case, our study of blindness would be in two discrete parts, the "philosophical" and the "literary," with no communication or interference between them. But literature, like other forms of discourse, is impure, neither purely representational nor self-referentially autonomous. In alluding to blindness, literature inevitably begins to represent the blind. Even Chateaubriand's presentation of the blind Indian Chactas, which seems to be primarily destined to bestow on the American wilderness the character of Homeric antiquity, contains echoes of eighteenth-century philosophical concerns and isolated elements of a psychological understanding of the blind. The allusions to blind seers in the work of Pierre-Simon Ballanche are accompanied by commentaries on the comparative mental faculties of the blind and of poets or thinkers. And in the works of Balzac, in particular in *Louis Lambert* and *Facino Cane*, the unseeing eyes of the mad and the blind become elements of the author's speculation on the relation between psychic functioning and narrative art. The old and blind Facino Cane is said to resemble Homer, but it is more important that he both resembles and fascinates the young creator-to-be of *La Comédie humaine*, who must take on himself the task of rescuing the old man's "Odyssey" from silence and oblivion. There may be only limited connections between the Enlightenment writings on blindness and Chateaubriand's presentation of Chactas, between descriptive modernity and allusion to tradition, but in Balzac (and Hugo) the two kinds of discourse can hardly be separated from one another. Our goal, in this book, is to explore the intersections of different ways of conceptualizing and presenting the blind, so that even if the writings of Mérian and

Chateaubriand, or Haüy and Ballanche, had nothing in common, we would need to consider both, since both are related to the literary figurations of blindness in the nineteenth century.

CHATEAUBRIAND

Chactas, the blind elder statesman of Chateaubriand's Natchez Indians, is best known to readers of French literature as the narrator and protagonist of *Atala*, published in 1801 and soon one of the new century's best-sellers. He also appears in *René*, where along with the missionary Father Souël he listens to the young European's melancholy confession. But it is worth recalling that both *Atala* and *René* were originally written as episodes in *Les Natchez*, Chateaubriand's youthful and extravagant epic of American savages in revolt against the colonists from Europe. In publishing them separately, Chateaubriand not only gave them literary status as well-made narrations in the classical French tradition, but also changed their ideological context radically. As companion pieces to *Le Génie du christianisme*, Chateaubriand's poetic rallying-cry to the Concordat of 1802, *Atala* was to be an illustration of the poetic beauties of Christianity, *René* a case study in "le vague des passions." But in the context of *Les Natchez*, the Christian missionaries and other European colonists are bearers of catastrophe, corrupters and destroyers of an authentic civilization still in the childhood of its development. *Les Natchez* was originally Chateaubriand's cry of protest against the claims of modern civil society, his lament for the destruction of a culture worthy of antiquity.[8] Even in the definitive version of *Atala*, there are echoes of a "philosophic" attack on Christianity, as when Chactas cries out to the missionary, "La voilà donc cette religion que vous m'avez tant vantée! Périsse le serment qui m'enlève Atala! Périsse le Dieu qui contrarie la nature! Homme, prêtre, qu'es-tu venu faire dans ces forêts?" (76).[9]

The blindness of Chactas cannot be studied without reference to this complex textual history of Chateaubriand's writings on America. Unfortunately, that history cannot be fully elucidated, for the manuscripts are lost, and we can read *Les Natchez* only in the published version of 1826, revised so as to be compatible with the published texts of *Atala* and *René*. We can, however, be sure of the role of Chactas in a long section of *Les Natchez* that resembles not the *Iliad* but *L'Ingénu* and the *Lettres persanes*, for Chactas, after his early initiation by his adoptive father Lopez into the ways of Europeans and after his adventure with Atala, was a captive and then guest of the French during the reign of Louis XIV. He encountered the ugliness of Paris, the grandeur of Versailles, the vanity and servility of courtiers, saw *Phèdre* and the execution of a Protestant, heard a sermon of Bossuet and conversed with Fénelon. In *René* he asks the young Frenchman for stories of Louis XIV and Versailles: "J'aimerai entendre parler de ce grand chef, qui n'est plus, et dont j'ai visité la superbe cabane" (125–126).[10] Like Voltaire's young Huron or Montesquieu's Persians, but also like Diderot's blind man of Puiseaux defining a mirror, Chactas applies to well-known objects a language that is strange to them, a foreign code that is fully capable of signifying them but that dissipates the illusion of natural referentiality. As a metaphor for his perceptions of society, Chactas employs an image of optical deformation: "La nature me semblait renversée; je ne la découvrais dans la société que comme ces objets dont on voit les images inverties dans les eaux" (269).[11] The young savage, like other philosophical outsiders, perceives the familiar as the unfamiliar, and thus invites the reader to question whether his own perception of French society is as unmediated as he might think.

Chactas the blind sage, however, is a quite different figure from Chactas the ingenuous visitor at the court. When René first encounters him in *Les Natchez*, the narrator describes him by referring to figures of antiquity: "Chactas, c'était son nom, ressemblait aux héros représentés par ces bustes antiques qui expriment le repos dans le génie, et qui semblent naturellement aveugles" (170–171).[12] A page later he becomes "le Nestor des Natchez," and in the prologue to *Atala* he appears guided by a young girl, "comme Antigone guidait les pas d'Oedipe sur le Cythéron, ou comme Malvina conduisait Ossian sur les rochers de Morven" (36).[13] Chactas, the ex-outsider in modern civilization, now resembles the sages and heroes of antiquity, the bards at the origins of literature. Although Homer is not mentioned directly, he is inevitably evoked by the presence of the blind sage in a work laden with pseudo-Homeric similes, invocations, and epic descriptions of warriors and battles.[14]

Blindness thus places Chactas at the center of Chateaubriand's attempt to identify the American tribes with antiquity and specifically with ancient Greece. This association is in at least one sense perplexing: what Chactas narrates is the least epic, least classical part of *Les Natchez*.[15] But for Chateaubriand, the candid gaze of the *sauvage* and the cultural origins figured by the blind sage are inseparable. In his *Voyage en Amérique* he writes that the New World, had Europeans not deformed it, could have rejuvenated the Old:

> Ecartant un moment les grands principes du christianisme, mettant à part les intérêts de l'Europe, un esprit philosophique aurait pu désirer que les peuples du Nouveau Monde eussent eu le temps de se développer hors du cercle de nos institutions. Nous en sommes réduits partout aux formes usées d'une civilisation vieillie . . . on a trouvé chez les Sauvages du Canada, de la Nouvelle-Angleterre et des Florides des commencements de toutes les coutumes et de toutes les lois des Grecs, des Romains et des Hébreux. Une civilisation d'une nature différente de la nôtre aurait pu *reproduire les hommes de l'antiquité, ou faire jaillir des lumières inconnues d'une source encore ignorée.* Qui sait si nous n'eussions pas vu aborder un jour à nos rivages quelque Colomb américain venant découvrir l'Ancien Monde? (857–858; emphasis added)[16]

"To reproduce the men of antiquity": Chateaubriand evokes the fleeting and unrealized possibility that a reproducible, perceptual origin (the arrival of the American Columbus) might provide the equivalent of a return to a cultural origin irretrievably lost through the passage of time. If the evocation of an old and spent civilization seeking rejuvenation seems to be a characteristic topos of romanticism, the metaphor of light, suggesting as it does a new genesis as a sudden opening of the eyes, reminds us that Chateaubriand the *enchanteur* was once

Chateaubriand the *philosophe*, the young man whose first literary project was an account of a Red Indian's voyage to Versailles.[17] The renewal of society through contact with something like its origin parallels the demystification of society through contact with its outside.

Chateaubriand realized, of course, that the colonial destruction of the Indian way of life was fast foreclosing this possibility of rejuvenation. According to Michel Butor, Chateaubriand's American writings are an attempt to preserve and transmit something of this narrowly missed rendezvous with an origin that is neither Greek nor Judeo-Christian:

> A European must "be reborn" an Indian, and make this voice heard, make heard this protest of an abolished race, this truth, this "genius"; then the text itself will become a fountain of youth. The epic, *Les Natchez*, will be able to be a veritable poem of foundation, the "Homer" of a truly new civilization, establishing it by this third tradition whose song *Les Natchez* makes heard.[18]

Chactas, figure of the blind bard, is also a figure of loss, of that bard's disappearance from the world. His blindness is constantly associated with his old age and infirmity (87, 170–171, 436), and the warriors see in his impending death the decline of wisdom and tradition in their tribe:

> Jamais on ne retrouvera un tel Sachem. Il sait la langue de toutes les forêts; il connaît tous les tombeaux qui servent de limites aux peuples, tous les fleuves qui séparent les nations. Nos pères ont été plus heureux que nous: ils ont passé leur vie avec sa sagesse; nous, nous ne le verrons que mourir. (193)[19]

Knowledgeable in the language of the forests, Chactas is at the center of Chateaubriand's efforts to preserve the poetic energy of that language. In the *Voyage en Amérique* he refers to the Natchez, Algonquins, and Hurons as "des peuples qui prêtent des sens à tout, qui entendent des voix dans tous les murmures, qui donnent des haines et des amours aux plantes, des désirs à l'onde, des esprits immortels aux animaux, des âmes aux rochers" (785).[20] The language of the Indians must express this animated and personified world, filled with symbolic objects that are signs of spirits or desires beyond themselves. Jean-Pierre Richard has noted that the image of the magnolia tree used by Chactas at the end of his *récit* attains "the overflowing voluminosity of the *symbol*" and thus participates in a remythification of the world, "the circulation of what Baudelaire will soon call *correspondances*."[21]

The most striking example of the blind elder's use of the symbolic language of his people occurs at the end of *René*, when, after his own cry of troubled sympathy and Father Souël's stern reproaches, Chactas provides a *poetic* response to the young man's confession, the apologue of the Mississippi:

> Un jour le Meschacebé, encore assez près de sa source, se lasse de n'être qu'un limpide ruisseau. Il demande des neiges aux montagnes, des eaux aux torrents, des pluies aux tempêtes, il franchit ses rives, et désole ses bords charmants. L'orgueilleux ruisseau s'applaudit d'abord de sa puissance; mais voyant que tout devenait désert sur son passage; qu'il coulait, abandonné dans la solitude; que ses eaux étaient toujours troublées, il regretta l'humble lit que lui avait creusé la nature, les oiseaux, les fleurs, les arbres et les ruisseaux, jadis modestes compagnons de son paisible cours. (145)[22]

True to Chateaubriand's description of Indian language in the *Voyage en Amérique*, personification abounds in this symbolic evocation of pride, destruction, solitude, and regret. The naïve authority of this passage stands in sharp contrast to the sentimental anguish that pervades the rest of the work, for the young René repeatedly evokes a sporadic and obsessive nature, capable of signification only as an echo of his own extreme and suffering subjectivity. All this might have very little to do with blindness were it not that at the beginning of *René* the Mississippi and its valley are designated as an example of the natural beauty that Chactas can no longer see (118). The poetry of Chactas appears to have its source in blindness: what he can personify and infuse with meaning is that which he cannot see.

The sympathy that Chactas displays to René brings us to another symbolic implication of his blindness: incest. The stories of Chactas and René have in common the theme of forbidden desire and impossible love between brother and sister. Although Atala is not related to Chactas by blood, and the actual obstacle to their union is her mother's vow that Atala will remain a virgin, Atala does reveal herself to be the daughter of Lopez, the adoptive father of Chactas. At the end of *René*, Chactas signals the parallel between René's life and his own by his initial empathetic reaction to the young man's tale: "Hélas, pour moi, tout me trouble et m'entraîne" (144). But the exile of Chactas has ended, and his return to his homeland signifies a partial resolution of conflicts and subsiding of passions. Chactas, we recall, is compared to Oedipus at the beginning of *Atala*. His blindness, by providing a specific symbolic punishment for incest, may in a sense make possible the old man's tranquillity and social reintegration. The narrator calls his infirmity the price paid for serenity and the return home: "Depuis plusieurs années, rentré dans le sein de sa patrie, Chactas jouissait du repos. Toutefois le ciel lui vendait cher cette faveur; le vieillard était devenu aveugle" (36).[23] For René, still tormented by regrets and impossible desires, there is no such reintegrative punishment and no end to exile, but Chactas, blind, is beyond the age of passions:

> La paix des passions éteintes se mêlait sur le front de Chactas, à cette sérénité remarquable chez les hommes qui ont perdu la vue; soit qu'en étant privés de la lumière terrestre nous commercions plus intimement avec celle des cieux, soit que l'ombre où vivent les aveugles ait un calme qui s'étende sur l'âme, de même que la nuit est plus silencieuse que le jour. (171)[24]

With its brief mention of an absence of desires, and the silent calm of darkness, this sentence is Chateaubriand's closest approach to a psychological representation of blindness in the *Natchez* cycle, his only use of an argument that could be found in a pedagogical treatise of the early nineteenth century. For Chateaubriand the blind bard was primarily a poetic topos, a figure of tradition, origin, and authority, a symbol of approaching death and calmed or expiated passions. The perceptions and language of Chactas were important to him not because they reflected the mental faculties of a blind person, but because they opened a modern window on an early age of civilization.

BALLANCHE

In the work of Pierre-Simon Ballanche, the image of the sightless bard functions both as a reference to tradition and as a pretext for psychological speculation about the mind of the poet or genius. In 1801, the year of *Atala*'s appearance, Ballanche published *Du sentiment*, a manifesto for "une nouvelle poétique," for a nonclassical aesthetic, and in its prologue he placed a reverential panegyric of Homer, "l'Aveugle de Smyrne." The prologue contains only passing references to Homer's blindness, but one of the book's chapters, "De la mélancolie," contains a theoretical discussion of blind poets, their emotions, and their relation to time and to the world around them. Ballanche begins the chapter by observing that melancholy is infrequently but charmingly portrayed by Greek writers; his first example is that of Oedipus at Colonus guided by Antigone. Melancholy, he writes, is the emotion of solitude, of exile, of submission to external laws, and it seeks places of isolation where "toujours errant hors du présent, elle double l'existence, tantôt par le souvenir des peines ou des plaisirs passés, tantôt par le pressentiment de la crainte ou de l'espérance, qui lui fait anticiper sur l'avenir."[25] The melancholic genius thus abandons an immediate, primary rapport with the world in favor of a historical imagination, a connection to past or future. Since the exterior world exists in the temporal present, the contemplation of past and future must take place in an interior world—what Ballanche calls the mind and heart—so that the melancholic turn to history coincides with autonomy and solitude. But his evocation of the solitary haunts of great thinkers and poets is interrupted when he reaches Homer: "Bientôt ce divin Homère trouva une solitude continuelle autour de lui; ses yeux, fermés à la clarté des cieux, cessèrent de voir la riante parure de la nature,

le front de l'homme . . ." (122).[26] Blindness, "une solitude con-
trainte et continuelle," radicalizes and renders irrevocable a sacrifice already made by every thinker, every poet who gives up
something of the present to sound the inner depths of past and
future.

The blind poet appears here as the most fully realized figure
of the melancholic or solitary artist, with the name of Homer
joined by those of Thamyris, Tiresias, Phineus, Ossian, and
Milton: "L'Homère anglais croyait que la privation de l'organe
extérieur de la vue rendait l'organe intérieur plus sensible à la lumière intellectuelle, qui est la vraie lumière" (122).[27] But Ballanche's speculation concerning the blind poet goes beyond the
idealistic substitution of one form of light for another:

> Cependant avouons qu'il y a quelque chose de bien pénible
> dans la pensée d'une solitude contrainte et continuelle:
> mais cet état même de privation et de chagrin, peint d'une
> manière si sublime par Ossian et Milton; cet état, dis-je, est
> encore favorable au génie, par l'intensité et la profondeur
> qu'une mélancolie habituelle lui fait acquérir. (122)[28]

The experience of blindness is described in this passage without
reference to optics, to light and darkness, and this description
makes it susceptible to metaphoric generalization, for it appears
as a set of exclusions in society, space, and above all time. To be
blind, for Ballanche, is to be imprisoned in the isolation of melancholy and thus to reap to the fullest the torments and rewards
of this intellectual and poetic apprenticeship.

When editing his *Oeuvres complètes* of 1833, Ballanche chose
to exclude *Du sentiment* but to conclude his general preface with
three early fragments. The first of these, "Mort d'un platoni-
cien," presents as narrator an old blind man, a surviving friend
of the philosopher whose death he recounts. The situation is repeated in *Antigone* (1814), with Tiresias reciting the misfortunes of Oedipus and his children at the court of Priam. And in
Ballanche's longest completed work, *Orphée* from the *Palingénésie sociale* (1829), the principal narrator is the blind poet Thamyris, a follower of Orpheus who after a long initiatory voyage
to Egypt reveals the Orphic teachings in conversations with

King Evander of Latium. The blind man thus occupies throughout Ballanche's work the role of a witness, of an initiatory narrator who interprets a predecessor or tradition to the future bearers of his historical mission. In his *Essai sur les institutions sociales* (1819), and especially in the *Palingénésie*, Ballanche elaborates a theory of social transformation in which linguistic and poetic traditions, and their interpreters, must play a decisive guiding role at critical moments of transition. Thamyris is said to have come to Evander at such a moment, when the Orphic initiation of civilization must be carried forward by the kingdom of Latium. The blind narrators assure the juncture of past and future, just as the melancholy (and blind) poets were condemned to an evasion from the present.

Ballanche's Thamyris is more than a narrator or even interpreter. He is himself a visionary poet, albeit on a less lofty and original plane than Orpheus. The Thamyris of antiquity was blinded by jealous muses whom he had rivaled in song, and Ballanche makes this loss of sight coincide with his visionary initiation and his encounter with the Orphic tradition, for his eyes grow cloudy as he deciphers the name of Orpheus on his tomb. He realizes that his blindness is "une véritable initiation," an initiation into a different understanding of time:

> Alors, Evandre, j'eus des notions moins confuses sur les objets les plus élevés; alors je conçus le temps faisant partie de l'éternité, identique avec elle. . . . Ainsi ma cécité m'apprenait les merveilles du monde où nous n'avons plus besoin de nos sens pour connaître; ainsi je comprenais comment, pour l'intelligence dégagée des organes, le passé, le présent, l'avenir sont contemporains.[29]

Even when not combined, as in the case of Thamyris, in a single figure, the blind visionary and the blind interpreter have in common their involvement with past and future, their separation from a present that was the object of their physical sight. The blind seer has sacrificed his visual, spatial perspective in favor of a temporal perspective from which he can perceive past, present, and future.

With Ballanche, then, and even in the early *Du sentiment*, we encounter for the first time an identificatory, psychological interest in the blind as romantic visionary figures. Blindness is more than the sign of venerable wisdom or of poetic models like Homer and Ossian; it is contiguously related to the isolation and melancholy said to be the condition of the modern poet or thinker. And yet Ballanche in his later works draws a sharp line between the visionaries of the past and the interpreters of the historical present. Under Christianity, he writes, poets need no longer fear the punishment of Thamyris, but this is a mixed blessing, for since no further religious revelation is necessary, there are no more true visionaries. The modern writer must attempt to carry out the function of his visionary predecessors, but he cannot claim the same kind of individual heroization; he must prepare the future without the aid of prophecy. The blind seer is thus tantalizingly close to but irrevocably sundered from the postrevolutionary writer who assumes the task of infusing something of poetry into a world of prose. Just as for the writers of educational treatises blind students could be characterized as alternately resembling and differing from the seeing, so there is a tension for the romantic writer between identification with and separation from the blind visionary. This tension will be central to our reading of Balzac, for what is most problematic in his writings concerning blindness is not the representation of the blind per se, but their relation to literature, their role with respect to the narrator or authorial persona.

BALZAC

An unwritten philosophical treatise haunts *La Comédie humaine*: it is the unfinished work of the young Balzac, the discarded work of Raphaël de Valentin, hero of *La Peau de chagrin*, the destroyed work of Louis Lambert, the author's fictive autobiographical double whose life ends in sterile madness. Balzac's presentation of the blind is inseparable from his fascination with the inner workings of the psyche, a fascination that predated his career as a novelist but never ceased to inform his fiction. The monomaniacs and mad artists of *La Comédie humaine* are but the most obvious manifestations of its author's early vocation as a speculative thinker. In fact, such problems as the economy of psychic energy and the nature of ideas are, for Balzac, central to narration, to character, and above all to the relationship between the author and his creations. In the preface to *La Peau de chagrin*, the very possibility of fictional representation appears to depend on the dynamics of energy and interior vision. That vision seems nowhere more vital or intense than in the blind, cut off as they are from the visible world. But the novelist *qua* visionary, however entranced he may be with the phantasmagoria of words and images in his brain, must also *see*. His creations, to be communicable, must be grounded in the substantial, visible world in which he and his readers live. When the young Balzac meets an old blind musician in the quasi-autobiographical story *Facino Cane*, the shock is that of the uncanny recognition of a double, an alter ego too familiar to cast aside and too estranging to embrace.

The narrator of *Facino Cane* evokes the philosophical origins of Balzac's literary career by recalling his life in the *mansarde* on the rue de Lesdiguières, where Balzac himself had lived at the age of twenty. "L'amour de la science m'avait jeté dans une mansarde où je travaillais la nuit, et je passais le jour dans une bibliothèque voisine . . ." (6:1019).[30] Balzac's ambition, when he first obtained his family's grudging permission to set himself up in a garret and become a man of letters, had not been to write novels. He wanted to write a verse tragedy, because he believed that the most prestigious of genres offered him the greatest chances of fame and success, and he wanted to write treatises on the soul and the nature of genius, because these were the intellectual problems that most intrigued him. His tragedy, *Cromwell*, need not concern us here, but in the fragmentary "Dissertation sur l'homme" and "Notes philosophiques" of this period we find the beginnings of Balzac's long speculation concerning the senses, the mind, and language. It is here that we shall begin our examination of the Balzacian writings on artistic creation and the mental universe, writings that provide the context for our readings of texts involving blindness—*Louis Lambert, Modeste Mignon*, and above all *Facino Cane*.

The earliest philosophical writings of Balzac display a tension between an uncritical acceptance of sensationalist epistemology and a lively interest in ideas that do not come directly from the senses. With the conviction of a disciple, Balzac writes: "Locke a prouvé d'une manière *irréfutable* qu'il n'y avait aucun principe inné."[31] In condemning innate ideas, Balzac uses familiar arguments from eighteenth-century philosophy concerning the consequences of sensory differences. In the "Notes" he evokes sensory deprivation in a passage that recalls Condillac's statue:

> Une preuve de la naissance, etc., de l'âme, c'est qu'il n'y a pas d'idées innées et qu'elles ne nous viennent qu'à mesure des sensations: car l'âme sans les sensations qui la frappent ne se manifesterait pas. Le prouver— Exemple d'un homme aveugle, sourd, muet, sans odorat, etc.[32]

And in the "Dissertation" he uses the familiar notion of contrasting climates to account for the variations in sense organs that produce, he claims, the different ideas found in different peoples and individuals.

Balzac's ambition as a thinker, however, leads him to reach beyond philosophic sensationalism to other ways of knowing, ways that he does not yet fully understand. The "Notes" marshal arguments against the immortality of the soul, and the "Dissertation" proposes an inquiry into the nature of genius, the putative cause of human scientific and cultural achievements. These projects lead him to investigate the meaning of abstract words such as "âme" and "génie." He distinguishes between words that signify ideas of perceivable objects or actions, and words that signify ideas for which there is no corresponding referent accessible to the senses. By taking the designation of sensible objects to be the primary mode of linguistic signification, Balzac was clearly taking as his starting point a classical view of language, one that stressed its mimetic or representational function. Now in classical theories of language as representation, the move from concrete designation to complex, relational concepts poses no problem. Balzac at one point even notes that Locke has said all that must be said on the subject, but for the young thinker anxious to pierce the mysteries of soul and genius, the abstract concept is more than just a set of concrete concepts compared, combined, or analyzed. The abstract word provides a semblance of understanding where no true understanding exists; thus, to investigate the abstract word is to investigate "les secrets de la Nature . . . les causes premières."[33] The abstract idea is for Balzac a function of what is *in* the mind, a product of the mind acting on its own contents. When the mind analyzes itself, it becomes an autonomous entity, cut off from the world: "un abîme sans fond, un labyrinthe inextricable."[34] In Balzac's dualistic view of man as a being of action and thought, outside and inside, ideas that do not refer to sensible objects belong clearly to the inner universe.

Balzac was not a philosopher, and his solution to the problem of abstract ideas and the mind's functioning were to be metaphoric and heuristic, never logical or rigorous. In the "Notes" and the "Dissertation," even the metaphors are poorly developed. The mind's power to act on its own contents may or may not be, he writes, a "sixième sens."[35] The concept of sensation is readily available and easily understood, but it can be applied only metaphorically to a process that is by definition beyond sensation. Without context or elaboration, the metaphor is weak, and it reveals little about Balzac's understanding of how the mind acts on itself. But in his earliest literary works, notions borrowed from such domains as mysticism and animal magnetism are beginning to provide a coherent set of images and figures to describe ways of knowing that are independent of sense perception. In an unfinished novel from 1821, *Sténie, ou les erreurs philosophiques*, dreams are said to be the privileged moment of mental autonomy, in which "l'âme réagit sur elle-même": the dreamer, by means of a "vue interne," sees objects that he has never seen or may one day see.[36] But it is in *Le Centenaire, ou les deux Béringheld*, a novel published in 1822 under the pseudonym of Horace de Saint-Aubain, that we find the first full-scale account of a Balzacian "visionary experience," an account surprisingly similar to those of mature works such as *Louis Lambert*. In this novel, an imitation of Maturin's *Melmoth the Wanderer*, the general Tullius Béringheld encounters his mysterious and diabolical ancestor, the *Centenaire*, a giant of prodigious strength who, thanks to vampirism, has lived for several hundred years. His ultimate victim is the general's hapless fiancée Marianine, whom he lures to his dwelling in the catacombs by promising her a vision of her absent lover:

> Là, une lueur surnaturelle, fruit de mon art tout-puissant, peut te le montrer, en quelque lieu qu'il soit. —Tu entreras dans l'atmosphère pur et vuide de la pensée, tu parcourras le monde idéal, ce vaste réservoir d'où sortent les *Chauchemars*, les *Ombres* qui soulèvent les rideaux des agonisans, cet arsenal des *Incubes* et des *Magiciens*; tu visiteras l'*ombre* qui n'est causée par aucune *lueur*, l'*ombre* qui n'a point de soleil!... tu verras, par un regard *hors les regards* de la vie![37]

Floating between life and death, trapped deep in the catacombs, Marianine "sees" the aboveground efforts of her fiancé and his soldiers to free her, as if she herself were standing among them. Marianine's experience has three notable features: it abolishes distance and spatial obstacles, it is a pure creation of thought, and it is a *vision* whose domain is not the same as that of ordinary sight. The vocabulary of occultism elaborates the metaphor of an internal sixth sense. Instead of being simply a faculty for abstraction and imagination, for the formation of ideas not directly attached to the substantial universe, the sixth sense of *Le Centenaire* provides a direct and immediate representation of a reality to which the subject would not have access through the physical senses.

Le Centenaire would hardly merit our attention if the visionary experience it describes were confined, in Balzac's works, to contexts of demonic giants and vampires. But the author of *La Comédie humaine* found the concept of psychic vision or second sight to be a remarkably adaptable one, and he turned to it on many occasions to explain his own powers of literary representation. Throughout his career Balzac was concerned with the relation between the work's author and the authorial persona that the reader might invent based on the work. Both his early use of pseudonyms and his later theoretical discourse on the nature of writing are attempts to prevent the author's own experience from being identified with the experiences he recounts. Since his novels had a referential vocation, Balzac could not claim that they were pure inventions in which his own experience and observation had no part. The relation between author and authorial persona was thus sometimes one of distance and difference, sometimes one of identity, very much like the relation between the blind and the seeing implicit in pedagogical treatises and in the writings of Ballanche. Unlike the pseudonyms, which simply distanced the author from his creation, the metaphors of second sight provided Balzac with a means of maintaining this dialectic of identity and difference while signing his works.

In 1828, with the "Avertissement du Gars," an abandoned preface to what was to become *Les Chouans*, Balzac presented for the first time the idea of an interior vision at the origins of the novelist's creation. The fictive author of *Le Gars*, Victor Morillon, had spent his youth

> s'abandonnant à une contemplation perpétuelle, possédé d'une haine curieuse pour les réalités et les corps, ignorant sa propre existence physique; vivant, pour ainsi dire, par les seules forces de ces sens intérieurs qui constituent, selon lui, un double être en l'homme, mais épuisé par cette intuition profonde des choses. (8:1672)[38]

This faculty of inner vision, we are told, accounts for Morillon's ability to invent stories such as the novel about to be read. The energy of his contemplations comes from the repression of worldly and bodily desires. The old professor who first discovers the young man's talents likens him to the monastic adepts of religious ecstasy, whose visions he attributes to "les ameublements dont la chasteté enrichissait leur cerveau" (8:1674).[39]

Balzac abandoned Morillon and signed *Les Chouans* himself, but the problem of authorial identity was by no means laid to rest. Once the game of a fictive creator has been rejected in favor of an author who is both proprietor and creator, this author must find a new way of preserving his personal image and his artistic freedom from contamination by each other. Balzac takes up the problem in the 1831 preface to *La Peau de chagrin* (henceforth referred to as "Préface"), noting that since he has admitted to writing the *Physiologie du mariage* he has been taken for an old doctor or a cynical veteran of eighteenth-century de-

139

bauchery. The usual strategy of a preface in this situation, he writes, would be to concoct an ingenious fictive autobiography, but that would not prevent the accusation from resurfacing (10:51). And so he turns to psychology, in a sentence that marks a bold new incorporation of science and philosophy into the discourse of fiction: "Mais pour terminer ce léger procès, en faveur de son innocence, il lui suffira sans doute d'amener aux sources de la pensée les personnes peu familiarisées avec les opérations de l'intelligence humaine" (10:51).[40] To create the space necessary to the authorial creation of narrative, Balzac proposes the scientific education of the reader. Whether or not the specific explanation to be presented is valid or even plausible, this is a significant step, for it places the relation between creator and creation inside the domain of fiction itself. Literature differs from the other arts, we are told, by its complexity, by the very fact that "ayant pour objet de reproduire la nature par la pensée," it cannot elude the mind-matter problem (10:51). The complementary foundations of literary art are thus dualistic—observation and writing, *conception* and *faire*, the movements of interiorization and exteriorization—but their balanced presence alone creates no dynamism, no driving force, "ne constitue pas la volonté qui engendre une oeuvre d'art" (10:52).[41] And so Balzac begins his justly famous presentation of the *seconde vue*:

> Outre ces deux conditions essentielles au talent, il se passe chez les poètes ou chez les écrivains réellement philosophes, un phénomène moral, inexplicable, inouï, dont la science peut difficilement rendre compte. C'est une sorte de seconde vue qui leur permet de deviner la vérité dans toutes les situations possibles; ou, mieux encore, je ne sais quelle puissance qui les transporte là où ils doivent être. Ils inventent le vrai, par analogie, ou voient l'objet à décrire, soit que l'objet vienne à eux, soit qu'ils aillent eux-mêmes vers l'objet (10:52).[42]

Like Marianine's vision in *Le Centenaire*, this literary second sight abolishes the constraints of space and permits the author to "see" what he wants to describe.

The term *seconde vue* accords to the eye and the gaze a dominant place in the metaphorics of literary creation, but it is to the more strictly literary implications of this passage that we must first turn our attention. This second sight provides more than the abolition of space, for it explains, according to Balzac, a classic property of literary language defined in Aristotle's *Poetics*: the presentation of a verisimilar possibility more general and truthful than historical reference. Since it is the power to name and describe what has not been seen or experienced, it guarantees the disparity between the historical author and the authorial persona of a work. In this the *seconde vue* may be taken to imply a second point of view; it describes the narrative process as one of mobile perspective.

But Balzac's theory does not simply provide a defense against the reductive biographical reading of his works, for *seconde vue* is not merely a name for literary use of language; it describes a transgressive faculty, the visual incorporation or penetration of an object. It is an imaginative faculty by which subject and object are made to coincide, by which identification with the other is accomplished, by which the narrative point of view can be transported to where it must be. As to the nature of this imaginative power, Balzac provides some suggestions that take us far beyond the simple problem of separating authorial identities:

> Les hommes ont-ils le pouvoir de faire venir l'univers dans leur cerveau, ou leur cerveau est-il un talisman avec lequel ils abolissent les lois du temps et de l'espace? La science hésitera longtemps à choisir entre ces deux mystères également inexplicables. Toujours est-il constant que l'inspiration déroule au poète des transfigurations sans nombre et semblables aux magiques fantasmagories de nos rêves. Un rêve est peut-être le jeu naturel de cette singulière puissance, quand elle reste inoccupée! (10:53)[43]

The ocultist discourse of *Le Centenaire* and the speculation on dreams from *Sténie* converge here in a more serious context, that of the artist's relation to his own brain. There is no need to assume that Balzac literally believed himself to possess parapsychological powers, but we must consider the implications of his choice of concepts and metaphors. For the modern reader, this transforming and transfiguring function akin to dreams suggests the unconscious dimension of the mind. Pierre-Marc de Biasi has proposed that the *seconde vue* refers to language itself in its rhetorical structure, to the use of language in relation to the unconscious.[44] This suggestive interpretation is compatible with Balzac's own speculation only if we take the language in question to be the signs actually stored within the psychic apparatus of an individual. The metaphor of second sight implies not an aleatory unconscious process but an exercise of conscious control over the energy and images of such a process.

After the "Préface" to *La Peau de chagrin* in 1831, Balzac's next major text on inner vision and literary creation was to be *Louis Lambert*, written and first published in 1832 and revised for subsequent editions in 1833 and 1835. Here the presentation of *seconde vue* is less theoretical than fictional, but to make matters more complicated the fiction is overtly autobiographical. The novel's hero, a fictive childhood friend of Balzac's, possesses extraordinary mental powers, but at the end of his life his eyes are those of a blind man, and he has withdrawn into a madness from which his once sympathetic friend, the narrator, can only draw back in troubled incomprehension. Although Lambert's genius resides in his ability to draw his gaze inward, away from the world and toward the objects of his thought and desire, his final appearance as a blind man unable to return his sight to the world reveals him to be insane, incapable of creating or communicating.

The text of *Louis Lambert* begins in as objective a biographical mode as possible: "Louis Lambert naquit, en 1797, à Montoire, petite ville du Vendômois . . ." (11:589).[45] The narrator passes quickly over childhood events to discuss the boy's precocious and voracious reading habits, and soon even this narrative gives way to lengthy discourses by the adolescent Lambert himself, quoted we are told, from memory. "Quand je le veux, me disait-il . . . je tire un voile sur mes yeux. Soudain je rentre en moi-même, et j'y trouve une chambre noire où les accidents de la nature viennent se reproduire sous une forme plus pure que la forme sous laquelle ils sont d'abord apparus à mes sens extérieurs" (11:593).[46] This description of interior vision clearly places Lambert in the series of Balzacian figurations of the intellectual creator. His mind functions as an instrument of representation, and does so in moments of voluntary blindness to the outer world. While reading intensely, "il perdait en quelque sorte la conscience de sa vie physique . . . il laissait, suivant son expression, *l'espace derrière lui*" (11:594).[47] In the dark chamber of his interior sight, the textual order of signs replaces the spatial order of sight, only to produce the impression of a clearer and more intense sight than that of the eyes.

The portrait of the visionary is soon interrupted, however, by a flustered narrator. "Malgré moi déjà, je viens d'intervertir l'ordre par lequel je dois dérouler l'histoire de cet homme qui transporta toute son action dans sa pensée, comme d'autres placent toute leur vie dans l'action" (11:594).[48] How, indeed, to narrate the life of such a man, to transport and translate the actions of his thought into actions capable of narrative representation? The narrator reproaches himself for abandoning an external, chronological account and for expressing directly his sympathetic fascination with Lambert's theories and mode of thought. Checking this indulgence, he recounts how he came to know Lambert, how they were the best of friends for two years at the Vendôme *collège des Oratoriens*. The institution, the dates, the narrator's age, and the reference to one of Balzac's real classmates—Ballanche's disciple and interpreter Barchou de Penhoën—all point to an autobiographical narration, an identification of narrative content with authorial experience that runs counter to the freedom of fiction that in the "Préface" had been theoretically founded on the *seconde vue*. In a manuscript prologue to *Louis Lambert*, Balzac acknowledges this situation and justifies it by according the work a scientific rather than purely literary status:

Je sais de quelle froideur un récit est frappé par l'emploi du *je* et du *moi*; mais si nous sommes en droit, si nous devons même cacher les sources où nous allons puiser certaines compositions romanesques, pourrait-il en être ainsi pour les faits susceptibles d'intéresser les sciences? (11:1502)[49]

While maintaining his opposition to the biographical fallacy in the reading of literature, Balzac leaves open the possibility of a scientific study of text and author. The first-person narrator will be no fictive Morillon arbitrarily distinguished from the author, but instead a voice contiguous to the author's, sometimes identical and sometimes differing. The *seconde vue*, rather than being the alibi of the first person, is projected to a character, a friend and hero with whom the narrator's identification could hardly be more intense. Their schoolmates even joined their nicknames into a singular term, *Le-Poète-et-Pythagore*. "Nous nous habituâmes, comme deux amants, à penser ensemble, à nous communiquer nos rêveries. . . . Il n'existait aucune distinction entre les choses qui venaient de lui et celles qui venaient de moi" (11:615, 618).[50] During their stay at the school, then, there is no discontinuity between Lambert and the narrator, merely a difference of degree in intensity and originality, as if Lambert were an extreme and concentrated projection of possibilities that the author-narrator once attributed to himself.

Yet there was one initial difference between the narrator and Lambert: the former was a materialist, the latter a spiritualist, and in their debates each came to recognize the validity of the other's position. "Peut-être les mots matérialisme et spiritualisme expriment-ils les deux côtés d'un seul et même fait" (11:616).[51] The most distinctive feature of the "theoretical" passages in *Louis Lambert* is the intermingling and juxtaposition of spiritualistic and materialistic discourse, the way in which explanations, metaphors, and analogies constantly cross over between the two. In one of Lambert's materialistic moments, he defines *volonté* to be a fluid or electric medium in which thought takes place and which constitutes "la masse de force par laquelle l'homme peut reproduire, en dehors de lui-même, les actions qui composent sa vie extérieure" (11:626)[52] *Volonté* is the internally stored energy whose release drives the representational act, the re-action, by which the subject realizes his desire. Desire, for Lambert, is an imbalance between interior and exterior, an excess of interior representation. Its satisfaction will consist of its reproduction in the exterior world, which restores the equilibrium of forces. The relation between interior and exterior is one of projection, both an optically projective reproduction of an interior image, and the projectile-like outpouring of energy that must accompany it. Lambert himself possesses to a high degree the power to project his *volonté* through the eyes. He even receives a flogging for casting on one of his teachers "un regard empreint de je ne sais quel mépris sauvage, chargé de pensée comme une bouteille de Leyde est chargée d'électricité" (11:612; cf. 11:633).[53] But if Lambert can at times project great energy outside himself, he can also concentrate his energy within his own psyche and thus withdraw all life or force from his eyes:

> Tantôt clair et pénétrant à étonner, tantôt d'une douceur céleste, ce regard devenait terne, sans couleur pour ainsi dire, dans les moments où il se livrait à ses contemplations. Son oeil ressemblait alors à une vitre d'où le soleil se serait retiré soudain après l'avoir illuminée. (11:605)[54]

When all his energy is concentrated on the contents of his mind, the visionary's eyes take on the inanimate gaze of one who no longer sees the world around him.

Lambert's visionary faculty in its purest form, given the name *Spécialité* in his fragments and in *Séraphîta*, unites transcendent insight and an analogical, metaphysical hierarchy of being. Lambert divides human activity into three spheres: first, Instinct, the sphere of unthinking, active, presocietal life; second, Abstraction, that of thought, speech, understanding, and social laws; finally *Spécialité*, as far above Abstraction as Abstraction is above Instinct. His explanation, in the sixteenth of his fragments recorded by the narrator, is one of the crucial Balzacian texts concerning the *seconde vue*:

> La Spécialité consiste à voir les choses du monde matériel aussi bien que celles du monde spirituel dans leurs ramifications originelles et conséquentielles. Les plus beaux génies humains sont ceux qui sont partis des ténèbres de l'Abstraction pour arriver aux lumières de la Spécialité. (Spécialité, *species*, vue, spéculer, voir tout, et d'un seul coup; *speculum*, miroir ou moyen d'apprécier une chose en

la voyant tout entière.) Jésus était Spécialiste, il voyait le fait dans ses racines et dans ses productions, dans le passé qui l'avait engendré, dans le présent où il se manifestait, dans l'avenir où il se développait; sa vue pénétrait l'entendement d'autrui. La perfection de la vue intérieure enfante le don de Spécialité. (11:688)[55]

To the dark, nonsensory, linguistic truths of Abstraction, Spécialité adds two new elements: first, light and vision, a phenomenal presence as if of the exterior world, and second, the perception of cause and effect, the linking of phenomena to an essential order extending over all space and time. A temporal as well as spatial view, *Spécialité* resembles the faculty of contemplating past and future that Ballanche attributed to the blind or melancholy poet. The life of pure *Spécialité* would be accessible only to the divine, but men of genius are those who approach it, who strive to give birth to it by perfecting their inner sight. *Spécialité* parallels and extends the *seconde vue* presented in the "Préface": second sight enables the writer to render the presence of absent or nonexistent objects and events, but a writer gifted with *Spécialité* could go beyond the presentation of the possible to the explanation of causes and effects. The theory of *Spécialité* thus corresponds to Balzac's ambition in the *Etudes philosophiques*: to present the *causes* of the social *effects* portrayed in the *Etudes de moeurs*.[56]

For the divine or angelic *Spécialiste*, Jesus or Balzac's own Séraphîta-Séraphîtüs, the passage beyond phenomena to essential causes poses no risk, but for Lambert, the all-too-human practitioner of *Spécialité*, inner vision leads to isolation. Lambert and the narrator, in their collective exposition of Swedenborgian doctrine, designate this peril by an analogy between geniuses and the blind: "Il peut exister entre les gens de génie et d'autres êtres la même distance qui sépare les Aveugles des Voyants" (11:617).[57] But what is the correct order of the terms here? Everything except the word order suggests that the genius is to the ordinary man ("dont l'intelligence inerte le condamne à une apparente stupidité") as the seeing are to the blind. The order of the terms, however, forces us to identify the geniuses with the blind, an interpretation consistent with the idea that the blind possess an inner vision superior to that of the seeing. Simultaneously analogy and chiasmus, the figure is unstable, indicating the risk that the superiority of genius may coincide with the solitude of blindness. For Lambert, who will take on the appearance of a blind man, the analogy of the seeing and the blind cannot be reassuring, for its reversed terms point to the sensory isolation that will engulf him.

Lambert's madness, though pathological, is at first presented according to the classical notion of madness as the departure of the soul from the body, a middle term between contemplation and death. References to the separation of soul and body occur throughout the text, in the words of the narrator, of Lambert's companion Mlle. de Villenoix, and Lambert himself (11:594, 617, 621, 629, 666, 683). But when Lambert's uncle informs the narrator of what has become of his old friend, he refers to contemporary psychiatric medicine: "Je l'emmenai promptement à Paris pour le confier aux soins de monsieur Esquirol. . . . A Paris, les médecins le regardèrent comme incurable" (11:679).[58] Jean-Claude Fizaine has advanced critical understanding of *Louis Lambert* by showing the significance of psychiatric discourse to its narrative structure. He notes that the connection between madness and genius can be interpreted in two ways: philosophically, as an essential relation (the madman as misunderstood genius in need of an interpreter), or scientifically, as a misleading resemblance awaiting demystification by the alienist. The narrator, of course, presents most of the account from the first point of view, but he abruptly shifts to the second on learning of the diagnosis, Lambert's attempt at self-castration, and his confinement to the care of Mlle. Villenoix. The narrator at this point replaces his initial identification with Lambert by a distanced perspective, from which he attempts to remain outside the madness.[59] *Louis Lambert* recounts the separation of the madman and the narrator—thus the formation of a narrator who, like Morillon and Lambert, has gone through the intense inner experience of language that is called *seconde vue* or *Spécialité*, but who has excluded and repressed the dangerous, alienating aspect of that experience. "Lambert exerça sur mon imagination une influence de laquelle je me ressens encore aujourd'hui,"[60] writes the narrator, but he maintains the distinction between such an influence and their former intimacy (11:616). The textual mediation posed by the narrator between himself and Lambert is extremely explicit, even for Balzac. The reader is constantly made aware of shifts in perspective, of difficulties in ordering, of the source of the narrator's information, of moments when the narrator embraces Lambert's point of view with passion and moments when he steps back and pronounces his judgments. It is as if in *Louis Lambert* Balzac were laying bare the mechanisms of identification and distancing in his narrative constructions, in his shifting points of view, leaving the difficulties and discontinuities in the open rather than minimizing them in the interest of the illusion of an innocently and ubiquitously mobile narrator.

The narrator's reaction when brought face to face with Lambert confirms that through his friend something of himself has been repressed, for with Lambert's appearance the repressed returns with uncanny force. On his way to see him, the narrator's heart trembles: "Je m'étais associé, pour ainsi dire, à sa vie et à sa situation . . ." (11:681).[61] Led into the dark room where at the doctors' orders Lambert lives with his maternally devoted companion Pauline, he is, like the platonic cave-dweller returning after beholding the sun, almost unable to see, just as he is unable to again enter into communication with Lambert's fantasmatic universe.

The image of blind eyes dominates the narrator's attempt to describe his old friend: "Hélas! déjà ridé, déjà blanchi, enfin déjà plus de lumière dans ses yeux, devenus vitreux comme ceux d'un aveugle" (11:682).[62] The image completes that of the lifeless *vitre* of Lambert's eyes during his meditations. The world of Lambert, of *seconde vue* and *Spécialité*, has become totally cut off from the possibility of referring to or knowing anything outside itself, and the analogy of the visionary superiority of genius has collapsed, leaving only the singular figure of the man of genius as blind. The narrator's quasi-medical description of him is an attempt to avoid joining his friend's madness. With tears in his eyes, tempted by the thought that Lambert may not in fact have lost his reason, or rather that he too could enter his intense private universe, the narrator tears himself away from him and his surroundings, from "cette vie d'enfant au berceau" (11:682): "Je redoutais de me retrouver dans cette atmosphère enivrante où l'extase était contagieuse" (11:691).[63] Lambert's infantile existence, a fantasy life so heavily invested as to exclude all external activity, exercises such strong attraction as to require continual renewal of its repression, to provoke continual disruptions of the narrator's mastery of his story.

In *Facino Cane* (1836), Balzac's only work centered around a blind character, the identification of narrator and author is less insistent but no less evident than in *Louis Lambert*, for the reference to the garret on the rue des Lesdiguières recalls, as we have noted, an episode in Balzac's life. Aside from his nightly intellectual labors, the young writer's only passion was to observe "les moeurs du faubourg" (6:1019), and the interpretation of this passion applies an autobiographical perspective to his development as the novelist of society: "Sachez seulement que, dès ce temps, j'avais décomposé les éléments de cette masse hétérogène nommée le peuple. . . . Je savais déjà de quelle utilité pourrait être ce faubourg" (6:1020).[64] Like *Louis Lambert*, *Facino Cane* presents a double of the autobiographical narrator, this time a symbolic rather than historical double, an old blind musician suddenly encountered at a working-class wedding feast. The old man tells how as a young Venetian nobleman he had murdered for love, how beneath his prison cell he had discovered a secret treasure, and how after his escape to the court of Louis XV he had been struck blind with amaurosis, then betrayed by his mistress and reduced to poverty. He proposes to his enthralled young listener that they go to Venice together in search of the gold. The narrator accepts, but he leads the old man back to the home for the blind, where two months later he is dead.

In the narrator's presentation of himself we can recognize elements of the Balzacian visionary as we have followed him from *Le Centenaire* to *Louis Lambert*. His studious habits obey an economy of sublimation, "toutes les conditions de la vie monastique, si nécessaire aux travailleurs." But as an observer his attention is directed more to the exterior, to others, than to the inner chamber of the mind; his *seconde vue* is expansive rather than concentrative:

> Chez moi l'observation était devenue intuitive, elle pénétrait l'âme sans négliger le corps; ou plutôt elle saisissait si bien les détails extérieurs qu'elle allait sur-le-champ au-delà; elle me donnait la faculté de vivre de la vie de l'individu sur lequel elle s'exerçait, en me permettant de me substituer à lui comme le derviche des *Mille et Une Nuits* prenait le corps et l'âme des personnes sur lesquelles il prononçait certaines paroles. (6:1019)[65]

What is here named intuition is described as a doubling or raising to a second power; it is a vision that goes beyond sensation and description, not only seizing the objects accessible to the senses, but also appropriating to a visual order the soul, the symbolic charge, the hidden essence. Like *Spécialité*, this intuition lifts the veil of words and phenomena, and penetrates the understanding of the the the Other. The narrator's faculty of observation parallels the structure of Balzac's referentially grounded symbolization in that both are second-order semiological systems, in which the signified image, or visual referent ("corps," "détails extérieurs"), becomes in its turn the symbolic or mythological signifier of an essence or meaning ("âme," "au-delà"). What must, however, strike us as different here from the second sight of Morillon and Lambert is the implied exteriority: rather than capturing and incorporating its objects, creating an inner stockpile of living visual memories, sight becomes the means by which the subject abandons his point of view as subject in favor of an identification with the Other, whose being is thus transgressed. This implies a kinship with madness, with the departure of the soul from the body, and yet no threat of madness seems to weigh on the narrator, for this dispersal of identity is balanced by the dark and solitary labors in the garret. The text's visual metaphors describe a narrator capable of adopting in turn the perspective of his several characters, and indeed of describing each as if from the inside of his or her psychic economy, or system of *volonté*. Baudelaire's famous statement that the souls of Balzac's characters are "chargées de volonté jusqu'à la gueule," that they are all Balzac himself,[66] suggests that the intuitive observation described in *Facino Cane*, far more than what is cited from other texts as proof of a "Balzac visionnaire," is a metaphoric description of the representational and signifying modes of *La Comédie humaine*, and that the narrator's autobiographical interpretation of this experience is profoundly true whether it is historically accurate or not.

Yet a trace of the fear of madness, which hangs over the narrator of *Louis Lambert*, surfaces here in another often-quoted sentence resuming the waking dreams of the future novelist: "Quitter ses habitudes, devenir un autre que soi par l'ivresse des facultés morales, et jouer ce jeu à volonté, telle était ma distraction"[67] (6:1020). In their widely used school manual, Lagarde and Michard quote this text, but they simplify matters by excising the words "et jouer ce jeu à volonté," thereby offering the *lycéen* a stable and secure Balzac whose own psychic economy remains unthreatened by the serious enterprise of creating realistic characters.[68] That this enterprise should be a game is perhaps scandalous enough, but still more serious is the apprehension indicated by the narrator, who insists on hanging on to his own will, his *own* psychic economy (*volonté*), in order to guard against a loss of self and to keep intoxication at the level of distraction. The narrator is engaged in transgressing the boundary of the Other, in seizing his soul, but he wants to remain in the place of an observer behind a protective barrier, behind his own anchored perspective as a subject. The gaze may circulate, but not be lost from the narrator's sight, for it must be brought back to its place after its distraction.

A chain of common circumstances and allusions marks Facino Cane as a double of the narrator. Both are autobiographical narrators, and both recount the adventures they had at the age of twenty. Both are likened to Dante, the narrator by his reference to Paris as the "ville de douleur" into which he descends in search of unsuspected dramas, and Cane by his appearance, "le masque en plâtre de Dante," and by his status as an exile. As young men, both Cane and the narrator perform intellectual labors in cell-like chambers, for Cane's escape depended on deciphering inscriptions in his dungeon and the narrator's attic room can be linked to the Venetian prison by a remark in *La Peau de chagrin* concerning Raphaël's *mansarde*, "cette cage digne des *plombs* de Venise" (10:137).[69]

The narrator meets Cane at a humble wedding feast in a wine merchant's building on the rue de Charenton and insists in his account on "la bizarrerie du cadre" (6:1021). The guests are dancing as if there were no tomorrow. The feast is a dissipation of meager savings, a discharge of sexual energy, a moment of innocent transgression to which the narrator opposes the regulated, hypocritical, and ultimately prostitutional libidinal economy of bourgeois society, "les timides oeillades des jeunes filles bien élevées." As Nicole Mozet has noted, the *fête populaire* in Balzac's work brings with it an oneiric atmosphere, a suspension of repression or rather the kind of prerepressive libidinal situation identified with the *Contes drôlatiques*.[70] In this atmosphere, so conducive to the return of repressed fantasms, the narrator encounters Cane and describes the event as a sudden and exhilarating displacement of self: "quand je m'en rapprochai, je ne sais pourquoi, tout fut dit, la noce et sa musique disparut, ma curiosité fut excitée au plus haut degré, car mon âme passa dans le corps du joueur de clarinette" (6:1022).[71] For the narrator this is an uncanny moment in the Freudian sense, "when the distinction between imagination and reality is effaced, as when something that we have hitherto regarded as imaginary appears before us in reality."[72] The narrator experiences immediately (though apparently without trauma) what the narrator of *Louis Lambert* had fought off in his final encounter with his onetime comrade: the outer world disappears beneath the fantasm of identification with the blind double. For Freud, the uncanniness of the encounter with one's double stems from a return or recurrence of something long ago repressed or surmounted.[73] In *Facino Cane*, this return of the repressed breaks through consciousness, subverts and threatens with dissipation the subject's concentrated *volonté*, and breaks down the separation between subject and object founded on visual perspective. The encounter with the blind man shifts the narrator from a phenomenal

152

order to a symbolic order, from the representations of sight to the blind figurations of the unconscious.

The narrator explains his fascination by presenting Cane's portrait, a description dominated by two elements: blindness and great poets. Cane's face resembles a bust of Dante, and the grandeur and force of his appearance suggests an old Homer, bearing within his mind a hidden "*Odyssey.*"[74] By referring to the blind founding figure of literature, Balzac lends seriousness and authority to the modern poetry of Paris, of which Cane is one of the hidden sources. But the narrator does more than allude to blindness; he describes it. The three musicians are first mentioned with reference to their status as institutional wards, as "trois aveugles des Quinze-Vingts." The two others are dismissed as being uninterestingly blind, as having "la figure si connue de l'aveugle, pleine de contention, attentive et grave" (6:1022).[75] The reference to a stereotype of respectable docility calls to mind the attempt, in pedagogical treatises, to present the public with an orderly and edifying image of the institution-alized blind. Dufau, in his *Revue de Paris* article of 1831, wrote: "Comme ils sont naturellement peu expansifs . . . nous les trou-vons froids . . . ils sont ordinairement dociles envers leurs maîtres."[76] Balzac thus emphasizes Cane's *difference* from the modern, desacralized representation of the blind fostered by the institutions devoted to their maintenance and education. But to lend verisimilitude to his claim that the narrator and Cane could share their thoughts, he turned to an idea which Defau, too, had propounded, the mental concentration of the blind: "Nos pensées étaient sans doute communes, car je crois que la cécité rend les communications intellectuelles beaucoup plus rapides en défendant à l'attention de s'éparpiller sur les objets exté-rieurs" (6:1025).[77] The presumed concentration and attentive-ness of the blind lend plausibility to the symbolic relation be-tween Cane and the narrator, and to the visionary powers of each.

Other aspects of Cane's description, however, have nothing to do with a "realistic" or psychological representation of the blind. His eyes, though sightless, radiate a powerful luminosity, suggesting pent up internal energy: "L'expression amère et douloureuse de cette magnifique tête était agrandie par la cécité, car les yeux morts revivaient par la pensée; il s'en échappait comme une lueur brillante" (6:1022).[78] Blindness intensifies Cane's appearance by offering a contrast between death and life, between a ruined exterior and an interior burning with desire. His infirmity, amaurosis or *goutte sereine*, leaves eyes that are clear and brilliant, that retain for the beholder the optical qualities of mirrors, windows on the soul, or radiant beacons. But if desire radiates from the eyes, its ravages are written on the forehead, and the landscape of Cane's face is that of a dormant volcano: "L'incendie du désespoir s'était éteint dans les cendres, la lave s'était refroidie; mais les sillons, les bouleversements, un peu de fumée attestaient la violence de l'éruption, les ravages du feu" (6:1023).[79] In the eyes, set like craters or caves in the face, lurks the danger of a new explosion, a new return of the burning desires whose repression has so scarred the outward visage. One fears the light of those eyes, says the narrator, "comme on craint de voir à la bouche d'une caverne quelques brigands armés de torches et de poignards. . . . Il existait un lion dans cette cage de chair . . ." (6:1023).[80] To the narrator, blindness and the ravaged countenance figure the repression of forces that are criminal, bestial, and indeed demonic, for Cane is a creature of Balzac's Parisian inferno.

But the significance of Cane's face can be read, discovered, or constructed only through the narrator's mediation. "Ces idées, réveillées par l'aspect de cet homme, étaient aussi chaudes dans mon âme qu'elles étaient froides sur sa figure" (6:1023).[81] The fire is first and foremost in the narrator; Cane provides a pretext for its bursting forth in open flames. In other words, the narrator's ability to decipher the pathological and geological text of the old Italian's face depends on the breakdown of his own well-ordered patterns of repression and requires him to lose sight of himself as subject and attach his own system of psychic energy to the prepresentation of his "object." Cane's initial distrust and the sarcasm of his companions make it clear that the narrator is alone in his fascination, in his willingness and ability to believe the old man's story and thus become its interpreter. Throughout the text, then, he translates Cane's gestures as if they are a language that he alone can understand, presenting no images of signifiers but proceeding directly to their meaning:

> Et il fit un geste effrayant de patriotisme éteint et de dégoût pour les choses humaines. (6:1024)
> A cette question il leva la tête vers moi, comme pour me contempler par un mouvement vraiment tragique, et me répondit: "Dans les malheurs!" (6:1025)
> . . . avec une pitié dédaigneuse, il fit un geste qui exprima toute la philosophie du désespoir. (6:1031)[82]

Once again an occultation or "blindness" is at work, this time in the service of the Balzacian narrative discourse. Sensory or phenomenal reality disappears, covered over by the interpretive fantasm that is allowed to surface when the subject, losing sight of his own *volonté*, hallucinatorily invests his passions in the hitherto merely observed object. The importance of blindness as the link between the writer's work and his fascination with Cane is confirmed by his description as "ce vieil Homère qui gardait en lui-même une Odyssée condamnée à l'oubli" (6:1023).[83] The old man is a poet, but an unrealized one. His double, the narrator, must save Cane's tale from oblivion through his mediation and interpretation, make literature out of the fantasies of a monomaniac.

Cane at twenty had killed the husband of his mistress; six months later he had severely wounded another high official who was courting her. Arrested and imprisoned, he managed to keep his broken sword, which was so much a part of his body that only by cutting off his fist could it have been taken from him. This totally improbable instrument, suggesting both castration and the preservation of the phallus, was to enable Cane to escape the decapitation he awaited in the dungeon. He dug a tunnel from his cell, guided both by Arabic relief inscriptions that he read in the dark with his fingers and by a hidden sense of attraction for gold, and thus reached the great secret treasury of Venice and was able to purchase his freedom. As a wealthy exiled nobleman, he established himself at the court of Louis XV "parmi les femmes les plus célèbres" (6:1027), but there he was struck blind. This series of events evokes the symbolic value of blindness as punishment for sexual transgression, but the transgression involved is complicated, and Cane's own explanation of his condition merits a close reading:

> Au milieu de mes voluptés, quand je jouissais d'une fortune de six millions, je fus frappé de cécité. Je ne doute pas que cette infirmité ne soit le résultat de mon séjour dans le cachot, de mes travaux dans la pierre, si toutefois ma faculté de voir l'or n'emportait pas un abus de la puissance visuelle qui me prédestinait à perdre les yeux (6:1030).[84]

Circumstantially related to pleasure and wealth, blindness is causally related to the decipherment and the *seconde vue* at work in the dungeon. Taken literally, this explanation describes a displacement of punishment from the most radical form of symbolic castration (decapitation) to an attenuated one (blindness). The darkness of the prison cell is decisive for both halves of Cane's account, since both describe ways of perceiving and knowing that go beyond, or function in the absence of, sight. The first way in which Cane directs himself to the gold is linguistic and archaeological: an unseeing order of codes and decipherment. The second is an order of transcendence, immediacy, presence, and sight, a second sight that goes beyond objects to that "transcendental signifier" of all modern objects, gold. The two "causes" of blindness, decipherment and *seconde vue*, are equivalent and may be said to be related metaphorically, since either would account for Cane's discovery of the treasure. *Facino Cane* thus leads by a different route to the conclusion of Biasi cited earlier: the Balzacian second sight is a metaphor for a process that is not perceptual but textual and linguistic in nature. As such it is an idealizing metaphor, reappropriating the effects of the symbolic order, of language in its relation to desire and the unconscious, to the visual order of perception-consciousness and representation.

But the sexual implications of the episode must now complicate our reading still further. Cane identifies his *seconde vue* for gold with his mother, and his work in the dungeon includes not only deciphering but also a blatantly sexual excavation and penetration. The second sight is an almost magnetic attraction to gold that functions in spite of, and even compensates for, physical blindness: "Je sens l'or. Quoique aveugle, je m'arrête devant les boutiques de joailliers" (6:1027).[85] Cane attributes this faculty to his mother's desire in a sentence that makes clear that there is no logical causality at work: "Que les fantaisies d'une femme influent ou non sur son enfant quand elle le porte ou quand elle le conçoit, il est certain que ma mère eut une passion pour l'or pendant sa grossesse"[86] (6:1026). The monomania for gold, then, is an identification with the desire of the mother, an expression of desire to return to the plenitude of the mother's body. This maternal origin of monomania and its fantasms can also be found in *Louis Lambert*, specifically in the image of thought or *volonté* as electric charge, for Lambert derives this image from a childhood memory of seeing, while lying in his cradle by his mother's bed, sparks fly from her hair as she combed it.[87]

If Cane's attraction to gold is a desire for a return to the lost presence of the mother, his excavation in the prison cell appears to be an attempt to realize this desire. The tunnel to the secret treasury of Venice is dug in a fantasy-sustained frenzy of penetration, its artisan entering it as if performing a sexual act and returning to the womb:

> Pendant que je travaillais, et dans les moments où la fatigue m'anéantissait, j'entendais le son de l'or, je voyais de l'or devant moi, j'étais ébloui par des diamants! Oh! attendez. Pendant une nuit, mon acier émoussé trouva du bois. J'aiguisai mon bout d'épée, et fis un trou dans ce bois. Pour pouvoir travailler, je me roulais comme un serpent sur le ventre, je me mettais nu pour travailler à la manière des taupes, en portant mes mains en avant. . . . (6:1028)[88]

Upon reaching the cave, Cane hears the voices of the Doge and another nobleman, paternal figures whose presence confirms the sense of Oedipal transgression and from whom he learns that this is in fact the treasury of the city. After a night ("Quelle nuit!") of orgiastic plunder, Cane escapes and sets off for other pleasures, but the memories of that night are too strong to be put aside: "Quand je me rappelai les sensations que j'avais éprouvées, que je revis cet immense trésor . . . il se fit en moi comme un mouvement de folie. J'eus la fièvre de l'or" (6:1029).[89] The gold and diamonds are in effect a reservoir of libidinal energy originally bound to the mother, identified as radiating from the mother. In carrying off this gold, this energy, to the court of Louis XV, which is referred to only as a scene of libertine pleasures, Cane reenacts the renunciation and reappropriation inherent in the Oedipal situation: he will not possess the mother, but he will possess other women. In other words, by performing a ritual of displacement and sublimation, Cane escapes from the decapitation to which his direct Oedipal transgression (intimacy with a woman possessed by a paternal figure) would seem to condemn him, but this would-be sublimation is in fact regressive because it involves the fantasmatic violation of the mother. He will never escape this fantasm. After bringing on fever and madness, it will blind him and leave him in a perpetual darkness lit only by his fantasies ("l'or et les diamants éclairent ma nuit"), an existence akin to Lambert's "vie d'enfant au berceau." The two causes of Cane's blindness, the monomania for gold and the tunneling to the treasury of Venice, now appear to be symbolically one and the same. His blindness is a symbolic castration, a punishment, but even more it is the inward collapse of a psychic system, an internally produced effect of overstepping the limits of fantasmatic vision.

To the young narrator, Facino Cane offers a fantasy of power, of boundless wealth, and twice the narrator accepts the old man's offers. The first acceptance is rewarded by the telling of Cane's story, the second by the resurgence of the volcanic fire on the old man's face: "J'ai donc trouvé un homme, s'écria-t-il le visage en feu" (6:1031).[90] Thus only by sharing to an extent in the old man's monomania does he obtain both the "histoire enfouie" of his life for his *étude de moeurs* and the confirmation of the energy hidden in his face (which had previously been cold, in contrast to the heat of the narrator's interpretation of it). By identifying with Cane, the narrator brings out what was hidden in him, or rather what the narrator describes in Cane is his own fantasm, whose release has been made possible by attaching it to an external representation. But the decisive mo-

ment that makes the narrator the narrator is his ultimate refusal
to follow Cane in pursuit of his desire, a refusal not stated but
implicit in the final paragraph of the text:

> Facino Cane mourut pendant l'hiver après avoir langui
> deux mois. Le pauvre homme avait un catarrhe.
> (6:1032)[91]

The speaker of this sentence has banished the promised trip to
Venice from his mind, condemned the fantasy of gold and
pleasure in favor of the activity of writing. By having gone up
to but not over the brink of Cane's monomania, the narrator becomes its interpreter. He has identified with the old man, invested his own psychic energy in the story so as to understand
its reasons and hidden meanings. His gaze, however, has not
been that of blind eyes illuminated only from within, but rather
a scrutinizing, quasi-medical gaze that has seen in Cane's face a
scarred ruin, in his blind eyes the image of a will powerless to
act in the exterior world.

The unspoken, radical break preceding that final paragraph,
by which the narrator irrevocably places the old blind man in
the position of the observed Other, is the turning point in *Facino Cane*, the pivot on which all else hinges, even the narrator's
vertiginous initial encounter with his double. At that meeting,
the narrator simply does what he has already said he would do:
embrace the life of the Other, transgress the boundaries of personal identity. Both the encounter with Cane and the old man's
visionary monomania are projections of the narrator's activity
as both *observateur des moeurs* and explorer of ideas. The narrator's and Cane's accounts of their *seconde vue* are parallel, though
differing in intensity and unreality. But in pulling back from
Cane, leaving him to die rather than joining him in a rejuve-
nating quest ("l'on est jeune quand on voit l'or devant soi"), the
narrator fixes, as if on a screen, this projected and distorted image of something of himself, an image that becomes *Facino
Cane*. By stepping back from his initial identification with
Cane's fantasm, the narrator confers objectivity on a figure animated by a subjectivity torn away from the self. The specificity
of *Facino Cane*, as opposed to *Louis Lambert* in which the prob-

lem of the narrator and his mad double is developed at far greater length, lies in the narrator's identity not only as the biographical Balzac but also as the self-conscious creator of what was soon to become *La Comédie humaine*, as the observer of society. Between *Lambert* and *Cane*, between 1832 and 1836, stand the great project of societal description, the *Etudes de moeurs*, and *Le Père Goriot*, with which the system of recurring characters so crucial to *La Comédie humaine* is established.

If it is to be part of a history of society, the novel cannot consist of the visions of a Lambert or the fantasms of a Cane; it must refer to the material world. The necessary referentiality of the novelist's work is conceived of by Balzac as above all a visual, ocular referentiality, just as in the sensationalist theories of language at his disposal sight was implicitly the dominant form, the formal model, of sensation. The attractiveness and danger of a nonreferential language thus find their most direct figuration in a blind man, for blindness implies a separation from reality that, for a sensationalist fascinated by the autonomous powers of mind, is akin to madness. In his encounter with his blind double, the Balzacian narrator faces the possibility that he too might lose contact with the world around him. Facino Cane appears to have been punished by blindness for realizing a regression into his most powerful fantasies, and he is henceforth cut off from communication with society; even his blind companions refuse to believe him. The narrator, in order to rescue and give voice to this regression, must cut himself off from it, make it the fantasy of the Other, write about it in a language that retains the referentiality conferred by a distinct point of view. This act of separation remains problematic in *Louis Lambert*, provoking explicit discontinuities that trouble the narrator and against which he feels powerless, but in *Facino Cane* it is accomplished in a single implicit stroke. *La Comédie humaine* must be written against Lambert and Cane, against the isolation of its creator into the blind world of fantasms, and yet it must appropriate the energy of this world in order to present "drames oubliés" such as that of the old blind musician, in order to go beyond mere description, mere seeing and naming.

In his "Avant-propos" of 1842, Balzac presents his ambition to go beyond descriptive realism in the following terms:

> S'en tenant à cette représentation rigoureuse, un écrivain pourrait devenir un peintre plus ou moins fidèle . . . mais, pour mériter les éloges que doit ambitionner tout artiste, ne devais-je pas étudier les raisons ou la raison de ces effet sociaux, surprendre le sens caché de cet immense assemblage de figures, de passions, et d'événements? (1:11)[92]

This is one of many passages in which Balzac presents the economy of his creation as parallel to that of the society that it claims to represent. The novelist must produce a surplus value capable of being exchanged ("mériter") for the status and gratification ("éloges") he seeks to acquire. This surplus value must derive from the penetration beyond events and images to reasons and hidden meanings. This quest for a hidden order beyond representable phenomena was not unique to Balzac or to literature, but was part of a fundamental transformation in the categories of knowledge and discourse. As Foucault has shown, nineteenth-century disciplines such as philology, biology, and economics differ from their predecessors—general grammar, natural history, and analysis of wealth—in that they locate the essential connections between phenomena not at the level of visible, representational structure but "in a sort of behind-the-scenes world even deeper and more dense than that of representation itself."[93] Whereas the natural history of the eighteenth century had attempted to define resemblances and differences between living beings in terms of the resemblances and differences of their visible structure, the comparative anatomists of the nineteenth century sought to base their analyses on the hidden architecture of each organism, the relation of its structures to the organic functions common to different species.

Balzac, fascinated by the work of Cuvier and Geoffroy Saint-Hilaire, was aware of this transformation. In celebrating Cuvier's reconstruction of a prehistoric animal from a single bone, he knew that he was praising not a feat of representational classification but a deciphering of seemingly hidden organic structure.[94] As far as language was concerned, however, Balzac had to grope toward his own attempts to go beyond an understanding of language as representation. Foucault has written of the philological understanding of language characteristic of the nineteenth century that "language is 'rooted' not in the things perceived, but in the active subject. And, perhaps, in that case, it is a product of will and energy, rather than of the memory that duplicates representation."[95] Balzac probably would have agreed with that statement, but he seems never to have acquired the intellectual background that would have enabled him to utter it. In borrowing what sometimes seems like a vague spiritualism from such marginal traditions as mysticism and animal magnetism, he was attempting to account for the nonrepresentational aspects of language, for the production of language by a desiring subject. And in creating the order of *Spécialité*, he sought to describe causalities that could not be reduced to Lambert's *Abstraction*, to the order of representation. Martin Kanes, in his study of the theory of language in Balzac's work, has likewise concluded that there are for him two kinds of language, the first turned outward, referentially, lending itself to unproblematic communication, and the second turned inward, poetically, identified with the spiritual, the ineffable, and the creative power of the mind.[96] The first of these linguistic functions corresponds to the sensationalist theories of language as representation inherited and adopted by Balzac; it corresponds as well to the novel as reproduction, the *conception* and *faire* that in the "Préface" are presented as the foundation of literary art. But the second function, for which Balzac possessed no adequate linguistic theory, corresponds to the formal interaction of signifiers, to language as a combinatory and energetic system. It is with this second type of language, Kanes argues, that Balzac claims to go beyond descriptive mimesis to reasons and hidden meanings. Having no theory of poetic language or of the unconscious working of signifiers, Balzac adopts the idealistic metaphor of a transcendent second sight.

But in *Facino Cane*, where the *seconde vue* is articulated in a fictional rather than theoretical context, it is shown to parallel a process of textual and nonvisual decipherment, the tactile reading of an inscription in the dark.[97] Moreover, the energy of this second sight is shown to be that of unconscious fantasms, the greatest possible source of *volonté*. To express causes and hidden meaning, then, Balzac must harness the energy of his unconscious to his literary "objects," thereby projecting (optically) "la volonté qui engendre une oeuvre d'art" into his creation, the realized representation of his desire. Within the mind, the electrical and fluid properties attributed to *volonté* create dynamic and energetic relations between ideas, as does psychic energy in Freud's successive metapsychological topographies. The causes and hidden meanings that Balzac claims to express are nothing more or less than the further representations to which initial representational contents are bound in a dynamic, energetic, or economic system. Such systems, for Balzac, include both the self and society, so that the desires and fantasms of the former may be used to give depth and dynamism to the representation of the latter. The narrated societal system is a projection, though by no means a linear or distortionless one, of the psychic system.

It is significant that in Balzac's most developed blind character after Facino Cane, visual deprivation should produce an ability to decipher hidden meanings, and that this ability should constitute her principal function in the plot and narration of the novel. In *Modeste Mignon*, written and published in 1844, Madame Mignon becomes blind while mourning the death of her older daughter, who had been abandoned by the Parisian adventurer who had seduced her. The girl's grave remains in her mother's eyes as an image replacing all others, so that here too physical blindness is in effect an occultation of the exterior world by an obsession. When the surviving daughter, Modeste, falls in love with the poet Canalis through her readings of his work and undertakes a secret correspondence with him, it is Madame Mignon alone who can detect the accents of passion in the girl's voice, a hidden meaning beyond the ordinary function of language. No visual sensations distract her from preoccupation with protecting her daughter's virtue. "Oh! elle n'est pas gaie pour vous," she tells her friends, "vous ne saisissez pas ces nuances trop délicates pour des yeux occupés par le spectacle de la nature. Cette gaîté se trahit par les notes de sa voix, par des

accents que je saisis, que j'explique" (1:494–495).[98] Once again
Balzac is making use of a notion that is common in descriptive
writings on blindness from his time, that of the special talent of
the blind for sensing the physiognomy and nuance of voices
(see above, pp. 111–112).[99] In Balzac's system, this commonplace takes on a particular importance: the obsessional concentration of psychic energy, drawn inward and away from reality,
is the means to superior decipherment and interpretation.
Moreover, it is through Madame Mignon that the reader learns
the causes and meanings of Modeste's actions. The blind
woman is an adjunct of the narrator, just as the narrator often
invokes a superior perspective (that of "les observateurs du
coeur humain," for example) as the basis of his explanatory remarks. What the blind person perceives is a second-order system of signs. Within the verbal signifiers, she notices the effects
of *volonté* that are the signifiers of her daughter's unspoken emotions.

Madame Mignon, metonymic surrogate of the narrator, may
be cured of her blindness by the great surgeon Desplein once a
fine marriage has been arranged for her younger daughter, but
Facino Cane, the narrator's metaphoric opposite, must be left
irreparably blind so that the narrator can be assured of his sight.
The narrator *must* be *figuratively* blind, blind to the fact that his
narration is the transformed projection of his fantasms, so that
the dynamic interaction of these fantasms may be imparted to
the narration. Balzac's "blindness" must be internal, an occultation of the "true" objects of inner sight by objects taken to be
external and visible, the objects to be represented in the novels.
The opposite blindness, that of Facino Cane, would hide potentially communicable outward reality behind the necessarily private screen of fantasms.

It could be argued that only the barest of comparisons links Facino Cane to the tradition of blind poets, that he is first and
foremost a creature of Balzac's speculation on madness, only in-
cidentally blind. Such an objection deserves consideration because it forces us to question the nature of nineteenth-century
interest in blind seers and rhapsodes, to examine the contexts in

which they appear in literary discourse. The blind are marginal figures in romantic literature. We do not find them, for instance, in the major statements on poetry made by such seminal figures as Lamartine, Vigny, and Hugo. Moreover, the myth of the blind seer, as presented, does not invite or require the reader's assent to its truth as myth. It is a construct from the past, to be alluded to or to be given a modern, often psychological, interpretation. The blind poet is a figure not of literature's direct link to the sacred but of its impossible look back to a putative lost origin. Thus for Chateaubriand the sightless elder of the Natchez provides a means of producing, textually, an "American antiquity," of evoking a youthful and vivid rapport with language and the world, now lost to an aged European culture. For Ballanche, the blind are initiatory figures, witnesses to an origin that can no longer be seen but from which have sprung the traditions that the initiators now transmit. At the individual level, blindness signifies the loss of a direct, perceptual relation to the world, and its replacement by an interiorized, melancholy contemplation, in which time replaces space and the understanding of the past provides a model for the prediction of the future.

The relation of blindness to literature's origins can help us understand the complexity of Balzac's portrayal of the blind, the connections he draws between the sightless seer and the madman. For Balzac, writing has a double origin: in the observation and description of the material world, and in the fantasies and desires that make up the inner life of the subject. The problem of a lost origin of Literature situated in an inaccessible past does not concern him; Dante can be compared to Homer, the *Human Comedy* to the *Divine Comedy*. Balzac can attempt to emulate, even appropriate, the prestige of Homer without defining his own stance as one of belatedness. Facino Cane is like Homer? Fine, Balzac will publish his "*Odyssey.*" But insofar as the novel takes *moeurs* and society as its objects, its origins must be in the visible, and the blind man must be the antithesis of the creator of fiction. Yet the novelist must also explain what he sees, and to do so he must draw on the experience of his own fantasms and desires. His double, the blind visionary, sees gold, the object of his desire. In other words, what he sees is what must be intuited in order to explain the interactions of individual subjects of desire in a society founded on money. The private fantasms of desire, represented by Cane's *seconde vue*, must animate the public narration of observable events. Blindness represents the risk that *La Comédie humaine* might collapse back into the private realm from which it draws its dynamism. The blind man is thus not a symbol of the narrator, but a figure who marks the limits between communicable narration and unspeakable fantasy.

· 6 ·

HUGO: BLIND SEERS,
BLIND LOVERS, AND
THE VIOLENCE OF HISTORY

Evoking the deaf Beethoven's creation of the nine symphonies, Victor Hugo wrote in 1863: "Il semble qu'on voie un dieu aveugle créer des soleils" (12:409).[1] The sentence is perhaps the most striking of Hugo's many aphoristic formulations of the relation between blindness and artistic creation, blindness and faith, blindness and love. Can we say that Beethoven has simply been annexed to the topos of the blind bard? To do so would be to reduce considerably the power of Hugo's metaphor. The blind god creating suns possesses not so much a second sight as the power to create *ex nihilo*, to bring the most dazzling light out of utter darkness. Moreover, the blind god acts selflessly, almost in a spirit of renunciation, creating for others something that he will never see. Yet the most striking feature of the remark is Hugo's own use of metaphor—sight for sound, blindness for deafness, suns for symphonies. The metaphor itself creates light, as if Hugo, contemplating Beethoven's achievement in sound, had pronounced: *Fiat lux*. Like Beethoven, he creates a moment of genesis; we may have understood the marvel of the deaf composer's work, but now we *see* it for the first time.

This sentence, the only mention of blindness in an essay that was itself no more than an unpublished fragment, is in at least one sense typical of Hugo's writings on the blind, for these writings are dispersed throughout his work. We shall have to consider, in this chapter, an odd collection of texts: a short poem from *Les Contemplations*, digressions in *Les Misérables*, personal letters, aphorisms, the late novel *L'Homme qui rit*. The contexts in which Hugo discusses blindness recall such disparate works as Diderot's *Promenade du sceptique*, Dorat's *Sélim et Sélima*, and Ballanche's *Du sentiment*; the blind are linked to religious belief, idyllic love, and poetic vision. The role of the blind in Hugo's work remains, nonetheless, marginal—there is no Hugolian *Lettre sur les aveugles*. Yet to say that a motif or figure is marginal implies that it is so with respect to something else, something more central, and thus we are led to the very heart of Hugo's poetic universe, to the act of seeing, to the eye and the gaze. In no writer are the thematics of seeing richer or more developed than in the author of *Les Rayons et les ombres*. The poet is an eye, he writes in the preface to *Les Feuilles d'automne*, and in the final poem of *Les Contemplations* the poet is enjoined to become "le grand oeil fixe ouvert sur le grand tout." The absence or loss of sight can be understood only with respect to the centrality of vision and the eye. But blindness is more than the absence of sight; it may also be a deformity or mutilation, a mark of punishment and violence, and it is no surprise to find blindness, in Hugo's work, linked to castration and to generational struggles for authority. The fascination with the gaze, likewise, cannot be free from prohibitions, menaces, and anxieties, because the exploring eye places itself in danger. An approach to Hugo's writings on blindness must be in large measure psychoanalytic: we shall explore the symbolic implications of sight and its absence in the context of the origins of sexuality and the strife between fathers and sons. There can be no better place to begin this exploration than Hugo's fantasmatic relation to an event that involves origins, spectacle, parricide, and the modern writer's claim to be present at a new genesis of literature: the French Revolution.

> Les écrivains et poètes de ce siècle ont cet avantage étonnant qu'ils ne procèdent d'aucune école antique, d'aucune seconde main, d'aucun modèle. Ils n'ont pas d'ancêtres. . . .
> Les poètes du dix-neuvième siècle, les écrivains du dix-neuvième siècle, sont les fils de la Révolution française. Ce volcan a deux cratères, 89 et 93. . . . Tout l'art contemporain résulte directement et sans intermédiaire de cette genèse formidable. (*Le Tas de pierres*, 12:1076)[2]

The walls of the Bastille fall to earth, the head of Citizen Louis Capet rolls into a basket, and from this chasm of destruction and blood is born a race of poets who will sing of the uni-

verse as for the first time. Theirs will be an unprecedented poetry beyond all tradition, rivaling even the sublime words of the
Book of Genesis: "Dieu la première fois a dit lui-même *fiat lux*,
la seconde fois il l'a fait dire. Par qui? Par 93. Donc, nous
hommes du dix-neuvième siècle, tenons à honneur cette injure:
—*Vous êtes 93*" (12:306).[3] In these and many other texts, the
Revolution becomes for Hugo the pretext to the writing of a
great fantasy in which the symbolic terrors that we now call the
Oedipus complex and castration anxiety can be eluded. Hugo
makes the claim that the modern poet has no father, that his
generative union with the mother, the Revolution, need not be
at the price of blindness. The cry *"Vous êtes 93"* is a rhetorical
accusation of regicide and thus of parricide, but Hugo's response, "tenons à honneur cette injure," is a call to put aside any
guilt over the desirability of the father's death by affirming a
new order in which there was no father to kill, no prior utter-
ances of a paternal God.

This new "Genesis" will be evoked again at the beginning of
Promontorium somnii, an exemplary work concerning sight and
perception in the Hugolian mythology of literary creation.
Through the astronomer Arago's telescope, Hugo observes a
lunar sunrise, the arrival of light in a sector that had been invisible in darkness, and then resumes the entire tradition of writing
about the moon to conclude, "Les poètes one créé une lune métaphorique et les savants une lune algébrique. La lune réelle est
entre les deux. C'est cette lune-là que j'avais sous les yeux"
(12:454).[4] Between these translations of the moon, between
poetic embellishment and scientific commentary, Hugo implicitly claims that there is a way—his own—to write of the real
moon, and he gives free rein to his powers of metaphoric description, of literal symbolization, as he evokes moment by moment the arrival of light to the lunar surface. Visual coming into
being and literary creation thus become one, and Hugo, satisfied with what he has seen and made, concludes: "Cela existait
magnifiquement. Là aussi la grande parole venait d'être dite;
fiat lux" (12:455).[5]

The nineteenth century, we read in Hugo's *William Shakespeare*, has no forefathers and needs no ancestors, not even the

great geniuses of humanity, for its mother is the French Revolution (12:305). Hugo is ostensibly discussing intellectual filiation, but the references to 1793 remind us that the absent father is the decapitated king, who has met his fate in that place where the body of the mother-revolution is terrible and fascinating and blinding to observe, that fiery crater or "bouche de bronze," 93 (12:306).[6] The Revolution permits the writing of an otherwise repressed Oedipal fantasy: the father is dead, the son is unchallenged in his possession of the mother. The poet, free from all predecessors, can fecundate the Revolution, create a new and revolutionary art, and cast his direct and immediate gaze on all things. Politically, the fantasy will be translated at least in part by the naïvely utopian current of Hugo's thought: France, the mother, becomes the place of origin for a new society in which the violent struggles of despotism and revolution will finally leave no traces.

In a famous poem from *Les Contemplations*, Hugo attempted to show that his own innovations in poetic style and diction were an expression of the postrevolutionary status of the modern writer. The poet's new freedom, in "Réponse à un acte d'accusation," takes the form of a language with which he can, like Adam, name things directly as they are seen, rather than through the oblique and figurative style of *préciosité* said to characterize the language of the Old Regime: "J'ai dit au long fruit d'or: Mais tu n'es qu'une poire!"(9:77).[7] Now this principle of linguistic demystification, of calling things naïvely by their name, is that of the Enlightenment, especially as it was portrayed (usually with negative connotations) during the early nineteenth century: implacably rational, egalitarian, utterly lacking in respect for aristocratic order and traditions. Speaking in this poem as a defender of the Revolution and its precursors, indeed, as a poetic terrorist,[8] Hugo ignores his own youthful royalism (which he will explicitly denounce in "Ecrit en 1846," also in *Les Contemplations*) and claims that *poetically* he has always stood on the side of the Republic. As the *philosophes*, with their rhetoric of enlightenment, are said to stand in relation to the obscurantist language of authority, so Hugo claims to be placing himself with respect to the old poetic diction. "Tous les mots à présent planent dans la clarté" (9:77).[9] The *clarté* is Hugo's, for he explicitly makes himself the God of a new "Genesis" in his ironic acceptance of the accusation that he has brought darkness and chaos to French verse: "J'ai dit à l'ombre: 'Sois!' / Et l'ombre fut" (9:74).[10] One party's enlightenment is of course another party's dark age, but the possibility that Hugo's new genesis would be a destructive one cannot easily be dismissed. If the directness of his poetic sight and diction, which Hugo declares to be a consequence of the Revolution, is the very stance toward authority that in the hands of the *philosophes* was a cause of the Revolution, then it becomes a cause of the regicide of 1793, and the poet-son cannot elude guilt over the father's death by presuming him to have been fortuitously nonexistent.[11]

A word of explanation is in order concerning the Hugolian symbolism of the Revolution as mother to the nineteenth century, because many readers will recall the poet's evocation of his parents in "Ce siècle avait deux ans . . . ": "Mon père vieux soldat, ma mère vendéenne" (4:375).[12] As a young royalist who wrote odes commemorating the official events of the Restoration, Hugo did identify his antirevolutionary vocation with his mother's Breton ancestry and her occasional role as a conspirator against Napoleon. And his "discovery" of first the Empire and then the Revolution as positive, even glorious, events in the history of France paralleled his recognition, during the 1820s, that his father, with whom he had earlier had distant and often troubled relations, was a figure worthy of admiration for his military achievements. There is a strong autobiographical aspect of the section of *Les Misérables* in which Marius Pontmercy, raised as an ultraroyalist by his maternal grandfather, reads the *Bulletin de la Grande Armée* and begins to worship his father and the Emperor. What Marius comes to admire are the military and administrative achievements of Napoleon, the patriotic victories of the Republic's armies; he stops short of identifying his father with 1793. The relation of the father figure to the Revolution was to remain ambiguous. On the one hand, the father could be identified with the Revolution as a unifying and patriotic event and, through Napoleon, with the codification of

1789 principles into laws and institutions. On the other hand, 1793 would always signify a rupture with the past, with ancestors, a new world in which the symbolic place of the father is absent.[13] The early association of the father with the Revolution, the mother with *chouannerie*, remains dominant in texts where Hugo refers to his real parents. The mother as Revolution and the father as victim of regicide are metaphors, but metaphors that have a significant place in the fantasmatic politics of Hugo's relation to his era.

In Hugo's postrevolutionary poetics, his fantasy of a modern genius unindebted to forefathers, nothing is more important than the poet's unmediated, unshackled *gaze*. Addressing the great geniuses of the past, he proclaims that the writers of the nineteenth century "observent directement l'humanité; ils n'acceptent pour clarté dirigeante aucun rayon refracté, pas même le vôtre" (12:310).[14] The directness of the gaze accompanies the liberation from the edicts of fathers and ancestors. This fantasy of direct, unthreatened sight is a response to the great uneasiness and anxiety that Hugo associates with the act of looking. The gaze, in Hugo's poetry, often involves transgression and is described by such words as *creuser, fouiller, plonger*. The objects of the gaze, in his metaphors, are pits, wells, chasms, abysses, *gouffres*. The desire to see becomes a desire to open up and enter into the abyss, and it entails for the gaze a risk of burial or submersion:

Tout se creuse sitôt que tu tâches de voir. (*L'Ane*, 10:398)

. . . j'ai souvent, d'un oeil peut-être expert,
Fouillé ce noir probléme où la sonde se perd!
(*Les Voix intérieures*, 5:629)[15]

These abstract images, in which the roving eye risks disappearing, encountering horror, or falling into darkness, cannot be interpreted without reference to another aspect of the Hugolian gaze: its libidinal energy. In Hugo's writings, sexuality is predominantly voyeuristic, the act of seeing more often than not eroticized. If the Revolution-as-mother is a volcanic crater, a "bouche de bronze," it is but one of a multitude of similar *abîmes* and *gouffres* that fascinate his gaze. When Gwynplaine, virginal hero of *L'Homme qui rit*, becomes preoccupied with a sensual woman he has seen, the narrator exclaims, "Toute la femme, quel gouffre!"[16] In his pioneering psychoanalytic study of Hugo, Charles Baudouin noted that the poet's earliest childhood recollections were of a voyeuristic experience with the schoolmaster's daughter (young Victor watched her put on her stockings) and of a courtyard whose description can be read as a screen memory or disguised remembrance of parts of the female body.[17] At the age of twenty, Hugo was horrifed by the possibility that his fiancée's leg might be seen when she raised her dress to avoid soiling it in the street, an emotion shared by Marius in *Les Misérables*.

If seeing and sexuality are so closely linked, then to the extent that sexuality is menaced—by the Oedipal prohibition, by the symbolic threat of castration—seeing is also menaced. It is an activity involving danger, the danger of punishment or loss. The gaze can be swallowed up by the abyss:

> Aux heures où l'esprit, dont l'oeil partout se pose,
> Cherche à voir dans la nuit le fond de toute chose,
> Dans ces lieux effrayants mon regard se perdit.
> *(Les Rayons et les ombres*, 6:57–58)[18]

In these lines poetic sight is neither direct nor assured of its position. It is exploratory and furtive, operating transgressively in a space of terrors and prohibitions. The clear vision of the modern poet in a universe without ancestors amounts to a denegation of this anxiety, an attempt to impose order on a complex and troubling process.

Blindness is but one of many dangers or obstacles to sight. Among the others are darkness, the vastness of the contemplated abyss, and the fact that the observed object may be veiled or terrifying, that it may flee or disappear. We need to consider the specific character of blindness with respect to the Hugolian problematics of seeing, which are inseparable from sexuality and revolution. Thematically, blindness appears in three not always distinct contexts: writings on doubt and religious faith, writings on innocent love, and writings on inner vision. Hugo's fragmentary writings on blindness in each of these contexts will provide a framework for our reading of *L'Homme qui rit*, the novel that contains his only developed blind character.

Hugo's use of metaphors of blindness in discussions of doubt, faith, and dogma often resembles Diderot's in the *Promenade du sceptique* and the *Lettre sur les aveugles*. For Hugo the anticlerical, priests who defend superstition and oppose philosophic or scientific innovations are myopic and blind. In "La Vérité" (*La Légende des siècles*), he has the guardians of tradition exclaim, "L'homme osant n'être pas aveugle, est un impie" (15:780). The priests in "L'Elégie des fléaux" are the "myopes de l'autel" (15:813). Sometimes the symbolism is historical, with the modern age portrayed as an age of light, so that those who deny this because of beliefs from the past can be dismissed as blind. In the chapter on convents in *Les Misérables*, we read: "Un couvent en France, en plein midi du dix-neuvième siècle, c'est un collège de hiboux faisant face au jour" (11:392).[19] Such images underscore Hugo's affinity for eighteenth-century philosophical criticism. The nest of owls and the nearsighted clerics who keep others from using their eyes are figures from Diderot's "Allée des épines."

The historical dimension of the debate on superstition and doubt, however, marks a crucial difference between Hugo's discussion of religion and the attacks of his eighteenth-century predecessors. The question of religion, in the romantic historical imagination, is linked to that of revolution and thus of regicide. During the Restoration, freethinking, impiety, and sacrilege were said to be far more important causes of the Revolution than economic crises or inequalities. In this matter, Hugo's thought long remained marked by his youthful royalism, although he has Gavroche mock the attack on the *philosophes* in *Les Misérables*: "C'est la faute à Voltaire. . . . C'est la faute à Rousseau." But throughout his work he insisted on belief in God as a condition of his attack on priests and religion—both victims of the Revolution. In a series of poems from the 1830s concerning doubt and faith, the inability to believe is often figured by a disorder or loss of vision:

O Dieu! considérez les hommes de ce temps,
Aveugles, loin de vous sous tant d'ombres flottants.
("Le Monde et le siècle,"
Les Rayons et les ombres, 6:48)[20]

Unlike the benighted priests or nuns who fail to see the direct, sensory evidence of science and philosophy, these contemporary doubters are "blind" to what lies beyond sensation; they have no insight into an essential, spiritual world beyond phenomena:

L'homme passe sans voir, sans croire, sans comprendre,
Sans rien chercher dans l'ombre, et sans lever les yeux
Vers les conseils divins qui flottent dans les cieux.
(6:47)[21]

Lack of faith, in "Pensar, Dudar" (*Les Voix intérieures*), becomes "notre cécité" (5:628); in "Que nous avons le doute en nous" (*Les Chants du crépuscule*), doubt appears as a "spectre myope et sourd" (5:480). The inability to "see" God is attributed, in the latter poem, to the revolutionary years lived through by the men and women of the nineteenth century. In the visual universe of doubt, veils and fogs hide the meaning of all that is, and the eye encounters only fleeting objects, clouds, and expanding chasms. The world, in "Pensar, Dudar," is a sphinx, and although the gaze of the doubter contains an element of blindness, this partial sight may be the only alternative to the punishment of Oedipus, which could accompany a more direct vision: "Plus de clarté peut-être aveuglerait nos yeux" (5:630).[22]

But it is in *Les Misérables* that this theme will receive its most direct expression, in the apology of prayer that concludes the denunciation of convents. Having condemned the convent as an institution of blindness and an affront to a modern age founded on the light of experience, Hugo does an about-face and affirms the religious principle underlying these places of prayer:

Il y a, nous le savons, une philosophie qui nie l'infini. Il y a aussi une philosophie, classée pathologiquement, qui nie le soleil; cette philosophie s'appelle cécité.

Eriger un sens qui nous manque en source de vérité, c'est un bel aplomb d'aveugle.

Le curieux, ce sont les airs hautains, supérieurs et compatissants que prend, vis-à-vis de la philosophie qui voit Dieu, cette philosophie à tâtons. On croit entendre une taupe s'écrier: Ils me font pitié avec leur soleil! (11:394)[23]

This argument is strictly platonic in that the self-evident brilliance of the sun, in contrast to the shadows of the cave or the unseeing darkness of the blind, should imply by analogy the existence of an infinite being in contrast to the finite world. For the Marquis de Sade, this kind of argument only indicated that atheism was logical for men of five senses (see above, p. 60), but Hugo attempts to defeat such a logic by appealing to a common-sense certitude that the sun exists, whether the blind see it or not. To affirm that we can "see the infinite," Hugo treats doubters and skeptics as infirm, as inadequately equipped to know the universe. Turned around, the analogy signifies that those who believe can see, in other words, that those who have not allied themselves with revolutionary parricide by denying God have not been blinded. The belief in God is thus a necessary safeguard for the direct gaze of the modern thinker who accuses priests of blind superstition and thereby participates symbolically in the revolutionary liquidation of ancestors and authority.

The dangers and risks of sight, and the desire to avoid punishment for a transgressive act of seeing, also structure Hugo's writings on blindness and love. Aside from *L'Homme qui rit*, to which we shall return later, the most notable text to consider here is a long paragraph in *Les Misérables* concerning the love of the venerable Bishop of Digne, Monsignor Myriel, for his sister. Nothing in the plot of the novel requires the presence of this digression, since the bishop had not yet become blind when Jean Valjean met him, and the narrator mentions his infirmity only after announcing his death and Monsieur Madeleine's mourning. The bishop, we are told, was happy to be blind, because his sister was with him: "Disons-le à présent, être aveugle et être aimé, c'est en effet, sur cette terre où rien n'est complet,

une des formes les plus étrangement exquises du bonheur"
(11:166)[24] The love in question is presented as innocent beyond reproach, given the age, relationship, and saintliness of
the couple. Blindness and love complement one another to create a plenitude, because the blind man lives in a state of total dependence and need, the complement of the total gift that is the
other's love. This relation is reciprocal, since it can stem only
from an equally radical, if less obvious, need on the part of the
seeing partner, "qui est là parce que vous avez besoin d'elle et
parce qu'elle ne peut pas se passer de vous" (11:166).[25]

The notion that blindness implies dependency and thus reinforces the sentimental exclusivity of the couple recalls *Sélim et
Sélima, L'Aveugle par amour*, and *Valérie*. The curable blindness
in these works possesses the same romantic interest that Hugo
attributes to the blindness of old age. Monsignor Myriel may
have died at eighty-two, but the presentation of his infirmity
follows the modern tradition of idealized blind children and ad-
olescents, not the ancient tradition of elders, sages, and seers,
for whom blindness was a sign of impending death, of communication with eternity. In fact, Hugo describes the total dependence of the blind person as that of a baby aware of the com-
ings and goings of its mother, self-centeredly believing "qu'on
est le centre de ces pas . . . si elle s'éloigne, c'est pour revenir."[26]
The digression, one might say, concerns not so much the
bishop of Digne as it does sexuality, or rather a concept of infantile love that excludes what is most threatening in sexuality.
Since the blind man's beloved must devote all her time to him,
he knows she is faithful. Moreover, the absence of sight means
that there is no demand for the beloved's visual presence, no
fear of her departure. It also sublimates love, making the soul
more important than the flesh: "L'âme à tâtons cherche l'âme,
et la trouve. . . . On est caressé avec de l'âme."[27] The blind lover
cannot be caught in the act of gazing immodestly or jealously.
The guilt that threatens love is so closely linked to the act of
seeing that in its absence reigns a marvelous sense of confidence
in which the beloved satisfies all the possible demands of the
ego. Love even takes on the attributes of religious belief in that
it is a second sight, truer and more ideal than the first: "Ce n'est

point perdre la lumière qu'avoir l'amour. . . . Il n'y a point de cécité où il y a certitude. . . . Dieu palpable, quel ravissement" (11:166).[28] The love of the blind appears to be free from the aggressivity and perils that are implied by the erotic gaze.

Direct, material sight entails, for Hugo, an element of transgression. It is the potentially murderous gaze of the rationalist who undermines tradition and authority, the voyeuristic gaze of the son fascinated by the forbidden body of the mother. In *William Shakespeare*, as we have noted, he attempts to remove these dangers by making the Revolution the fatherless origin of the nineteenth century, but this was not his only imaginative solution to the problem. In opposition to the direct gaze of the eye, Hugo also propounded the idealization of sight, its passage from the material to the spiritual, or the substitution of pure form for observed phenomena. In this context the topos of the blind poet or visionary is of the utmost importance, but we need to begin by considering some of the implications of genius and form in Hugo's writings about poetic creation. In *William Shakespeare* the English dramatist stands at the end of a series of fourteen "geniuses," all equal, none greater or loftier than any other, and equally unbeholden to any ancestors. The rhetoric of progress and enlightenment describes their political mission; visionaries, they illuminate the path to greater and greater liberty. They are, in other words, the nonviolent bearers of revolutionary ideas and principles, forefathers outside the realm of generational strife, without ancestors or descendants. Yet they can have successors, and in particular are followed by the nineteenth century, Hugo's grandiose metonymy for himself: "Etant génie, il fraternise avec les génies. Quant à sa source, elle est là où est la leur: hors de l'homme" (12:305).[29] The source of genius is beyond mankind, both genealogically and intellectually, for what the geniuses discover, or receive, are insights beyond human experience, beyond the horizons of sense perception and individual reason. And yet this capacity for discovery is described in optical terms: "Ces hommes qu'on appelle les révélateurs fixent leur regard sur quelque chose d'inconnu qui est en dehors de l'homme. Il y a là-haut une lumière, ils la voient. Ils dirigent un miroir de ce côté. . . . Ce révélateur est un voyant" (12:1085).[30]

Hugo also evokes this vision beyond the visible, this extension of the eye's power beyond the phenomena that are its object, in discussing the role of form in aesthetic experience. He cites a passage from Virgil that presents only odious characters and actions, and describes how, while reading it, the formal beauty of the verses makes him forget their vile subject matter:

> Je lis ces vers, je subis cette forme, et quel est son premier effet? j'oublie Auguste, j'oublie même Virgile; . . . j'entre en vision; le prodigieux ciel s'ouvre au-dessus de moi, j'y plonge, j'y plane, je m'y précipite, je vois la région incorruptible et inaccessible, l'immanence splendide. . . . (12:367)[31]

The passage from content to poetic form, from what is named to how language is articulated beyond mere naming, implies a move from material sight to the idealized sight of the invisible.[32] It thus purifies the evil that can be its initial object—and not just any sort of evil, but one particularly dear to the Hugolian gaze: "La nudité d'une femme devenue la nudité d'une statue fait taire la chair et chanter l'âme. Sitôt que le regard devient contemplateur, l'assainissement commence" (12:413).[33] Contemplation is to voyeurism as artistic form is to female flesh. The significance of *contempler* has been discussed at length by Jean Gaudon, who takes as his point of departure the line from *La Légende des siècles*, "Eve qui regardait, Adam qui contemplait" (10:439). Eve is more sensual, Adam an "être complet": contemplation involves going beyond the limits of the visible, extending the gaze beyond its initial domain.[34] Like the turn to form, the move to contemplation implies a sublimation of the sensory world, a turning away from direct sight and naming. In this sense the "direct vision" of the nineteenth-century poet is sharply restricted. He will gaze directly and write without the obscuring veil of of the old "poetic" diction only at the price of turning his gaze away from its forbidden material origins. And yet this sublimated, redirected gaze will still be said to be original, the poetry a translation of first sight. For this to be so, the forms explored must themselves constitute a hitherto unseen and unheard of territory. And so from the *Préface de Cromwell* to *William Shakespeare* resounds a message of refusal: for the nineteenth century there can be no models, no masters, no separation of styles. The poetic and dramatic forms are to be discovered, unveiled for the first time. The new genesis of literature will be a genesis of what is most autonomous in literature, its forms. At the price of an initial turning of the eye away from the female body and the visible world, the genius of the nineteenth century reaches a poetic realm where he has no father or precursor, where no paternal edict can bend or detain his gaze.

Small wonder, then, that in *Littérature et philosophie mêlées* the poet's task should be described as a separation from the material world:

> Il faut qu'il se soit isolé de la vie extérieure, pour jouir avec plénitude de cette vie intérieure qui développe en lui comme un être nouveau; et ce n'est que lorsque le monde physique a tout à fait disparu de ses yeux, que le monde idéal peut lui être manifesté. (5:145)[35]

This interior sight is like that of Louis Lambert, or of Ballanche's melancholy geniuses. For Hugo, as for Balzac and Ballanche, blindness radicalizes and intensifies a visionary experience also undergone by the seeing writer.[36] The notion of inner vision is no more unique to Hugo than to anyone else, so that what must interest us in his treatment of the blind poet is the degree of identification or distancing with which he relates the unseeing bard to his own narrative or poetic persona. This relation dominates the little poem "A un poète aveugle" from *Les Contemplations*, here quoted in its entirety:

> Merci, poète! —au seuil de mes lares pieux,
> Comme un hôte divin, tu viens et te dévoiles;
> Et l'auréole d'or de tes vers radieux
> Brille autour de mon nom comme un cercle d'étoiles.
>
> Chante! Milton chantait; chante! Homère a chanté.
> Le poète des sens perce la triste brume;
> L'aveugle voit dans l'ombre un monde de clarté.
> Quand l'oeil du corps s'éteint, l'oeil de l'esprit s'allume.
>
> (9:99)[37]

The commonplaces associated with the blind poet—evocation of Homer and Milton, antithesis of light and darkness, displacement of sight from the material to the spiritual—fail to account for this text, which must be read in terms of both internal and external reference. The study of manuscripts and outlines has revealed the identity of the blind poet: Ossian's translator, Baour-Lormian, who died in 1855 during the preparation of *Les Contemplations* and who, as a "classic" pitted against the "romantics," had long opposed Hugo's election to the French Academy. Written in May 1842, the poem appears to be the fruit of a reconciliation of the two following Hugo's reception among the "immortals."[38]

Now at the age of fourteen Hugo had written several satiric pieces against Baour, a well-established poet of the Empire. In one of these poems ("Conte") he describes Baour as the creation of all the worst poets, the sum of all their literary vices. In another, "Sur Baour-Lormian," he specifically attacks the older man's poetic diction, which is that of *préciosité* and visually absurd metaphors:

> Puisque tu nous as fait, Baour,
> De la lune un glaçon, du soleil une croûte,
> Ne sois pas étonné d'entendre chaque jour
> Tes lecteurs (s'il en est que l'ennui ne dégoûte),
> En déchiffrant ton style obscur et lourd,
> S'écrier: —C'est si clair, ma foi! qu'on n'y voit goutte!
>
> (1:47)[39]

Hugo's youthful attack on Baour thus anticipates precisely his general attack, identified as revolutionary in "Réponse à un acte d'accusation," on the poetic language of the *ancien régime*, a language that blinds and obscures by refusal of direct sight and naming. This would make of the now blind and aged Baour a figure of the revolutionary victim, and specifically a victim of the Hugolian poetic revolution, which excludes predecessors and relegates them to blindness. With their reconciliation, Baour enters the circle of Hugo's forebears and unveils himself as a member of the cult of poetry now glorifying its new idol, Hugo. This constitutes a kind of paternal pardon of transgression, an interpretation supported by Baour's appearance among the *lares*, the souls of ancestors who now as domestic divinities protect their descendant. As to the fantasmatic interest of such a pardon, the apparently unremarkable location of the poem in *Les Contemplations* enables us to hazard a guess, for it is placed between two rustic poems about the erotic appearance of young women. In the first, "Vieille chanson du vieux temps," the young speaker is naïvely "blind" to his friend's charms, whereas in the second his visual seduction meets with immodest success. Between the two, then, with the homage to the blind poet, a liberation of the amorous gaze has occurred, an end to the figurative blindness of the would-be lover.

According to his correspondence and a fragment initially destined for *William Shakespeare*, Hugo was personally fascinated by blindness and at times felt that he would lose his sight to the eye diseases from which he suffered periodically from 1824 to 1843. Sometimes his references are merely to the discomfort, sometimes they are to the possibility of blindness. On November 1, 1837, he wrote to J. G. Charpentier, "Il y a en effet, monsieur, un gros nuage sur mes yeux, une ophtalmie qui m'aveugle."[40] To Saint-Valmy he wrote, on May 15, 1824, "Imaginez-vous que depuis votre départ environ, je me pique de ressembler singulièrement à Homère, à Milton, à Ossian et à tous les sublimes aveugles qui ont chanté. . . . Je ne sais quand cela passera, mais je vous assure que j'ai déjà tout mon saoul de cet échantillon de cécité"[41] (2:1440). The tone of offhanded pleasantry is perhaps the only one that could offer a defense in the face of a possibility that was both genuinely troubling and secretly attractive, and Hugo returns to it in a digression in the fragment "Du génie":

> Il [Sainte-Beuve] regarda mes yeux, et me dit doucement: *C'est une amaurose commençante. Le nerf optique se paralyse. Dans quelques années la cécité sera complète.* Une pensée illumina subitement mon esprit. *Eh bien*, lui dis-je, *ce sera toujours ça.* Et voilà que je me mis à espérer que je serais peut-être un jour aveugle comme Homère et comme Milton. La jeunesse ne doute de rien. (12:412)[42]

The context of this anecdote indicates that Hugo imagined blindness as an exemplary punishment. He was writing about blindness or other infirmities as signs of genius, marks of initiation: "Etre foudroyé, c'est être prouvé Titan. C'est déjà quelque chose de partager avec ceux d'en haut le privilège d'un coup de tonnerre. . . . Etre infirme ainsi que les forts, cela tenterait volontiers" (12:412).[43] Hugo often evoked the myth of the Titans, the race of giants overthrown by Zeus and the other Olympian gods. Pierre Albouy, in his fundamental work *La Création mythologique chez Victor Hugo*, noted that the oppression of the Titans by the Olympians becomes, for Hugo, a myth of the oppression of the people by kings.[44] Hugo's reference to the blind or infirm genius as Titan implies participation in the struggle of generations, the symbolic Oedipal rivalry, from which the *génies* were supposed to be free. "L'infirmité ou la difformitée infligée à ces bien aimés augustes de la pensée fait l'effet d'un contrepoids sinistre, d'une compensation peu avouable là-haut, d'une concession faite aux jalousies dont il semble que le créateur doit avoir honte" (12:412).[45] Compensation, concession, counterweight: the spiritual vision of geniuses is given only in exchange for material weakness or deformity. For the creator, participation in this exchange appears scandalous and unavowable; it is even more so for the genius himself. Hugo declares the nineteenth-century poet to be untouched by rivalry with his ancestors, but he describes, through the myth of the rebellious and stricken Titan, a poet locked in just such a struggle. The Titan Phtos of *La Légende des siècles*, imprisoned in the earth, rebels, escapes, and denounces the Olympians ("ces parvenus") in the name of a higher principle: "O Dieux, il est un Dieu" (15:686). In a similar vein, Hugo always insisted on the "principles of 1789" as a condition of his acceptance of the Revolution and 1793, just as his affirmation of God was a condition of his attacks on priests and religion. The modern poet or genius cannot escape this tension between revolt against tyranny and acceptance of authority. The Revolution gives birth to genius, but genius performs the work of revolution or prepares its arrival. This last alternative is crucial, for if the work of the genius takes the place of revolution, the violence is sublimated or abolished and the next revolution will not take place, but if he prepares yet another revolution, then the wheel of conflict is merely given another turn. At the center of Hugo's great poem "La Révolution" stands the figure of the prerevolutionary artist, the sculptor Germain Pilon, who by creating the cariatides of the Pont-Neuf unknowingly prepares the Revolution: "Etre, sans le savoir, Titan; est-ce possible?" (10:231).[46] The artist or poet may be unknowingly, unconsciously, a revolutionary and even a regicide, as Hugo indicates in his apostrophe to Germain Pilon:

> Et ta fatale main, ô grand tailleur de pierre,
> Dans Trivelin sinistre ébauchait Robespierre. (10:230)[47]

The problem becomes particularly intense during restorations, which scandalize Hugo both because they undo the progress that justified, or at least redeemed, revolutionary violence, and because they imply that regicide can be repeated, that the artist who denounces suffering and oppression may be the Titan of a new revolt.[48]

These problems of deformity, Oedipal rivalry and violence, revolution and restoration dominate *L'Homme qui rit*, the enormous, convoluted, and troubling novel in which Hugo placed his only true blind character, the saintly adolescent Dea, beloved of the fallen lord Gwynplaine, whose monstrous laugh is forever scarred upon his face. In this couple, a comic motif from the *commedia* plays about lustful old occulists becomes a serious, romantic situation. Gwynplaine finds love because Dea cannot see his hideous deformity. Her existence places him in a little universe of forgetfulness in which, for a time, he can live without reference to the mask of his own flesh. As in *Les Misérables*, blindness produces a sentimental paradise. But unlike the second childhood of Monsignor Myriel or the untroubled love of Dorat's Sélim and Sélima, the idyll of *L'Homme qui rit* is a paradise whose occupants are doomed to expulsion. Dea may be providentially blind, but Gwynplaine is a visionary pursued by fatality, a son of a revolution who must discover his titanic vocation and be struck down in his revolt.

The novel's action takes place following the English Restoration. The return of the Stuarts in 1660 suggests more recent restorations of despotic rule: Bonaparte's *18 brumaire*, the return of Louis XVIII and the White Terror, and of course the *2 décembre* of Napoléon III, railed by Hugo as *Napoléon-le-petit*. On a stormy winter night, Gwynplaine, a boy of ten, is abandoned on a rocky coast by a band of people who then embark in a small ship, only to meet their death at sea. They are the *comprachicos*, child kidnappers who had stolen, disfigured, and raised the boy. Stumbling over a range of hills in the darkness, Gwynplaine encounters first death, in the form of a tarred and rotting hanged man, and then life, in the form of a baby girl whose impoverished mother had just died in the snow. He hears a voice that he is not sure of hearing, a voice that may not be a voice. "C'était du bruit, mais du rêve" (240): the baby's cry is an amalgam (the term is Hugo's) of presence and absence, matter and spirit, strength and weakness, life and death. The girl will grow up to be Dea, and it is this cold night that both unites her with Gwynplaine and costs her her sight: "La fatale nuit d'hiver . . . avait tué la mère et aveuglé la fille" (284).[49] Dea's origin, the moment of her blinding and of her entry into the text, coincides with the origin of the human voice, at a moment of undifferentiated transition: "C'était quelque chose comme une souffrance qui appelle, mais sans savoir qu'elle est une souffrance et sans savoir qu'elle fait appeal" (240).[50] But this nascent appeal suffices to reach the nascent intelligence that is Gwynplaine's on this night, which will form the first layer of his conscious memory—he is born to consciousness as Dea half forms her cry, for he forgets everything that took place during his stay with the *comprachicos*.[51] He takes the little girl in his arms amid the tempest's winds, and together they seek refuge against the chaos of the universe.

They find their shelter with Ursus, a *philosophe* who has outlived his age, an ironist who exchanges proper names, confounds the order of things, speaks ill of everything and does only good. A precursor of revolution, he becomes to them a father whom they know not to be a father. Together they grow and prosper, providing for each other happiness and prosperity.

Gwynplaine, a ridiculous monster to the world, which judges him by the mask of his face, is to Dea simply himself: "C'est que Dea, l'aveugle, apercevait l'âme" (285).[52] With her second sight, she perceives the soul in exchange, as it were, for the loss of the visible body, but neither of them experiences this as renunciation. What Dea "sees" and is named *âme* are simply the words, deeds, and tactile presence of Gwynplaine. For these "amoureux assortis," the topos of the blind seer seems to be nothing more than a description of their way of life together—far from implying a radical sublimation or an incidence of the supernatural, the topos is transformed into a novelistic situation. But while thus avoiding a visual objectification of Gwynplaine, Dea, like Monsignor Myriel, creates for herself a myth of his absolute presence—"la présence, profond mystère qui divinise l'invisible et d'où résulte cet autre mystère, la confiance" (287),[53] and Gwynplaine becomes her "religion." The ability not to see his face is the sole reason for her clairvoyance, and her second sight is for no one but him. Robed in white, Dea will appear as a visionary priestess, gifted with clairvoyance, but Hugo explains her insights in a manner that recalls eighteenth-century philosophy rather than myth or illuminism. When Gwynplaine tells her that he is ugly, she answers with a definition worthy of Diderot's blind man from Puiseaux: "Etre laid, qu'est-ce que cela? c'est faire du mal. Gwynplaine ne fait que du bien. Il est beau"[54] (290). Hugo's mythic use of Dea takes as its foundation an understanding of blindness fostered by sensationalist philosophy: to be blind is to lack visual referents and thus to use words and understand reality in ways different from those of the seeing. Since Dea's status as a blind seer depends on Gwynplaine's need not to be seen, her function in the text can be explained only with reference to her lover's deformity. *L'Homme qui rit* is the novel not of a blind *woman* but of a disfigured man who receives a miraculous second chance at acceptance beneath the gaze of a woman incapable of seeing him.

Gwynplaine, by birth an heir to a peerage, was kidnapped and disfigured by royal order so that his exiled father's title could be given to his bastard half-brother. Condemned by sight and mirrors to reflect upon his face, he must find there "quelque chose d'absent qui est soi-même" (284). His physical appearance is the product of reinscription, suggesting an origin prior to present bodily form and a true, hidden nature that can only come into its own secondarily, belatedly. Defaced by the surgeon of the *comprachicos*, his mouth has become a slit running from ear to ear. "Gwynplaine vivait dans une sorte de décapitation, ayant un visage qui n'était pas à lui" (286).[55] Narrative allusions to castration confirm the symbolic import of this wound: Saxon law, we are told, substituted facial mutilation, blinding, and removal of the genitals for the death penalty (332), and the sultan's eunuch and the pope's *castrati* head the list of human productions of the *comprachicos* (198). A manuscript variant even contains a direct reference by Ursus to the link between Gwynplaine's deformity and castration: "Tout en le déshabillant, il le voit nu. Il grommelle: —Allons! ils l'ont laissé homme. Quelle bêtise! Pendant qu'ils étaient en train, ils auraient bien dû le faire monstre tout à fait. Il eût pu gagner sa vie en chantant chez le pape" (Massin, 14:404).[56]

A son punished by order of the king, one of countless victims of aristocratic cruelty, Gwynplaine also has a revolutionary father. During the English Revolution of 1642, Lord Linnaeus Clancharlie had opted for the Republic, and stubbornly so, going so far as to choose exile under the Restoration. His lineage in the tribe of King Charles, indicated by his name, shows the gravity of his role as a son in revolt against the father. Since the execution of Charles I in 1649 follows closely on the heels of 1642, Lord Clancharlie was almost a regicide, and the narrator leaves no doubt as to the significance of these dates:

> La statue équestre, réservée aux rois, figure très bien la royauté; le cheval, c'est le peuple. Seulement ce cheval se transfigure lentement. Au commencement, c'est un âne, à la fin c'est un lion. Alors il jette par terre son cavalier, et l'on a 1642 en Angleterre et 1789 en France, et quelquefois il le dévore, et l'on a en Angleterre 1649 et en France 1793.
>
> Que le lion puisse redevenir baudet, cela étonne, mais cela est (266).[57]

Restorations—1660, 1815, and not least 1851—astonish and scandalize, for they begin the cycle anew, thereby proving that it is a cycle, an endless combat. Fermain Clancharlie, alias Gwynplaine, is punished during a restoration for his own father's part in a revolution. The Oedipal desire to remove the political father has been accomplished and punished, and yet the agent of that desire is the biological father. Like Marius in *Les Misérables*, like Hugo himself, Gwynplaine has a revolutionary vocation through his father's example.

As a fallen young nobleman, son of a revolution and of an absent father, adopted son of a *philosophe*, Gwynplaine resembles, by his origins, the figure of the nineteenth-century poet as elaborated by Hugo in *William Shakespeare*. He is not a poet per se, but he becomes a visionary spokesman for the suffering people, a prophet of revolution. A court intrigue and the arrival of a message in a bottle from the doomed *comprachicos* bring about Gwynplaine's restoration to his father's peerage. Upon realizing what has happened to him, he undergoes an experience akin to that of the romantic visionary: "Il lui sembla qu'il voyait tout, le passé, l'avenir, le présent dans le saisissement d'une clarté subite" (347).[58] This transcendence of chronological time also characterized the visionary experience of Ballanche's blind Thamyris ("pour l'intelligence dégagée des organes, le passé, le présent, l'avenir sont contemporains")[59] and of the adept of *Spécialité* as defined by Louis Lambert. Gwynplaine's attributes as a visionary artist do not differ essentially from those of the blind seer, and moreover both blindness and disfigurement are equated, in the text, with castration. As symbolic punishment, or as condition for second sight, blindness implies a renunciation of the material world in exchange for serenity or wisdom, but this kind of trade-off does not characterize Gwynplaine. Despite the symbolic equivalence implied between his disfigurement and blinding, it is Dea, not he, who cannot see. Through her love, and later through his restoration to the peerage, he receives second chances at happiness in the material world, and between his dizzying changes of position it appears for brief moments that for him some kind of solution other than that of total sublimation can be realized. The price of such a solution is *to be unseen*—whence the blindness of a woman to whose shining eyes he will remain invisible, whence the darkness of a night session at which Gwynplaine will be escorted into the House of Lords by two old nearsighted peers.

By displacing the loss of sight from the visionary hero to his female companion, Hugo links the topos of the blind seer to the psychological fascination with a blind person as a partner in love. *L'Homme qui rit*, and specifically the relation of Dea to Gwynplaine, thus lay particular claim to our attention, for in them the sentimental, literary, and psychological aspects of blindness coincide. Founded on intense reciprocal need, with each in effect occupying the position of the blind beloved with respect to the other, Gwynplaine's and Dea's love attains a state of near-perfect complementarity, and the narrator's ecstatic commentaries constitute a veritable theory of sexuality, the theory of a sexuality defined by innocence, undifferentiation, and symbiosis. A brief comparison of these ideas to those of Freud, elaborated in the *Three Essays on the Theory of Sexuality*, will show how Hugo both evokes and denies the phenomena of childhood sexuality, phenomena without which such concepts as the Oedipus complex and castration would have no meaning.

Freud argued that our first choices of love objects are made in earliest childhood and that these choices form models for object choices in our adult lives. Gwynplaine and Dea learn their love while she is a baby, he a preadolescent without prior affective experience ("dans ce groupe qui l'abandonnait [the *comprachicos*] rien ne l'aimait, et il n'aimait rien" (205).[60] Thus, as in Freud's theory, object choice takes place in two stages; when the drives specific to puberty appear, sexuality has already been learned. Bedded down together by Ursus, the boy and the baby girl enjoy "une nuit de noces avant le sexe" (249). The irreducible difference here between Freud and Hugo is that in *L'Homme qui rit* the two object choices coincide, so that there is no displacement from an original love object to an adult love object.

As in the *Three Essays*, Dea's initial object choice develops by means of what Freudians call anaclisis (*Anlehnung*, leaning on, *étayage*) from the infant's relation to the mother. When Gwynplaine first takes her in his arms, she attempts to use his body as a maternal breast: "les lèvres violettes du nourrisson se rapprochèrent de la joue du garçon comme d'une mamelle" (241); "elle ne criait pas, croyant à une mère" (243). Later, Dea will know that for her Gwynplaine "s'est fait mère et nourrice" (285). There is even a suggestion of the Freudian *Lutschen* or "sensual sucking," by which the transition from nurture to pleasure is accomplished, for when Ursus gives Dea a bottle, she sucks it "voluptueusement" and then softly shuts her eyes, "signe de plénitude" (247, 248). For Freud, the pleasure obtained by the nursling "persists as a prototype of sexual satisfaction in later life."[61]

But according to the founder of psychoanalysis, this derivation of sexuality proper from self-preservation drives implies a process of differentiation, a displacement of drives and a loss of the primordial plenitude that was their point of departure. The Hugolian "theory" of infantile sexuality proposes a pure and simple continuation of the state of absolute presence and need. Everything disconcerting in Freud's account is missing here. There is neither autoeroticism (for the love object was present from the beginning) nor castration (for in symbolic form—mutilation, blindness—it has already taken place and cannot therefore be a threat or source of anxiety) nor Oedipus complex (for Gwynplaine and Dea are mother and daughter, brother and sister, yet without really being so; their "incest" need not be prohibited because it is not incestuous). Gwynplaine's and Dea's love is stable, eternal, and forever locked in the form of an original symbiosis. Together they constitute a little monadic space shielded from the universal chaos without. In Freudian terms theirs is no sexuality, for they experience no derivation of sexuality, its childhood manifestations already taking the form of adult (romantic, bourgeois) love, its adult manifestations still retaining both the objects and the so-called innocence of their childhood play. Speaking as Freudian critics, we might say that Gwynplaine's and Dea's love is "blind"—to the derivation of sexuality, to the mechanisms and cleavages that it involves. It represents a reactional fantasy, a denegation of the castration and Oedipus complexes so important to Hugo's texts on revolution and notably to *L'Homme qui rit*. With this providentially blind woman, Gwynplaine lives in a microcosm of innocent incest and inconsequential castration.

Their unlikely love is described as an exception to the antithesis of matter and spirit; each is for the other an ideal made palpable. "Il y avait du rêve en Dea. Elle semblait un songe ayant un peu pris corps . . . elle était tout juste assez femme" (286).[62] More even than Dea herself, their situation as a couple constitutes an amalgam of the visible and the invisible: "Gwynplaine voyait descendre vers lui en pleine lumière, *dans un arrangement de destinée qui ressemblait à la mise en perspective d'un songe*, une blanche nuée de beauté ayant la forme dé femme" (287; emphasis added).[63] To describe this union beyond all categories of description, Hugo turns to a language of synesthesia, an amalgam of heterogeneous and disaggregated images. "Ils se serraient l'un contre l'autre dans une sorte de clair-obscur sidéral plein de parfums, de lueurs, de musiques, d'architectures lumineuses, de songes . . ." (287).[64] This is no sensory evocation of synesthetic experience, but a juxtaposition of images that can coexist and be reconciled only by their idealization, only if their sensory particularity is evaporated in a movememt of formal distillation. The same procedure is used by the narrator to evoke the world of dreams, thus confirming the oneiric quality of the lovers' existence: "Au-dessus de ces paupières où la vision a remplacé la vue, une désagrégation sépulcrale de silhouettes et d'aspects se dilate dans l'impalpable" (244).[65] Here *la vision* designates a second sight in which visual forms persist, but in an order that is no longer that of the observing, representing, mastering eye. Such is also the form of Dea's mental universe, "l'inexprimable abstraction où vit une pensée que n'éclaire pas le soleil" (285).[66] The idyllic life of the "Green-Box," the ambulatory home and theater where Gwynplaine and Dea live with Ursus, is animated by the desire to materialize this dreamlike fusion of opposites.

It is the appearance of Dea and Gwynplaine as a couple that creates this effect of a floating, ineffable vision descended to earth in "Chaos vaincu," the "interlude" written by Ursus and performed each night by the little family on the stage of their green wagon. The couple forms a mystery between knowledge and ignorance, a nonvisual mystery suggestible only by a totally abstract language of light and vision:

> On sentait qu'elle aimait son monstre. Le savait-elle monstre? Oui, puisqu'elle le touchait. Non, puisqu'elle l'acceptait. Toute cette nuit et tout ce jour mêlés se résolvaient dans l'esprit du spectateur en un un clair-obscur où apparaissaient des perspectives infinies. (294)[67]

Together, Dea's blindness and shining beauty seem to form a transition between all opposites, between heaven and earth, spirit and matter, the sublime and the grotesque. That the material existence of a blind girl should imply the fusion of so many antitheses stands as an index of the inextricable bond between sight and the guilty fascination of matter in Hugo's imaginative universe. Dea's presence gives the play a mysterious dimension, for the audience perceives her spirituality and her clairvoyance: "On voyait qu'elle était aveugle et l'on sentait qu'elle était voyante. Elle semblait debout sur le seuil du surnaturel. Elle paraissait être à moitié dans notre lumière et à moitié dans l'autre clarté" (294).[68] Dea, as Léon Cellier was the first to point out, is an initiatory figure, leading Gwynplaine (and the audience) from the material to the spiritual.[69]

The subject of "Chaos vaincu" is nothing less than the triumph of spirit over matter, man's escape from the destructive forces of nature through mind and speech. This allegorical presentation of the origin of the logos begins with the sound of Dea's voice, with a reenactment of the cry with which she enters both the novel and Gwynplaine's nascent consciousness. There is first a song, a voice in the darkness, "Des musiques mystérieuses flottaient, accompagnant ce chant de l'invisible,"[70] and then she appears, at the very moment when Man, Gwynplaine, was about to succumb to "les forces féroces de la nature, les faims inconscientes, l'obscurité sauvage,"[71] Ursus and Homo as bear and wolf (293). The "description" of the floating voice and music recalls that of the dream-world, of Dea, of Gwynplaine and Dea, the fantasy of a reconciliation of all conflicts and oppositions. At first undifferentiated and inarticulate, as on the nights when Gwynplaine found her, Dea's voice becomes

speech and recounts the creation of light and reason out of
song. Saved for the moment from the ageless cycle of violent
struggle, Gwynplaine strikes down the beasts and raises his
body erect toward Dea, who places her hand on his woolly
head. In the eyes of the audience, Dea saves Gwynplaine, but
Dea, troubled by the rumor of the crowd around the Green-
Box, feels that Gwynplaine is saving her. The mythical effect of
the play thus depends on the symbiosis of the couple. As Cellier
puts it, "Beyond the advent of joy, a more distant perspective is
unveiled: that of a world in which it can no longer be known
who saves and who is saved."[72] To Dea, Gwynplaine in this moment is a figure of strength and virility: "Dea touchait un mou-
ton qu'elle savait être un lion" (294).[73]

But for those who see, for audience and reader, a ray of light
falls upon Gwynplaine's face, and the play passes from the sublime to the grotesque in a single stroke. Before "le monstre
épanoui," the Man Who Laughs, the assembled populace bursts
into an orgasmic "convulsion d'hilarité"—provoked by the unexpected, says the narrator, but this is a particular kind of unexpected, what Freud would call the return of the repressed, the
violence of castration reappearing at the moment when the divine priestess has inspired Gwynplaine's virile triumph. The
crowd's laugh is joyous and liberating and does not humiliate
Gwynplaine. Nonetheless, this nightly reminder of his deformity marks the limits of the Green-Box idyll, of his first chance at
reconciliation with himself and the world, at escape from his
marred destiny.

More than his appearance, however, it is Gwynplaine's roving eye that fractures the harmony of his life with Dea. Ursus
senses the danger and warns him: "Tu me fais l'effet d'un observateur, imbécile! Prends-y garde, cela ne te regarde pas. Tu as
une chose à faire, aimer Dea" (297).[74] But Gwynplaine cannot
resist gazing out at the masses of humanity surrounding his little island paradise, and he sees on all sides misfortune and misery, everything that the world of the couple in the Green-Box
had shut out. "Ses yeux parfois, curieux d'une curiosité émue,
cherchaient à voir jusqu'au fond de cette obscurité où agoni-
saient tant d'efforts inutiles et où luttaient tant de lassitudes. . . .

Lui il était au port, il regardait autour de lui ce naufrage" (296, 297).[75] Now what was shut out, repressed, was above all sexuality, as absent from Gwynplaine's and Dea's chaste adoration as it was from the theory of idyllic infantile love, and one night sexuality explodes before Gwynplaine's bedazzled eyes—the Duchess Josiane appears in the box "for the nobility" of their crude theater, transforming what had been a "trou noir" into a flood of light, displaying herself "la plus nue qu'elle pouvait" (312-313). "Toute la femme, quel gouffre!" The voyeuristic attraction to the forbidden female body will reach its paroxysm when Gwynplaine, exploring his palace after his restoration, beholds Josiane asleep and naked. Like 1793, the Stuart duchess is a volcanic crater, and in gazing at her Gwynplaine risks being blinded: "Ce qui arrive sur vous, c'est trop de lumière, qui est l'aveuglement, c'est l'excès de vie, qui est la mort. . . . Monde de lave et de braise. Dévorant prodige des profondeurs" (368).[76]

But at first this carnal spectacle appears at an insurmountable distance from Gwynplaine, at the distance of an apparition, of an ideal. The objects of first and second sight seem to have exchanged places, and "Destin ironique, l'âme, cette chose céleste, il la tenait, il l'avait dans sa main, c'était Dea; le sexe, cette chose terrestre, il l'apercevait au plus profond du ciel, c'était cette femme"(315).[77] With Dea, the material and the ideal converged, united, and came to rest in an amazing harmony, but with Josiane they become dialectical poles threatening to tear Gwynplaine apart. To the fascination of woman is added the danger of a transgressive "second sight." But this situation, which the narrator calls ironic, is ultimately that of the menaced erotic gaze, which can be direct and assured only by turning away from its first, carnal object and which must transgress to return to it, risking separation and loss. Life with Dea embodied an extraordinary fantasy of reversal, of escape from this predicament, for with her the first and most immediate object of sight was ideal and therefore not forbidden, and sublimation and deferment had no place. For Gwynplaine, "castration" had taken place; it was no longer a menace and, thanks to Dea's blindness, could be forgotten. But Josiane desires him not in spite of or aside from but because of his deformity—"Gwynplaine était flatté dans sa vanité de monstre" (320)[78]—and she tells him to gaze at her as in a dazzling mirror in which to know himself: "Vois comme je te ressemble. Regarde dans moi comme dans un miroir. Ton visage, c'est mon âme" (370).[79] This specular relation brings Gwynplaine closer to an awareness of the irreconcilable conflict between his inside and his outside, between his once whole and now mutilated selves, an awareness that he had kept hidden by the superficial symbiosis of his life with Dea.

The fantasy of Gwynplaine and Dea, however much it may express a profound longing to escape from the structures of castration, violent rivalry, and antithesis, can be allied objectively only with the instance of repression, against the voyeuristic sexuality that returns with Josiane. Seeing her, Gwynplaine is reminded of his deformity, which he could forget when the only gaze that mattered to him was Dea's. He remembers as well the long-forgotten inscriptions in Ursus's little shack explaining the power and privileges of the nobility. A *textual* image, that of the palimpsest, figures this resurfacing of what had been submerged. Gwynplaine's seduction by Josiane takes place in several stages. After he first sees her, he is troubled, but forgets her totally—"une dissipation de rêverie . . . ne laisse point de trace" (316)[80]—only to remember everything and more when he receives her message of desire: "et ses premières pensées tumultueuses sur cette femme reparaissaient, comme chauffées à tout ce feu sombre. L'oubli n'est autre chose qu'un palimpseste. Qu'un accident survienne, et tous les effacements revivent dans les interlignes de la mémoire étonnée"[81] (320).

The reappearing text accompanies the fantasy-shattering returns of the repressed throughout *L'Homme qui rit*. Two distinct processes, both working by means of the palimpsestic mechanism, pull Gwynplaine away from his happiness with Dea and toward the nobility of his origins. The first is Josiane's desire, which appears in Gwynplaine's mind as reappearing letters in a manuscript. The second is the arrival on shore, after fifteen years in the waves, of the parchment written by the shipwrecked *comprachicos* (on the verso of the royal order bearing the words "*jussu regis*. Jeffrys") in which they confess their crime and reveal Gwynplaine's identity. Precipitated to wealth and power by the resurfacing of this text, Gwynplaine meets Josiane face to face and enters the House of the Lords. But from his father he has inherited not only titles and possessions but also a revolutionary vocation. He sees himself as a political visionary capable of warning the Lords of the suffering of their subjects and thereby averting the coming revolution (1793), preparing an escape from the circle of violence. He decides to resolve the contradiction between his inner and outer selves by speaking as both a lord and a victim, as one who has both the right to speak in high places and the experience to tell of misery and injustice. But the fantasy of this second reconciliation will likewise be shattered by the palimpsestic reappearance of texts, for his face is a double text, the product of a "monstrueuse superposition" (395). Through an intense effort of will and muscular control, Gwynplaine makes his face appear almost normal as he begins his speech to the Lords. The content of the speech is itself a palimpsest, for when the boy Gwynplaine, abandoned by the *comprachicos*, survived his encounter with the tarred hanged man, the narrator remarked that children can stop at first impressions but that later "les souvenirs du jeune âge reparaissent sous les passions comme le palimpseste sous les ratures, ces souvenirs sont des points d'appui pour la logique, et ce qui était vision dans le cerveau de l'enfant devient syllogisme dans le cerveau de l'homme" (212).[82] In Gwynplaine's discourse before the Lords, the memories of that night reappear as logical arguments in his denunciation of oppression: "La première chose que j'ai vue, c'est la loi, sous forme d'un gibet" (392).[83] But with the resurfacing of that memory comes another reappearance, this one catastrophic: "Gwynplaine, pris d'une émotion poignante, sentit lui monter à la gorge les sanglots, ce qui fit, chose sinistre, qu'il éclata de rire" (392).[84] With this rending of the serious rewriting that Gwynplaine had for a moment been able to superimpose on the textual mask of his face, the Lords explode in laughter and drive him from their midst. Gwynplaine before the Lords is a Titan appearing before the Olympians, but unlike his mythic counterparts in Hugo's work—Phtos and the *Satyre* of *La Légende des siècles*, Mirabeau of *Littérature et philosophie mê-*

lées, Germain Pilon and his caryatids in "La Révolution"—
Gwynplaine does not have the last laugh. In the words of Albouy, "Gwynplaine is the most pained of Hugo's Titans. He
failed."[85]

With the resurfacing of his indelible laugh, Gwynplaine must
face not only political failure but also the implications of the
contrast between outside and inside, surface and depth, that Josiane has first revealed to him: "Etre comique au dehors, et tra-
gique au dedans, pas de souffrance plus humiliante, pas de co-
lère plus profonde. Gwynplaine avait cela en lui" (393).[86]
Renouncing his title and seeking to return to Dea, to a new reconciliation on the private level, he finds the Green-Box gone
and his universe vanished, and again the palimpsest shatters his
hopes, for he remembers words spoken to him by the court
schemer Barkilphedro:

> Cet homme lui avait écrit dans le cerveau quelque chose
> d'obscur qui à présent reparaissait, et cela avait été écrit
> d'une encre si horrible que c'était maintenant des lettres de
> feu, et Gwynplaine voyait flamboyer au fond de sa pensée
> ces paroles énigmatiques, aujourd'hui expliquées: *Le destin
> n'ouvre pas une porte sans en fermer une autre.*[87] (400–401)

Despite this devastating triumph of antithetical logic, the novel
does not end without a final stroke of melodrama. The wolf
Homo interrupts Gwynplaine's preparations for suicide and
leads him to Ursus, fleeing England on a ship about to depart.
Dea, whose existence had given Gwynplaine a chance at happiness, is dying of a broken heart in his absence. In her farewell to
Ursus she explains her own status as a character, as Gwynplaine's creature ("il m'avait ramassé"), who has no life without
him: "Gwynplaine, c'était tout simple, je vivais. Maintenant
Gwynplaine n'y est plus, je meurs. C'est la même chose"
(409).[88] As always, she redefines words as a function of her perceptions: Gwynplaine is a synonym of *je vivais*. Left to herself,
she at last discovers her blindness: "C'est à présent que je suis
aveugle" (409).

The ending of *L'Homme qui rit* is a turn to the spiritual, to an
afterlife, an attempt to conquer the triumphant chaos with a fi-

nal vision of order, to show that the union of Dea and Gwynplaine was not an accident or a deluded fantasy but the most ultimate of realities. At the moment of her death, the blind girl cries that she sees the light, a profession of faith that suffices to make of Gwynplaine a smiling and accepting suicide. "Le Paradis retrouvé ici-bas," the penultimate chapter title announces, to be succeeded by "Non. Là-haut." But the succession is belied by Dea, who just before her final agony exclaims with poignant lucidity, "C'est ici qu'était le paradis. Là-haut, ce n'est que le ciel" (414).[89] Paradise cannot be won through sublimation, Dea tells us; it is not the substitution of the spiritual for the material. Hugo attempts to say at the end of the novel that her second sight is of the immortal realm that she enters on her deathbed, but throughout the novel Dea's vision has existed only in the context of the Eden of innocent pleasure that she formed with Gwynplaine. Their love, for all its excessive sentimentality, embodied a powerful and moving project: to escape from the violent effects of psychic conflict and the psychic terrors of historical violence. Such an escape required forgetfulness, the merciful effacement of the scar left by history and the strife of generations. It required a blindness that would be insightful by the simple act of not seeing. But Dea's blindness was not enough. The project failed, and the novel's final words tell of that failure. With the blind virgin gone, the beast called man regresses. Light and speech, the triumph of "Chaos vaincu," give way to an inarticulate cry in the darkness, and the gaze, which had been sublimated, reverts to (a homonym of) its first object. Ursus the *philosophe*, having outlived all his progeny, must take in these final images: "Il aperçut près du bord Homo qui hurlait dans l'ombre en regardant la mer."[90]

EPILOGUE

The writings of Hugo demonstrate that even within the work of a single author blindness appears in multiple contexts, in different kinds of discourse. There are the blind of superstition and the blind of doubt; there are lovers whose blindness brings them innocent bliss; there are blind bards and visionaries, figures of fascination and anxiety for the poet of the nineteenth century. In the preceding chapter, I attempted to use a psychoanalytic approach to show a certain coherence of preoccupations behind these Hugolian approaches to blindness, but it is also necessary to remember the differences, for they show Hugo working in several modern traditions of representing the blind. Even within a single character, Dea, we can identify different strategies of presentation. Dea's language and ideas are presented along the lines established by Diderot with the man from Puiseaux; her innocent love for Gwynplaine follows what we might call the modern idyllic tradition of presenting the sentiments of the blind; her ability to see Gwynplaine's soul, while grounded in her perceptual faculties, is described in the language of illuminism and with reference to the tradition of blind prophets and seers.

This multivalent character of Hugo's references to blindness make of Dea something of a microcosm of the strategies for writing about the blind examined in this book. The types of discourse by which Hugo characterized Dea—the philosophic, the sentimental, and the visionary—correspond to the principal ways in which blindness, since the early eighteenth century, had been conceived of and represented. These three representations can be distinguished, quite simply, by their distance from the Molyneux problem, from the origin of Enlightenment writing on the blind. With that problem, the perceptual and mental faculties of the blind became an object of intellectual interest and began to be compared with those of the seeing. What we may call the "philosophic" mode of writing about blindness stems directly from this interest, since in it the blind are described by means of an analysis of their perceptions. Most of the material treated in Chapters 1, 2, and 4 can be placed in this category, for the pedagogical writings on blindness were, above all, writings on perceptual abilities or handicaps and their impact on personality and intellectual aptitude.

The second type of representation, the "sentimental," is a derivative of the first, a product of modern interest in the experience of those who see for the first time, but here the focus of attention shifts from the description of mental processes to the imaginative postulation of moral and emotional states specific to the blind and those close to them. In the literary works examined in Chapter 3, but also in *L'Homme qui rit*, the cured or curable blind person is described in terms of emotions presumed to be entailed by visual deprivation. More precisely, the blind are idealistically imagined as being free of every sort of ethical, spiritual, or psychological defect that can be associated with the act of seeing.

In contrast to the philosophic and sentimental presentations of blindness, the "visionary" or "romantic" mode derives not from modern developments in medicine or philosophy but from a deliberate turn to myth and tradition. Here the individual implications of being sightless are less important than the symbolic implications of the blind figure. In this third type of representation there is not so much a direct link to the Molyneux problem, to modern ideas, as there is an interference of discourses: the figure of the blind poet or seer is not presented without some speculation or discussion concerning perceptions and the workings of the mind. The notion that the blind are gifted with compensatory faculties, for example, although drawn from ancient myth, is given verisimilitude for the modern reader by being presented as the not wholly implausible consequence of a particular kind of mental organization.

My intention is not to erect these three modes of discourse concerning blindness into absolute categories, or to claim that such a simple classification does justice to the complexity of the material in question. It is simply to show that such categories exist, however difficult it may be to define them or establish their exact limits. These categories cannot be reduced to literary genres, even though at times, as in the comic theater, a particular representation of the blind flourishes in a given literary form. When we move between such works as Diderot's *Lettre*, Balzac's *Facino Cane*, Hugo's *L'Homme qui rit*, and Dufau's *Des aveugles*, the discourses concerning blindness do not so much change their meaning as recombine in changing contexts. That is why great difficulties would arise if one attempted to make global comparisons between authors and to produce articles with titles like "L'Aveugle chez Diderot et Hugo." We cannot say that blindness means X to Diderot, and Y or perhaps X plus Y to Hugo. We can only define, as Foucault suggested, "limited spaces of communication." We can only say that certain aspects of the way in which the *Lettre sur les aveugles* presents the blind person's relation to language can be found, still functioning, in *L'Homme qui rit*, a text in most respects quite incommensurable with the writings of Diderot. Similarly, it is possible to explore in depth the way in which Balzac made blindness a term of his speculation on the creative mind and the act of narration, but it is not possible to leap from the function of blindness in Balzac to the function or meaning of blindness in romantic literature. Writings on blindness are simply too disparate, too different from one another, to lend themselves to general interpretations or sweeping conclusions.

It might be argued, then, that even such loose categories as the three kinds of representation outlined above are simply figments of the interpreter's imagination, that the differences observed among writings on the blind stem from individual, historical, and generic factors that have nothing to do with "blindness" as such. I would respond by claiming that these representations, in the middle of the nineteenth century, were distinct enough to be falsifiable through parody or systematic inversion. To give an example: If we can find a parody of sentimental representations of the blind, then such representations must have existed in the eyes of the parody's author and public. What is more, such parodies, inversions, or negations may signal the discredit of certain kinds of representation and thus help to explain why the subject of this book has not only a beginning, the Molyneux problem, but also an end, a zone beyond which philosophic, sentimental and romantic representations of the blind fail to be of immediate literary or cultural interest. We will conclude, therefore, with brief readings of three works: Charles Nodier's *Histoire du roi de Bohême et de ses sept châteaux*, Baudelaire's "Les Aveugles," and Flaubert's *Madame Bovary*.

Published in 1830, the *Histoire du roi de Bohême* is a nineteenth-century antinovel, a literary parody hailed by Balzac as one of the masterpieces of the "Ecole du désenchantement," along with his own *Physiologie du mariage*, Jules Janin's *La Confession*, and Stendhal's *Le Rouge et le noir*. Spread out among the fifty-eight chapters of this "délicieuse plaisanterie littéraire"[1] is a simple novella about a pair of blind adolescents in the Alps. The novella appears to be an incident of the first leg of the putative voyage to Bohemia, the tale that the narrator is supposed to be telling amid the endless digressions and discussions in which his friends don Pic de Fanferluchio and Breloque involve him. In fact, it is almost the only part of the voyage ever recounted. Each chapter is titled with a single word ending in *-tion*. At the end of "Protestation" the narrator announces that he intends to recount the advantages of Gervais and Caecelia and asks his listeners for approval. The next chapter, "Dubitation," begins as follows:

> "Je n'y fais aucune objection," dit don Pic, "moyennant que votre Caecelia ne soit pas aveugle."
> (Elle l'est.)[2]

Breloque's warning suggests that the blindness of a young heroine has become a literary cliché. In response to his objection, the narrator changes not her condition but her name, and begins to tell the sad tale of the blind Gervais and the once-blind Eulalie.

Traveling through the Savoie, the narrator meets a young blind man, Gervais, who tells him—following a ten-chapter interruption—of his lost love, Eulalie, the blind daughter of a rich foreigner who had mysteriously settled in the region. Their blindness reinforced their love, and Gervais, like the heroes and

heroines of so many plays and novels, placed Eulalie above the
pleasures of seeing:

> O! si je jouissois de la vue, je supplierois le Seigneur d'é-
> teindre mes yeux dans leur orbite, afin de ne pas voir le
> reste des femmes; afin de n'avoir de souvenir que toi, et de
> ne laisser de passage vers mon coeur qu'à ces traits que j'au-
> rois vu sortir des tiens! (135–136)[3]

Their idyll came to an end with the surgical restoration of Eulalie's sight. Gervais realizes that she has seen when she tells him
that she is wearing a green ribbon—whereupon for six chapters
we are treated to don Pic de Fanferluchio's monograph on the
expression "ruban verd," a parody of Latinate academic discourse. When the story picks up again, we learn that after her
cure Eulalie and her father left the Savoie and Gervais for Geneva and then Milan. As in *L'Aveugle qui refuse de voir*, the cure
is a catastrophe, the disruption of individual happiness by the
logic of wealth, ambition, and vanity. The narrator is so moved
that he gives Gervais his dog Puck and goes immediately to
Milan to plead with Eulalie on his behalf. After a hundred pages
of unrelated incidents, he confronts her at a reception:

> Gervais, repris-je avec véhémence en la saisissant par le
> bras, qu'en as-tu fait?
> Elle tomba. Je ne sais pas si elle était morte. (311)[4]

Any sense of an authentic sentimental crisis disappears with this
absurdly indifferent reaction to a grossly melodramatic *dénoue-
ment*. But the parody continues. Upon returning to the Savoie,
the narrator learns that Gervais, informed by a traveler of Eulalie's life (or death!) in Milan, has committed suicide. As if the
tale were not by now sufficiently maudlin, the dog Puck, who
had gone blind like his new master, throws himself into the
gorge of the Arveyron as well. Breloque judges the story
harshly: "De l'affectation pour de la grâce, du sentimental pour
du tendre, de la déclamation pour l'éloquence, du commun
pour du naïf" (361).[5] The very choice of a blind couple as the
subject of the ridiculed narration shows that Nodier considered

it to be a sentimental commonplace. The cure of blindness, in his antinovel, has fallen from modern myth to modern cliché.[6]

In "Les Aveugles," Baudelaire writes not a parody but a thoroughgoing negation of the romantic notion of the blind visionary. Like its companion sonnet, "A une passante," and many others of the "Tableaux parisiens," the poem evokes a disconcerting urban encounter:

> Contemple-les, mon âme; ils sont vraiment affreux!
> Pareils aux mannequins; vaguement ridicules;
> Terribles, singuliers comme les somnambules;
> Dardant on ne sait où leurs globes ténébreux.
>
> Leurs yeux, d'où la divine étincelle est partie,
> Comme s'ils regardaient au loin, restent levés
> Au ciel; on ne les voit jamais vers les pavés
> Pencher rêveusement leur tête appesantie.
>
> Ils traversent ainsi le noir illimité,
> Ce frère du silence éternel. O cité!
> Pendant qu'autour de nous tu chantes, ris et beugles,
>
> Éprise du plaisir jusqu'à l'atrocité,
> Vois! je me traîne aussi! mais, plus qu'eux hébété,
> Je dis: Que cherchent-ils au Ciel, tous ces aveugles?[7]

At the outset, the blind are horribly separated from the poem's speaker. Although they may be objects of contemplation, they are so in a ridiculous manner, not even authentically grotesque or sinister. Their uncanny somnambulism, worthy of Hoffman or the early Balzac, is both intensified and subverted by the uncertainty of their shadowy eyes, which possess neither divine spark nor diabolical flame. The eyes of Facino Cane, it may be recalled, had been likened to a cavern filled with outlaws bearing torches and daggers. The faces of the blind in Baudelaire's poem reveal neither dignity nor serenity nor energy. Instead of an extinguished gaze suggestive of a lost origin, they possess the vacant gaze of creatures lost in a limbo without origin or end. A comparison with one of the preceding poems in the "Tableaux parisiens" confirms the peculiarity of their eyes. "Les Aveugles" follows the three great lyrics dedicated to Hugo: "Le Cygne," "Les Sept Vieillards," and "Les Petites Vieilles." The seven identical old men resemble the blind by their uncanny, unstoppable movement through the streets, but the gaze of the *vieillards* is diabolical, loaded with menacing signification: ". . . la méchanceté qui luisait dans ses yeux, / . . . On eût dit sa prunelle trempée / Dans le fiel; son regard aiguisait les frimas."[8] The eyes of "Les Aveugles" will finally terrify not by their fury or intensity but by their void, the absence that seems to be their only feature.

Commentators have proposed that the image of blind eyes raised upward, which obsesses the poem's speaker, can be traced to Breughel's famous painting or to Champfleury's 1856 translation of Hoffmann's *Contes posthumes*, where the upturned face of a blind man is identified with the second sight of a visionary: "Son oeil intérieur tâche d'apercevoir l'éternelle lumière qui luit pour lui dans l'autre monde."[9] But in Baudelaire's poem there is no transcendent inner vision, and the blind are figures of delusion. The possibility of sight beyond sight disappears in a contrary-to-fact hypothesis, "Comme s'ils regardaient au loin. . . ." The blind search in vain for insight, just as the exiled swan of "Le Cygne" bends his head skyward as he searches for water in the arid center of Paris. The blind appear deluded because they act as if they were going to see, as if a "seconde vue" would be granted them from above, but instead even sound and hearing reinforce their darkness, for "le noir illimité" is "Ce frère du silence éternel." The human voices around them are only the cries of the city's collective orgy, so that the social and sexual exclusion of the blind closes the circle of their isolation. As in the writings of Ballanche, Balzac, and Hugo, the blind of Baudelaire's sonnet become the doubles of the poet or speaker, but their likeness is one not of shared insight or communion but of numbed stupidity and movement without direction. The speaker heaps his hatred of this degraded condition on the blind, even as he concedes his own participation in it. More than the poetic transformation of an incident in the day of a *flâneur*, "Les Aveugles" is a systematic undermining of the romantic figure of the blind visionary.

The blind beggar of *Madame Bovary* first appears at Emma's return from one of her trysts in Rouen with Léon, and the sight of him plunges her into "L'espace d'une mélancolie sans bornes."[10] Unlike most of the blind figures studied in this book, this "pauvre diable" has occupied the attention of a multitude of critics and scholars. Interpreters of the novel have tradition-ally considered him a symbolic figure, but they have disagreed as to what he symbolizes: Nemesis, Death, the Devil, Blind Fate, Damnation, Retribution.[11] More recent commentators have seen the blind man as simply a figure of reality opposed to Emma's fantasy view of herself and the world[12] or as a meaning-less figure, symbolic for the deluded Mrs. Bovary but not for Flaubert or the subtle reader.[13] All these critics, however, treat him as a kind of absolute object in the text, symbol or antisym-bol. None has attempted to read Flaubert's presentation of the beggar as a response to or in the context of prior discursive and textual treatment of the blind. The following remarks, then, though strictly speaking extrinsic to the central interests of Flaubert criticism, offer a new kind of approach to a long-stand-ing interpretive problem.

Unlike the blind of philosophy, vaudeville, or romantic fic-tion, the beggar of *Madame Bovary* has a frightfully deformed face: ". . . à la place des paupières, deux orbites béantes tout en-sanglantées" (272).[14] The contrast with the august dignity of Chactas, or even of Facino Cane, with the serene beauty of ad-olescents, could hardly be more striking, for the romantic blind were almost without exception the victims of amaurosis and thus retained the beauty of their eyes. The beggar has neither the grandeur of the aged blind seer nor the concentration and docility attributed to blind students, for he never ceases to move, to dissipate his energy, to implore passersby and roll the bluish and greenish remains of his eyes. "L'aveugle s'affaissa sur ses jarrets, et la tête renversée, tout en roulant ses yeux et tirant la langue, il se frottait l'estomac à deux mains, tandis qu'il pous-sait une sorte de hurlement sourd, comme un chien affamé"[15] (306). Flaubert does not imply that either these raucous move-ments or the beggar's diseased appearance are consequences or corollaries of his being blind, but it is worth noting that any suggestion of repugnant appearance or disconcerting physical behavior was scrupulously avoided by the educators and caretakers of the blind. The beggar of *Madame Bovary*, recalling the medieval tradition of representing the blind as grotesque social outcasts, seems to be made up of elements that modern forms of discourse on blindness had excluded.

It could be argued that this beggar, who is not blind in Flaubert's earliest scenarios,[16] simply bears no relation to the exalted blind of romantic literature or to the gravely attentive blind of philosophy and pedagogy. However, two distinct sequences of actions, both mentioned by Flaubert in the scenarios only after he had changed the beggar from a legless cripple to a blind man, suggest that there is a relation and that as in Baudelaire's poem it is one of subversion or denial. When the beggar first appears, and again as Emma agonizes on her deathbed, he sings a simple licentious song, whose text Flaubert took from a novel by Restif de la Bretonne. The beggar becomes, in effect, a degraded blind minstrel. The song is hardly romantic poetry, but its lines are not without bearing on Emma's own "romanticism":

> Souvent la chaleur d'un beau jour
> Fait rêver fillette à l'amour.
> Pour amasser diligemment
> Les épis que la faux moissonne,
> Ma Nanette va s'inclinant
> Vers le sillon qui nous les donne.
> Il souffla bien fort ce jour-là
> Et le jupon court s'envola! (273, 332)[17]

Just as the song's coarse message demystifies Emma's idealization of her *baisades*, its performance by the beggar creates a low-comic parody of the inspired and idealized figure of the blind bard.

Flaubert's use of the blind man does not stop, however, at the degradation of a romantic figure, for in a second series of events we find a debased version of the scientific and humanitarian projects of the Enlightenment. The key figure here is that inveterate practitioner of Enlightenment rhetoric, Homais, who earlier in the novel had stormed against "cet aveuglement à se refuser aux bienfaits de la science"[18] and had hailed Bovary's inept operation on the hotel boy's club foot as the occasion to proclaim "que les aveugles verront et que les boiteux marcheront!" (180, 183).[19] The pharmacist wants to eliminate the blind man's begging in the name of progress: "On devrait enfermer ces malheureux, que l'on forcerait à quelque travail" (305).[20] After mumbling a few medical terms such as *cornée opaque* to impress his listeners, Homais announces that he could cure the blind man by a diet and a pomade—ludicrous folk remedies, given the condition of the man's eyes. When this "cure" produces no results and the beggar begins to recount the pharmacist's failure to all who will listen, Homais wages a successful press campaign to have the hapless beggar incarcerated (350–351).

Medical and social interest in the blind is thus shown in its most degraded possible form, motivated only by professional vanity and by a violent desire to cleanse a supposedly rational society of imperfections. The troubled fascination of the seeing with the blind, which educators and social reformers so carefully sought to control and convert to sympathy or pity, turns ugly in the novel's final pages. Emma makes of the beggar a ghastly symbol of fate or death, and Homais, worse, represses him. In Flaubert's presentation of the blind man, the heritage of the Enlightenment is as contaminated as that of romanticism. With its return to grotesque and low-comic traditions, and its denunciation of pseudo-progressive attempts to eliminate society's imperfections, Flaubert's use of the beggar in *Madame Bovary* amounts to a clinical autopsy of Enlightenment and romantic approaches to blindness.

Of course, literary interest in blindness does not end with this autopsy, or with the parodies and negations of Nodier and Baudelaire. Any reader of literature can think of modern works in which the theme of blindness plays a major role, and readers of French literature are likely to think immediately of André Gide's novella, *La Symphonie pastorale*. But after the era of Flaubert, it seems that the philosophic, sentimental, and romantic modes of writing about the blind are no longer of direct or immediate literary interest. These kinds of writing can still be found in literary texts, to be sure, but they cease to confer, in and of themselves, a literary dimension of the theme of blindness. *La Symphonie pastorale*, where these kinds of writing about the blind are clearly in evidence, can serve as an example of this transformation.

Gertrude, the heroine of Gide's novella, is not only blind but completely untrained and inarticulate when the narrator, a Protestant minister, takes on the task of educating her. Like the blind child as theorized by Guillié, she is completely cut off from society. The narrator and his friend, a doctor, refer to Condillac, to philosophic theories of mind and education, to the special alphabet developed for the blind. The doctor proposes to teach her in a manner that recalls the pedagogy of Haüy or of Itard, the teacher of deaf-mutes and of the wild boy of Aveyron: "Il s'agit, pour commencer, de lier en faisceau quelques sensations tactiles et gustatives et d'y attacher, à la manière d'une étiquette, un son, un mot. . . ."[21] Like Haüy's first students, Gertrude soon becomes a teacher of other blind children (112).

The sentimental mode of discourse concerning blindness is no less important in *La Symphonie pastorale* than the philosophic mode. At the beginning of his journal, the narrator announces his project as follows: "J'ai projeté d'écrire ici tout ce qui concerne la formation et le développement de cette âme pieuse, qu'il me semble que je n'ai fait sortir de la nuit que pour l'adoration et l'amour" (12).[22] Thus destined to be brought from darkness to adoration, Gertrude's first moments of intellectual comprehension are attributed by the narrator not so much to intelligence as to love (41–42). He repeatedly evokes the blind Gertrude's innocence, her ignorance of evil. But when her blindness is cured by an operation, the minister, now Gertrude's lover, admits that the idea of being seen by her torments him (125–126). His apprehension is well founded, for like the blind heroines of vaudevilles and melodramas, Gertrude, her sight restored, loves not the man who has planned her education and cure but a younger man, the minister's son Jacques: "Quand j'ai vu Jacques, j'ai compris soudain que ce n'était pas vous que j'aimais; c'était lui. Il avait exactement votre visage; je veux dire celui que j'imaginais que vous aviez" (137–138).[23]

But any but the most superficial reading of the novella shows that its center of interest lies not in a philosophic or sentimental approach to a blind girl's education, but in what that education and the pastor's account of it reveals about him as character and as narrator. Germaine Brée noted, "It is not the method of education in itself that interests Gide: the account of the blind girl's education reveals only the strange intellectual blindness of the pastor himself."[24] In describing the difficult beginnings of Gertrude's mental awakening, the narrator in fact emphasizes his own conflict with his wife and family, their resistance to his interest in the girl. He dismisses as unworthy of note any aspects of her progress that he believes to be common to the education of all blind people (49). Even Gertrude's innocence is revealed to be a creation not of her blindness but of the minister's manipulative delusions. He has attempted to keep Gertrude in a false state of innocence by describing to her the world as he wishes it were, devoid of what he considers evil.

Enlightenment and early romantic approaches to blindness function as topoi in *La Symphonie pastorale*. Gide uses them, but he does not rely on them for his central literary effects. The novella certainly does not derive its power from philosophic or sentimental representations of the blind, and it does not ask its reader to assent to such representations. What power it has stems from the reader's progressive realization of the deluded character of the narration, the moral and religious bankruptcy of the narrator. Far from being presented to the reader for direct effect, as they were in so many works of the late eighteenth and early nineteenth centuries, the topoi of blindness are either treated in passing or revealed to be part of the narrator's delusions. Unlike Nodier, Baudelaire, and Flaubert, who seemed to be self-consciously negating representations that had become little more than clichés, Gide appears to have been relatively indifferent to them, capable of evoking them while keeping his main interests elsewhere.

It would be inappropriate to conclude with the suggestion that all modern writing about the blind is somehow related to what was written by the *philosophes*, their popularizers, or the romantics, whether that relation be one of imitation, negation, or coolly calculated thematic borrowing. What I have tried to describe in this book is a small and partially interrelated group of modes of writing about the blind, a discursive space that made possible, at certain moments in history, a particular set of representations of blindness. It would appear that for Gide this discursive space was essentially a thing of the past, but a useful and familiar thing of the past. But it is quite possible to write about blindness from a vantage point from which the philosophic, sentimental, and romantic topoi are simply absent, irrelevant. This is precisely the situation of a recent short novel, *Des aveugles*, by the writer and photographer Hervé Guibert.[25]

Set in a tradition-bound institution for the blind established in the early nineteenth century, Guibert's novel seems an obvious place in which to seek contemporary echoes of earlier writing about blindness. But nothing in *Des aveugles*—neither the institution, nor the blind lovers, nor the narrator's obvious fascination with the sensory and sensual world of the blind—links it to the kinds of writing we have studied here. The origin of ideas is of no concern to Guibert's characters or to his narrator; at most the memory of fleeting childhood sight is a pretext for imagining and storytelling on the part of the blind. The reader is constantly made aware of the different kinds of perceptions and thoughts experienced by the blind, but these differences are unrelated to questions of origin, and no attempt is made to use them to demystify the supposedly natural worldview of the seeing. There is nothing innocent about these characters, of whom it might be said that they realize the worst fears of administrators such as Guillié concerning the effects of sex and marriage in a community of the blind, and yet their very perversity is not defined in opposition to any sort of innocence, nor does it appear as a moral consequence of blindness. Guibert invents an eroticism based neither on the pleasures of seeing nor on the putative charms of being protected from sight.

Des aveugles presents a perceptual universe that is fascinating because of its radical incommensurability with that of seeing, not because it can be compared to the sighted world in a series of reassuring contrasts and resemblances. A blind boy confounds the distinction between those who see and those who do not by obtaining a job as a sighted guide and reader for the blind. His activities, which at the turn of the nineteenth century could have been described either as comic fakery or as manifestations of visionary powers, are for Guibert a kind of living fiction, a continual inventive game in which he navigates through busy streets, describes buildings and pedestrians, and extemporizes letters from relatives.

Volumes could be written about blindness in twentieth-century literature or in literatures other than that of France. I mention *Des aveugles* only to remind the reader, at the close of this study, that the topic of blindness does not in itself imply the presence of anything like the kinds of writing we have been considering here. The philosophic, sentimental, and visionary representations of blindness are indeed specific and constraining discursive formations, ways of writing that may have once seemed natural and well-nigh universal, but that from the perspective of our modernity appear definable and strange.

NOTES

INTRODUCTION:
UNSEEING IN THE EYE

1. *Sophocles*, trans. F. Storr, Loeb Classical Library (London: Heinemann, 1928), 1:125.
2. Hesiod, *Melampodia*, 3; Ovid, *Metamorphoses*, III.316–338; Apollodorus, *The Library*, III.vi.6–7.
3. Apollonius of Rhodes, *Argonautica*, II.178–186; Apollodorus, *The Library*, I.ix.21 and III.xv.3.
4. Apollodorus, *The Library*, trans. J. G. Frazer, Loeb Classical Library (London: Heinemann, 1921), 1:21 (I.iii.3–4).
5. "Règlement donné aux Quinze-Vingts par Michel de Brache, aumonier du roi Jean (1351–1355)," in *Le Garçon et l'aveugle*, ed. Jean Dufournet, Traductions des Classiques français du moyen âge (Paris: Champion, 1982), pp. 121–122.
6. For the foregoing summary of early attitudes toward and presentations of blindness, I have relied on Jean Dufournet, "Après *Le Garçon et l'aveugle*" and "L'Aveugle au moyen âge," in *Le Garçon et l'aveugle*, pp. 27–84; Michael Monbeck, *The Meaning of Blindness* (Bloomington: Indiana University Press, 1973), passim; Stith Thompson, *Motif-Index of Folk Literature*, 6 vols. (Bloomington: Indiana University Press, 1955–1958), passim. Less reliable, though drawing on a wide range of sources, is Berthold Lowenfeld, *The Changing Status of the Blind: From Separation to Integration* (Springfield, Ill.: Charles C. Thomas, 1975).
7. G.W.F. Hegel, *Phenomenology of Spirit*, trans. A. V. Miller (Oxford: Clarendon Press, 1977), p. 5.
8. *The Works of George Berkeley*, ed. A. A. Luce and T. E. Jessop (London: Nelson, 1948), 1:209 (sec. 92).
9. Michel Foucault, *Birth of the Clinic*, trans. A. M. Sheridan Smith (New York: Pantheon, 1973), p. 65.
10. *The Republic of Plato*, trans. A. Bloom (New York: Basic Books, 1968), p. 187 (507c).
11. For a discussion of the *épistémè* based on language as representation, see Michel Foucault, *Les Mots et les choses* (Paris: Gallimard, 1966), esp. the chapter "Représenter."

12. "We never go outside ourselves; and it is never anything but our own thought that we perceive." Etienne Condillac, *Essai sur l'origine des connaissances humaines* (Paris: Galilée, 1973), p. 107.

13. "Perception, or the impression caused in the soul by the action of the senses, is the first operation of understanding. The idea of it is such that it cannot be acquired by any use of language." Ibid., p. 115.

14. Michel Foucault, *The Archaeology of Knowledge*, trans. A. M. Sheridan Smith (New York: Pantheon, 1972), p. 32.

15. Ibid., pp. 32–33; see also pp. 40–41.

16. Ibid., pp. 178–181.

17. Ibid., p. 126.

18. Ibid., p. 47; see also pp. 76, 135–140.

19. "Because the metaphorical is inevitable, must one say nothing?" Judith Schlanger, *Les Métaphores de l'organisme* (Paris: Vrin, 1971), pp. 261–262.

1 • "SUPPOSE A MAN BORN BLIND . . ."

1. "This problem occupies a distinguished place in modern Philosophy. The Lockes, the Leibnitzes, the most famous men of our century have made it the object of their research. It has been the seed of important discoveries, which have produced considerable changes in the knowledge of the human Mind, and above all in the Theory of Sensations." Jean-Bernard Mérian, "Sur le problème de Molyneux," *Nouveaux Mémoires de l'Académie de Berlin* (1770), p. 258.

2. John Locke, *An Essay Concerning Human Understanding*, ed. Peter H. Nidditch (Oxford: Oxford University Press, 1975), p. 127 (II.v).

3. Ibid., pp. 135, 137 (II.viii.9, 15).

4. Ibid., pp. 143, 149 (II.ix.1–3, 15).

5. Ibid., p. 145 (II.ix.8).

6. Ibid., p. 146 (II.ix.9).

7. Ibid., p. 146 (II.ix.8).

8. Mérian, "Sur le problème de Molyneux," p. 264.

9. Molyneux first proposed the problem in a 1688 letter to the authors of the *Bibliothèque universelle*, where a summary of Locke's *Essay* had appeared in French. Locke was unaware of this letter. He learned of the problem only when Molyneux wrote him directly in 1693 following the *Essay*'s publication. At this time, in fact, the two men

were regular correspondents, and Locke had asked for corrections and suggestions for the second edition of his work. Only once again did they mention the problem in their letters. Molyneux passed on to Locke a letter containing an affirmative solution to the problem that both considered erroneous. See *The Correspondence of John Locke*, ed. E. S. de Beer (Oxford: Oxford University Press, 1976–1982), 3:482–483; 4:651, 666; 5:493–496, 596.

10. Locke, *Essay*, p. 146 (II.ix.8).
11. Ibid., pp. 146–147 (II.ix.9).
12. Etienne Condillac, *Essai sur l'origine des connaissances humaines* (Paris: Galilée, 1973), p. 107: "Considérons un homme au *premier* moment de son existence. . . . *Suivons-le* dans les momens où il com-*mence* à réfléchir sur ce que les sensations occasionnent en lui" (emphasis added). See also Jacques Derrida's prefatory study to that volume, "L'Archéologie du frivole," esp. pp. 15–28.
13. *The Works of George Berkeley*, ed. A. A. Luce and T. E. Jessop (London: Nelson, 1948), 1:209 (sec. 92).
14. Ibid., p. 210 (sec. 95).
15. Ibid., p. 226 (sec. 136).
16. Ibid., p. 239.
17. *The Tatler*, no. 55 (London: J. and R. Tonson, 1759), 2:37–38.
18. Ibid., p. 38.
19. Ibid., p. 39.
20. Ibid.
21. Ibid., p. 42.
22. Berkeley, *Works*, 2:276 (sec. 71).
23. William Cheselden, "An Account of some Observations made by a young Gentleman, who was born blind, or lost his Sight so early, that he had no Remembrance of ever having seen, and was couch'd between 13 and 14 Years of Age," *Philosophical Transactions* 35, no. 402 (London: Royal Society, 1729), p. 448.
24. Ibid., p. 449.
25. Ibid., p. 450.
26. Ibid.
27. "He could not at first distinguish what he had judged round, with the help of his hands, from what he had judged cornered." Voltaire, *Oeuvres complètes* (Paris: Garnier, 1879), 22:470.
28. . . . "a thumb-sized object, placed in front of his eye, which hid a house from him, seemed to him as large as the house." Cheselden, "Account," p. 449; Voltaire, *Oeuvres*, p. 469.
29. "But where to find the blind person on whom depended the indu-

bitable resolution of this question? Finally in 1729, Mr. Cheselden.
. . ." Voltaire, *Oeuvres*, p. 469.

30. "The blind person had a hard time agreeing to it. He didn't have
much of an idea that the sense of sight could greatly increase his
pleasures. If the desire to read and write hadn't been instilled in him,
he would not have wanted to see. By this indifference he confirmed
that one cannot be made unhappy by being deprived of goods of
which one has no idea: a truth of no small importance." Ibid.

31. . . . "one of these famous surgeons who joins skill of hand with the
greatest lights of the mind." Ibid.

32. Jean-Jacques Rousseau, *Oeuvres complètes* (Paris: Pléïade, 1959–
1969), 4:1092–1093; Montesquieu, *Oeuvres complètes* (Paris: Seuil,
1964), p. 1071; Sade, "Pensée inédite," *Le Surréalisme au service de
la révolution*, no. 4 (December 1931), p. 1; Buffon, *Oeuvres complètes*, 2d ed. (Paris: Rapet, 1819), 10:268–273.

33. ". . . these judgments would have been of no use to him in distinguishing by sight the globe from a cube: he only needed to be given
the time to open his eyes, and to look at the composite tableau of the
universe." La Mettrie, *Oeuvres philosophiques* (Amsterdam, 1774),
1:208.

34. "Now a globe attentively considered by touch, clearly imagined
and conceived, need but show itself to open eyes; it will conform to
the image or idea engraved in the brain." Ibid., p. 207.

35. Ibid., pp. 206–207.

36. "I venture to assert one of two things: either the disturbed dioptric
organ was not given time to get back in form, or by means of tor-
menting the new seer, he was made to say what people were content
to hear him say." Ibid., pp. 207–208.

37. . . . "by whatever sense extension comes to our understanding, it
cannot be represented in two different ways. . . . This person born
blind will therefore distinguish by sight the globe from the cube,
since he will recognize in them the same ideas he had gotten of them
by touch." Condillac, *Essai*, p. 187 (I.vi.14).

38. . . . "don't light and colors necessarily outline different distances,
different sizes, different situations?" Ibid., p. 186 (I.vi.12).

39. . . . "the order, beauty, and grandeur of the universe." Ibid., p. 187
(I.vi.13).

40. "It is thus because odors and sounds are transmitted without being
mixed with colors, that [the statue] separates so well what belongs
to hearing and to smell. But as the sense of sight and that of touch
act at the same time . . . we have difficulty distinguishing what be-

longs to each of these senses." Etienne Condillac, *Oeuvres philoso-phiques*, ed. Georges Le Roy (Paris: Presses Universitaires de France, 1947), 1:288.

41. On the relation between Condillac's distinction of *voir* from *regar-der* and modern theories of perception, see Michael Morgan, *Moly-neux's Question: Vision, Touch, and the Philosophy of Perception* (Cambridge: Cambridge University Press, 1977), pp. 68–79. Morgan's survey of the question omits La Mettrie, Leibnitz, and Mérian, but is informed by current research in perceptual psychology.

42. Leibnitz, *Nouveaux essais* (Paris: Garnier-Flammarion, 1966), p. 106 (II.v).

43. "And these two geometries, that of the blind person and that of the cripple, have to meet and agree, and even come down to the same ideas, although they have no images in common." Ibid., p. 114 (II.ix).

44. "I would like to outline a tableau that would represent these subtle and abstract matters in all their forms, and with all the clarity that can be given to them." Mérian, "Sur le problème de Molyneux," p. 259.

45. "This connection is purely symbolic. It is the same as between words and things, or between written words and articulated sounds. Visible and tangible objects resemble one another no more than sounds resemble thoughts, or written words resemble sounds. But once the connection is established, the presence of the former awakens at once the presence of the latter." Mérian, *Nouveaux Mémoires* (1774), p. 445.

46. "It is thus far more important to us to be warned by Sight of the effect that tangible objects will have on us, than to be warned by Touch of the effect that visible objects will have on us." Ibid., p. 447.

47. "Articulated sounds interest us very little by themselves; they interest us only insofar as they portray for us perceptions and ideas; and when the latter are present in our soul, we can do without the former. It is thus natural that the former serve as signs with respect to the latter. As for written characters, it is even more natural that with respect to sounds they should be signifiers rather than signi-fieds; since in its origin the language of speech preceded that of writ-ing." Ibid.

48. "This plan would be to take children from the cradle, and to raise them in profound darkness until the age of reason." Ibid. (1780), p. 407.

49. "In a word, as their minds would be, so to speak, in our hands, and as we could shape them like soft wax, and develop understanding in

them in whatever order we pleased, we would be in a position to take all precautions, and to vary the experiments in all imaginable ways." Ibid.

50. "I answer that my project is addressed to philosophers inflamed by the love of Knowledge, who know that we move toward greatness only by trampling popular prejudices underfoot." Ibid., p. 409.

51. *The Forbidden Experiment: The Story of the Wild Boy of Aveyron* (New York: Washington Square Press, 1981), pp. 52–57, 208.

52. "With what a torrent of delights will they be flooded, what will be their movements of joy, when they shall be brought from night to day, from shadows to light, when a new universe, an absolutely brilliant world, will come forth for them as from the womb of Chaos? Is there anything comparable to such a moment?" Mérian, *Nouveaux mémoires* (1780), p. 411.

2 · DIDEROT: PHILOSOPHY AND THE WORLD OF THE BLIND

1. "He speaks so well and so justly about so many things that are absolutely unknown to him, that exchanges with him greatly weaken that induction that we all make without knowing why, from what goes on in us, to what goes on inside others." Diderot, *Lettre sur les aveugles*, ed. Robert Niklaus (Geneva: Droz, 1951; 3d ed. 1970), p. 4. Hereafter, numbers in parentheses refer to pages in this edition.

2. Michel Foucault, *The Order of Things* (New York: Vintage, 1973), p. 65.

3. "The observations of such a famous man have less need of spectators when they are made, than of listeners once they have been made."

4. . . . "an experiment in which I hardly saw anything to be gained for my instruction or for yours."

5. Georges May suggests only that although the *Lettre* abandons the simple allegorical mode of the *Promenade*, "le personnage de l'aveugle-né est bien encore le moyen d'un transfert métaphorique." Georges May, "Diderot et l'allégorie," *Studies on Voltaire and the Eighteenth Century* 89 (1972): 1052.

6. See Roland Mortier, *Clartés et ombres du siècle des lumières* (Geneva: Droz, 1969); and Aram Vartanian, "*Fiat Lux* and the Philosophes," *Diderot Studies* 16 (Geneva: Droz, 1973): 375–387.

7. "Those of the new creation claim to be exclusively favored over those of the old, whom they look down on as blind people." Diderot, *Oeuvres complètes*, ed. Roger Lewinter (Paris: Club français du livre,

1969–1972), 1:327. Subsequent parenthetical references to volumes and pages of this edition are signaled by "*OC.*"

8. "How delighted I would be to pull you from the labyrinth in which you are going astray! Come here, so that I may take that blindfold off you."

9. . . . "find themselves suddenly in the situation of a person born blind whose eyelids are opened. All the objects of nature appear before him in a form very different from the ideas that he would have received."

10. May, "Diderot et l'allégorie," pp. 1052–1053.

11. "People are trying to restore the sight of persons born blind; but if we looked closer, we would find, I believe, that Philosophy can profit every bit as much from questioning a sensible blind person."

12. "One would learn how things go on in him; one would compare it with how they go on in us."

13. "If he attaches no idea to the terms he uses, he at least has this advantage over most men: that he never pronounces them inappropriately."

14. . . . "a machine . . . which puts things in relief, far from themselves."

15. "There are no questions for which his comparison would not have sufficed."

16. "It's quite surprising how easily we learn to talk."

17. . . . "a succession of subtle and profound combinations of the analogies that we notice between nonsensory objects, and the ideas that they excite."

18. "Madame, one must be without a sense to know the advantages of the symbols destined for those one still has."

19. . . . "whence there results a double illumination for the person spoken to: the true and direct light of the expression, and the reflected light of the metaphor." For the notion of "expressions heureuses" Diderot refers to Saunderson's biography in his *Elements of Algebra* ("Ceux qui ont écrit sa vie disent qu'il étoit fécond en expressions heureuses"). While calling attention to Saunderson's use of language, the English text uses no equivalent term: "His Discourse was so enlivened with frequent Allusions to the Objects of Sight, that there appeared no Defect of the blind Man. . . . The force and Spirit of his Expression surprised and fixed the Attention of all that heard him." Saunderson, *The Elements of Algebra* (Cambridge: Cambridge University Press, 1740), 1:xviii.

20. . . . "forced to say everything with a very small number of terms, which obliges them to use some of them very felicitously."

21. "What is the function of the geometer? To combine spaces, setting aside the essential qualities of matter; no colors; great mental concentration, no emotion in the soul. What is the function of the poet, the moralist, the eloquent man? To portray and to move."

22. "If a pedant makes off with an argument of Cicero or Demosthenes, and reduces it to a syllogism with its major and minor premises and its conclusion, shall he have the right to claim that he has just eliminated words, without having altered the content?"

23. . . . "Beauty for a blind person is but a word, when it is separated from usefulness."

24. . . . "less extended, but sharper than those of seeing Philosophers."

25. See esp. the articles "Beau," "Beauté," and "Génie" in the *Encyclopédie*, and the *Mémoires sur différents sujets mathématiques*.

26. "It seems to me that a blind person has ideas of relation, of order, of symmetry, and that these notions have entered his understanding by touch, as they enter ours by sight; they are less perfect perhaps, and less precise; but that proves at most that the blind are less affected by the *beautiful* than are we seers."

27. "Nurses help them acquire the notion of the permanence of absent beings, by having them play a little game of covering and then suddenly revealing the face. In this way they experience, a hundred times in a quarter-hour, the fact that what ceases to appear does not cease to exist: whence it follows that we owe to experience the notion of the continuous existence of objects."

28. "It must then be agreed . . . that consequently one sees nothing the first time one uses one's eyes . . . that experience alone teaches us to compare sensations with what provokes them; that sensations having nothing that essentially resembles objects, it is experience that must instruct us concerning analogies that seem to be purely man-made."

29. "To deny it . . . would be to hide from one's self the fact that there is no Painter skillful enough to approach the beauty and exactitude of the miniatures that are painted at the back of our eyes, that there is nothing more precise than the resemblance of the representation to the object represented."

30. See *Eléments de physiologie* (*OC* 13:790): "Les aveugles ont de l'imagination, parce que le vice n'est que dans la rétine."

31. "I have never doubted that the state of our organs and of our senses has a large influence on our metaphysics and our ethics, and that our most purely intellectual ideas, if I may say so, stick very closely to the form of our bodies."

32. "He asked us, for example, if only those called Naturalists could see

with the microscope, and if Astronomers were the only ones who could see with the telescope; if the machine that magnifies objects was larger than the one that makes them smaller; if the one that brings them closer was shorter than the one that makes them farther away."

33. "Each one had brought signs of his vocation with him at birth; thus, in general people there were what they ought to be. . . . Those that nature had destined to geometry had fingers stretched into compasses; my host was one of these. An individual fit for astronomy had helical eyes; for geography, a globe head; for music or acoustics, trumpet ears; for surveying, staff legs. . . ."

34. . . . "someone who sees no more than a mole spends his life making observations."

35. "Diderot's Optics," in *Studies on Eighteenth-Century French Literature Presented to Robert Niklaus* (Exeter: n.p., 1975), p. 20.

36. . . . "would tell them every day of some new mystery which would be a mystery only for them."

37. "It is claimed [that] . . . far from taking away sight, one sees, through it, an infinity of marvelous things, which cannot be seen with the eyes alone. . . . multifaceted lens . . . covered lantern."

38. . . . "the presence of an object in several places at the same time . . . to see him ceaselessly and to be always as amazed as if one were seeing him for the first time."

39. The blind man's discourse on optics has the same antithetical associations as the optical instrument. In the case of Saunderson, it provides "la lumière réfléchie de la métaphore," but in the *Promenade* it is an object of ridicule, the title of a religious work: "*Théorie physique et morale de l'existence et des propriétés de la lumière, par un aveugle espagnol, traduite et ornée de commentaires et de scolies par le marguillier des Quinze-Vingts*" (*OC* 1:367–368). The blind man's "view" opposes that of ordinary sight, but it may be the opinion of the dogmatic ignoramus as well as of the philosopher.

40. "This great argument drawn from the marvels of nature is indeed weak for the blind."

41. Jacques Chouillet, *La Formation des idées esthétiques de Diderot* (Paris: Armand Colin, 1973), pp. 133–134.

42. "I repeat to you: all that is not as beautiful for me as for you."

43. "He would tell them every day of some new mystery which would be a mystery only for them, and that freethinkers would be happy not to believe."

44. "Couldn't the defenders of religion use to great advantage such a

stubborn incredulity, so just indeed in some respects, and yet so unfounded?"

45. "Therefore God no more exists for man than do colors for a person born blind; man is as much in his right to affirm that there is no God, as the blind person is to assert that there are no colors." "Pensée inédite de D.A.F. de Sade," *Le Surréalisme au service de la révolution*, no. 4 (December 1931): 1.

46. "If you accept this supposition, it will remind you in borrowed guise of the story and persecutions of those who have had the misfortune of encountering truth in ages of darkness, and the imprudence to unveil it to their blind contemporaries."

47. "Take a good look at me, Mr. Holmes, I have no eyes. What had we done to God, you and I, one of us to have this organ, the other to be deprived of it?"

48. See Jacques Roger, *Les Sciences de la vie dans la pensée française du XVIIIe siècle* (Paris: Armand Colin, 1963), p. 592: "Devant le monstre, toutes les arguties sont inutiles. Si Dieu n'est pas bon, il n'existe pas. La révolte du sentiment entraîne la conviction morale." See also Emita B. Hill, "The Role of 'le monstre' in Diderot's Thought," *Studies on Voltaire and the Eighteenth Century* 97 (1972): 156.

49. See Robert Mauzi, *L'Idée du bonheur dans la littérature et la pensée françaises au XVIIIe siècle* (Paris: Armand Colin, 1960), p. 26: "Ils ouvrent un univers sans limite où tout devient possible. Le monstre humain n'est en somme qu'un homme libéré, qui n'est plus tenu d'obéir à la 'nature,' ce mythe dangereusement équivoque qu'on invente pour justifier une révolte et qui bientôt devient plus tyrannique que cela même contre quoi il fut conçu."

50. . . . "it is perhaps because you're in the habit of treating everything that appears to you beyond your capacity as a marvel."

51. See the eighteenth of the *Pensées philosophiques*: "Ce n'est que dans les ouvrages de Newton, de Musschenbroek, d'Hartzoeker et de Nieuwentyt qu'on a trouvé des preuves satisfaisantes d'un Etre souverainement intelligent. Grâce aux travaux de ces grands hommes, le monde n'est plus un Dieu: c'est une machine qui a ses roues, ses cordes, ses poulies, ses ressorts et ses poids" (*OC* 1:280).

52. "Is a phenomenon, in our opinion, beyond man? Right away we say it's the work of a God, our vanity is content with nothing less: couldn't we speak with a little less pride and a little more philosophy?" La Mettrie, referring also to human pride and the investigation of nature, had chosen an image of blindness in *L'Homme machine* (1747): "Nous sommes de vraies taupes dans la nature: nous

n'y faisons guère que le trajet de cet animal, & c'est notre orgueil qui donne des bornes à ce qui n'en a point." La Mettrie, *Oeuvres philosophiques* (Amsterdam, 1774), 3:86.

53. . . . "that the testimony of Newton was not as strong for him, as that of all nature for Newton."

54. See Diderot, *Lettre sur les aveugles* (ed. Niklaus), p. 100, n. 38.

55. M. L. Perkins, "The Crisis of Sensationalism in Diderot's *Lettre sur les aveugles*," *Studies in Voltaire and the Eighteenth Century* 174 (1978): 167–188.

56. "The voice of nature is sufficiently heard by [Saunderson], via the organs that he has, and for that his testimony will be all the stronger against those who stubbornly close their ears and their eyes."

57. "As they see matter in a far more abstract way than we, they are less far from believing that it thinks."

58. "But if it is all the harder for a blind man seeing for the first time to judge correctly objects that have a larger number of forms, what would prevent him from taking an observer, all dressed up and immobile before him in an armchair, for a piece of furniture or a machine; and a tree, whose leaves and branches were stirred by the wind, for a moving, animated, thinking being? Madame, how many things do our senses suggest to us, and how hard it would be, without our eyes, to suppose that a block of marble neither thinks nor feels."

59. "Here you have no witnesses to set against me, and your eyes are no help to you."

60. François Jacob, *The Logic of Life*, trans. B. E. Spillmann (New York: Pantheon, 1973), p. 61; see also pp. 28, 57.

61. Ibid., pp. 146–158.

62. . . . "former and first state concerning which you are no less blind than I."

63. "from which he emerged only to cry out: 'O God of Clarke and Newton, Have pity on me!' and die."

64. "*Bordeu*: For example, if the origin of the network draws all its forces to itself, if the whole system moves, so to speak, backward, as I believe happens in the man who meditates profoundly, in the fanatic who sees the heavens opened, in ecstasy, in voluntary or involuntary madness.
Mlle de l'Espinasse: Well?
Bordeu: Well, the animal becomes impassive, it exists only in a point."

65. See Perkins, "Crisis," p. 174: "Saunderson . . . is not Diderot's

porte-parole; he is more accurately to be taken as his puppet, who gives the speeches needed to make a point."

66. ". . . several others who appeared to be so far above the rest of men, with one less sense, that the Poets could have pretended without exaggeration that jealous Gods deprived them of it, out of fear of having equals among mortals. For was this Tiresias, who had read in the secrets of the gods and possessed the gift of predicting the future, anything other than a blind Philosopher whose memory has been preserved by Fable?"

67. . . . "the discoveries of a Philosopher who would have meditated well on his subject in darkness; or, to speak to you in the language of Poets, who would have put out his eyes to know more easily how vision occurs."

68. "I give up without pain a life that has been for me but a long desire and a continual privation." In calling his life a *privation*, the blind man can be said to be using poetic language, if Diderot's reference in the *Lettre* to Condillac's theory of metaphor is applied to his statement. Diderot writes that a person who has always suffered will not necessarily equate the concepts of living and suffering (as Condillac had said such a person would) and that at least he may have the two words, "*j'existe* et *je souffre*, l'un pour la prose et l'autre pour la poésie" (61–62).

69. "It is night at high noon in the streets for someone who is thinking deeply, deep night."

70. "We have distinguished two kinds of philosophies, the experimental and the rational. The former has blindfolded eyes, always feels its way along, and in the end encounters precious things. The latter gathers these precious things, and tries to make a torch of them, but this so-called torch has until now done less good than the groping of its rival, and that is as it should be."

71. "It's usually at night that the vapors that obscure in me the existence of God arise; the rising of the sun always dissipates them, but the shadows last for a blind person, and the sun rises only for those who see."

3 • CURING BLINDNESS:
A MODERN MYTH

1. After appearing in the *Encyclopédie*, the French translation of the *Tatler* article turned up in the *Gazette littéraire de l'Europe*

(March 21, 1764), in *Variétés littéraires*, 1776, pp. 511–517, in *Pot-Pourri* 4, no. 20 (1782): 91–96, and in the *Encyclopédie méthodique*, published by Panckoucke in 1791.

2. "Mind, graces, nobleness, sensitive and pure soul, / Sélim had everything, except that happy organ, / That sees, traverses, embraces both the Earth and the Heavens, / And without which man, alas! is dead to Nature." Claude-Joseph Dorat, *Recueil de contes et de poëmes* (Paris, 1775), pp. 119–120.

3. "I, whom you have not seen, and who knows but to love, / What then is my secret by which I could charm you?" Ibid., p. 127.

4. "You ceased, and I thought that I would cease to be. / How many tears and sighs came forth from me! / I sought that voice that had made me be reborn; / I had, in losing it, lost all my pleasures. / I thought I recovered it, I thought I heard it again. / My heart, given over to my illusion, / Cherished an error which increased its love, / And it seemed surprised at its emotions." Ibid., p. 128.

5. "By day and night hovered around me the image / Of the voice, which my heart in its ecstasy / Enveloped in a body. Even in dreams / The lovely singer visited me, / Took my hand, drew me gently toward her / And sang the song; I sat at her feet / And hearkened, silently entranced, until dream and image / Disappeared." Christoph Martin Wieland, *Werke* (Berlin: Gustav Hempel, n.d. [1879]), 39:274.

6. "Well, she said, Well, my Friend, take courage, / Hope slips again into my loving heart; / You are perhaps not far, at least I foretell it, / From obtaining, from tasting this sweet present from the Heavens." Dorat, *Recueil de contes et de poëmes*, p. 131.

7. Sigmund Freud, *Standard Edition* (London: Hogarth, 1953–1974), 11:181–208. See also Jean Laplanche, *Problématiques II. Castration. Symbolisations* (Paris: Presses Universitaires de France, 1980), pp. 91–101.

8. "My gazes have seen your youth grow and bloom, / And guiding your steps, though absent from your eyes, / I have, from the cradle, given you my affection, / While you were playing at your mother's breast, / Yes, it is I, Sélima, I whom you were caressing." Dorat, *Recueil de contes et de poëmes*, p. 132.

9. "I feel bedazzled . . . Ah! turn away their flames / Stop . . . what are you doing? . . . I've lost the light . . . / Hide them from me no longer . . . Do you want my death? / Better that the sun, which lights my way, should go out! / My soul is in the night, when I don't see

them." Ibid., p. 160 (pagination of this edition skips from page 134 to 155).

10. "O my friend, what delightful pleasures, what divine ravishments, what pure enjoyment! Nothing can exist beyond the happiness I am tasting. Yes, yes, my universe is in your soul; close to you, I possess it fully. Eh! do you think that I envy the rest of humankind the light that you can't get over seeing me deprived of? There is, there is, for the heart where you reign, a sweeter illumination, stronger and more durable." Beauharnais, *L'Aveugle par amour* (Amsterdam, 1781), p. 51.

11. "O wonder! O ravishment unexpected, and still more inexpressible! . . . Eugénie calls his name, she sees him, their cries answer one another; they throw themselves in each other's arms; their kisses, their tears, their intoxicated hearts unite. . . . Never, never, Love, did you have so much Ardor. . . ." Ibid., p. 253.

12. "The eyes of Eléonore are still beautiful, and now see only what ought to be seen; those of Sophie are still closed, but her heart supplements them: it feels all, foresees all, and she is truly our guardian angel, the bond of our happy society." Montolieu, *Douze nouvelles* (Paris: Paschoud, 1812), 1:130.

13. "The expression of her physiognomy and all her movements had something singular and interesting." Montolieu, *La Jeune Aveugle* (Paris: Bertrand, 1819), p. 280.

14. J.-F. Lepitre, *L'Aveugle supposé* (Paris: Masson, 1803).

15. "Yes, in these circumstances, / Do not doubt / That your acquaintances / Will arrive here; / Women, women especially, / Who for some time now, so as to shine in everything, / Have managed to develop a taste for experiments." *Cassandre oculiste* (Paris: Vente, 1780), p. 7.

16. "You think that concerning her, / Glory sets me on fire. / But know that my plan / Is to deserve the hand of this object." Ibid., p. 28.

17. "You will see me, I swear to you, / As well as I see you. / Permit my enraptured soul this quotation: / You will be the Galathea / Of a new Pygmalion." Ibid., p. 23.

18. Michael Monbeck, *The Meaning of Blindness* (Bloomington: Indiana University Press, 1973), p. 140. See also Luce Irigaray, *Speculum. De l'autre femme* (Paris: Minuit, 1974), pp. 184–185, 409–415.

19. Monbeck, *Meaning of Blindness*, pp. 137–138.

20. "And I've become an oculist, I've promised to cure him . . . and he, as a reward, has promised me his daughter's hand." Chazat, Du Mersan, and Moreau, *Cassandre aveugle* (Paris: Huet, 1803), p. 12.

21. Courcy and Carmouche, *Les Deux Aveugles* (Paris: Huet, 1823).
22. "But, different indeed from those generous scientists who would believe that hiding a useful discovery would betray the cause of humanity, my master was speculating on his talents. . . . He saw but fortunes, treasures; and, stingy with the knowledge that procured them for him, he'd have thought that to share it with me would be to impoverish himself . . . ! Well then, that knowledge . . . I stole it from him!" Scribe and Mélesville, *Valérie* (Paris: Ladvocat, 1822), pp. 69–70.
23. "But I was proud enough to believe in myself! . . . And shall I tell you, Madame, I would have been jealous had the one I love received from a hand other than mine such a favor. . . . It seemed to me that this prize was owed me!" Ibid., pp. 70–71.
24. "*Ernest*: Having reached this moment that I had so desired, I no longer know myself . . . ! all my resolution gives way . . . ! I tremble. . . ." Ibid., p. 75.
25. "*Ernest*: For a moment . . . I thought I had succeeded.
   Henri: Well then . . . ?
   Ernest: At the scream she let loose . . . I fled in terror."
   Ibid., p. 78.
26. "If my courage doesn't leave me, if my hand doesn't tremble . . . I should succeed." Carrion-Nisas and Sauvage, *Valérien ou le jeune aveugle* (Paris: Pollet, 1823), p. 30.
27. . . . "it will only be out of gratitude, and I'm not responsible for what follows." Desaugiers and Adolphe, *M. Oculi* (Paris: Huet, 1823), p. 39.
28. "Zounds! think to what extent / A belle who doesn't see / can make mistakes, even if she's not naughty." *Cassandre oculiste*, p. 28.
29. "Marry a blind man! Ah! the very idea makes me shudder with horror." Legrand, *L'Aveugle clairvoyant* (Paris: Fages, 1802), p. 4.
30. "Refuse a husband because he doesn't see a thing! / Alas, your late husband saw all too clearly, / Always going crazy over the slightest suspicions." Ibid.
31. "The oculist possesses a very rare talent, / Which is ardently desired everywhere. / His hand performs a striking miracle on Sight, / Causing its recovery when it is believed lost. / . . . / Beautiful operation! inestimable cure, / That makes the eye suddenly clear, chases dark night away! / O admirable talent, O precious talent, / That gives to humankind the light of the heavens!" Gleize, *Nouvelles observations pratiques sur les maladies de l'oeil et leur traitement*, 2d ed. (Orléans: Guyot aîné, 1812), p. xvi.

227

32. Armand-Croisette and Chateauvieux, *Les Aveugles de Franconville* (Paris: Barba, 1802).

33. Montolieu, *La Jeune Aveugle*, p. 281.

34. *Flanelle*: Young man, I hope that you'll never forget that you owe your sight to me, I operated on you.
    Nicolas: Yes, a fine oculist you are!
    Brazier, Mélesville, and Carmouche, *Les Trois Aveugles* (Paris: Quoy, 1824), p. 35.

35. . . . "charlatans lacking required knowledge." Guérin, *Essai sur les maladies des yeux* (Lyon: Berthoud, 1769), p. x.

36. See Steven Kaplan, Introduction to *"La Bagarre": Galiani's "Lost" Parody*, International Archives of the History of Ideas 92 (The Hague: Martinus Nijhoff, 1979), pp. 3–29.

37. "I shall say nothing about the splendor of the Sovereign and of the principal dignitaries of the State. . . . I shall speak only of those pleasures that are within reach of all orders of citizens. There is one of these that each individual can enjoy at will and without spending a thing: that of going out walking. I only wish you could see at an appropriate hour these boulevards, these gardens devoted to public amusement: you could no longer decide to deprive yourself of the sight. The tumult, the din, the dust. . . ." [Cerfvol], *L'Aveugle qui refuse de voir* (Londres [Paris]: Jean Nourse, n.d. [1771]), pp. 22–23.

38. "You strike me as too well informed not to know about the diverse systems of Physiocracy that hardworking writers have given us, and in accordance with which, morals and the good order will soon be reestablished." Ibid., p. 52.

39. "Concentrated in us, almost all our study is limited to the development of ourselves: your attention, to the contrary, divided by all that surrounds you, exhausts itself elsewhere; and, perhaps, the lovely faculty of sight serves only to corrupt you by the abuse you make of it." Ibid., p. 42.

40. "As a blind man, I judge things only by the relations they have to me. I call them beautiful or ugly, good or bad, according to the way they affect me. The privilege of sight would necessarily generalize my judgments, by multiplying my perceptions and my sensations, and it would force me to take a position on a multitude of phenomena that wouldn't touch me at all." Ibid., p. 57.

41. Each object that will strike my sight will become for me an inexhaustible source of chagrins; I'll want to possess them, at least know them: the impossibility of satisfaction will irritate my self-esteem,

humiliating it, and will procure for me, continuously, the regret of having seen. Ibid., pp. 49–50.

42. "Far then from believing happiness to be attached to your condition, I presume on the contrary that, for you who see, life is but a web of pleasures that aren't really yours and of very real regrets, of desires ceaselessly renewed and never satisfied." Ibid., p. 77.

43. G. Grente, A. Pauphilet, L. Pichard, and R. Barroux, *Dictionnaire des lettres françaises. Le Dix-huitième siècle* (Paris: Fayard, 1960), 1:284.

44. "Blind, I am but a useless burden to Society; do you want to make me its scourge?" Cerfvol, *L'Aveugle qui refuse de voir*, pp. 74–75.

4 · A Modern Project: Educating the Blind

1. "The intellectual world does not exist for this child of nature; most of our ideas are without reality for him: he acts as if he were alone; he relates everything to himself. It is from this deplorable state that one must try to draw him, by teaching him that there are relations and bonds of communication between him and other men." Sébastien Guillié, *Essai sur l'instruction des aveugles* (Paris: Imprimé par les aveugles, 1817), p. 13. Further references to this volume signaled by "*G*" in parentheses in the text.

2. Robert Scott, *The Making of Blind Men: A Story of Adult Socialization* (New York: Russell Sage, 1969).

3. "To contribute to their subsistence is doubtless considerable; but wouldn't it do still more for them to found their subsistence on their own labor?"

4. "You see, Sirs, that there are occupations for Blind People of all stations: and that these occupations, by making their fate better and more fortunate, would provide society with new wealth by putting into action ordinarily useless arms, and heads—among which there could be some well-organized ones." *Journal de Paris*, no. 51 (1784): 234

5. Guillié was to castigate the philanthropists for failing to emphasize work and self-sufficiency: "On se coalisa, pour ainsi dire, contre la mendicité qu'on cherchait à dissiper par des moyens plus propres à la perpétuer qu'à la détruire." *Notice historique sur l'institution des jeunes aveugles* (Paris: Les Jeunes Aveugles, 1819), p. 8.

6. "We will not fail to profit as much as we can from the useful views that this same letter presents." *Journal de Paris*, no. 111 (1784): 488.

7. "It is to the letter that M. de la Blancherie wrote you last April 24, Sirs, to that of M. Diderot, printed in 1749, that I owe the idea of an educational plan for the blind." *Journal de Paris*, no. 274 (1784): 1158.

8. "Eight to ten poor blind men, glasses on their noses, placed along a stand where the music was placed, were performing a discordant symphony, which seemed to provoke joy in those present. An altogether different sentiment overcame our soul; and we conceived at once the possibility of giving these Unfortunates real possession of capabilities that they only seemed, ridiculously, to have. Does not the blind man, said we ourselves to ourselves, know objects by the diversity of their shapes?" Valentin Haüy, *Essai sur l'instruction des aveugles* (Paris: Les Enfans-Aveugles, 1786), p. 119.

9. . . . "this was so that the sight, reproduced before my eyes, bearing into my heart a profound affliction, should fire my genius. Yes, I said then to me myself, seized by a noble enthusiasm, I shall put truth in the place of this ridiculous fable." Valentin Haüy, "Troisième note," *Trois notes du citoyen Haüy* (Paris: Les Aveugles-Travailleurs, 1801), p. 10.

10. "There was a throng of subscriptions for the new school, and by the magic effects of fashion, the blind became the objects of every conversation." Alexandre Rodenbach, *Lettre sur les aveugles faisant suite à celle de Diderot* (Brussels, 1828), p. 4.

11. Gleize, *Règlement de vie* (Orléans: Jacob l'Aîné, 1787), p. 96.

12. "In outlining the plan for the Education of the blind, we at first regarded music as but an accessory, suitable for relaxing them after their work. But the natural dispositions of most blind people for this Art, the resources that it can furnish many of them for their subsistence, the interest that it seemed to inspire in those who deigned to attend our exercises, all these forced us to sacrifice our own opinion to the general advantage." Haüy, *Essai*, pp. 83–84.

13. Galliod, *Notice historique sur l'établissement des jeunes aveugles* (Paris: Aux Quinze-Vingts, 1829).

14. *Journal de Paris*, no. 363 (1784): 1539.

15. Haüy, *Essai*, pp. 37–38.

16. "Under the reign of despotism, Charity had taken them in. What should they not expect under the joys of Equality!" "Adresse du citoyen Haüy . . . Aux 48 sections de Paris," December 13, 1792.

17. Concerning the difficulties of the Institution during these years, see

Dora B. Weiner, "The Blind Man and the French Revolution," *Bulletin of the History of Medicine* 48 (1974): 60–89, and "Les Handicapés et la Révolution Française: Aspects de Médecine sociale," *Clio Medica* 12, No. 2/3 (1977): 97–109.

18. Léon Cellier, *Fabre d'Olivet* (Paris: Nizet, 1953), p. 54.

19. "Since my son must give up light, / At least open to him the path of wisdom; / And may the radiance of Virtue at the bottom of his heart / Compensate him, alas! for the daylight he has lost." Fabre d'Olivet, *Le Sage de l'Indostan* (Paris: Les Aveugles-Travailleurs, 1796), p. 13.

20. Ibid., p. 25.

21. "But the only happiness to which I aspire, / By learning in this place, / Alas! is to be able to write to you / How much I love you." Ibid., p. 28.

22. "The intermingling of the sexes is now meticulously forbidden; marriages among the blind are no longer encouraged, as they once were, and couples, a continual source of discords and misunderstandings, are no longer tolerated in the institution. A paternal and just government has thus replaced the capricious and weak regime that, for such a long time, prevented good from being carried out." Guillié, *Notice historique*, pp. 25–26.

23. "Ah! SIRE, quel serait le bonheur des Aveugles si, le ciel ouvrant un instant leurs paupières, ils pouvaient contempler les traits de leur Bienfaiteur!" Guillié, *Essai*, pp. 7–8.

24. . . . "unfortunate bearers of the spirit of insurbordination and licentiousness that they had drawn from their first stay, and whose tradition would have been preserved by them."

25. "Like us, they desire what is hardest to obtain. All blind people have a pronounced taste for independence and freedom. Yet nothing is more contrary to their true interests than the use of a thing that they could only abuse. So, we indeed realize, the art of those around them consists less in satisfying them than in letting them believe that they are satisfied."

26. Rodenbach, *Lettre*, 16–17.

27. "Here the American author indulges in a series of recriminations against the Paris Institution des Jeunes Aveugles, which we shall not reproduce, because they struck us as equally unseemly and ill-founded." Howe, "De l'éducation des aveugles et des perfections dont elle est susceptible," *Revue brittanique*, 3d ser. (November 1833): 86–87.

28. Howe, "Education of the Blind," *North American Review* 37, no. 80 (1833): 45.

29. "[The blind] to be sure find sympathetic humanity in some, but more often cruel refusals in others, because man naturally flees that which shows him human infirmities, or reminds him of them: it is, for him and for his soul, a mixture of compassion and loathing that makes him dread the possibility of the same fate." Desmonceaux, *Traité des maladies des yeux et des oreilles* (Paris: Méquignon, 1806), 2:257.

30. "As we customarily use only the quick but none too faithful means of sight to discern the objects that surround us, it is believed that the blind must not know anything of what exists. . . ."

31. "Shouldn't they, like us, adore him in spirit and in truth? . . . Sensitivity does not have, for them, the charms that make us place it among the sweetest and most agreeable of virtues."

32. "We have all more or less felt it; when all is darkness around us, when night is deep, there are more vivid, more colored ideas in our minds. . . . Often we are afraid of our thoughts, for they go too fast and too far! Solitude frightens us, we call for daylight. Wearily we push away this profound darkness that isolates us from everything, for we are weak, we want to see! . . . What we thus feel sometimes, the blind person always feels; thus fear accompanies him everywhere." Eugénie Niboyet, *Des aveugles et de leur éducation* (Paris: Krabbe, 1837), p. 60.

33. . . . "the benefits of education, by making him judge all things better, come to distract him from himself." Ibid., p. 61.

34. Rodenbach, *Lettre*, p. 20.

35. "The faculty of Sight is correctly regarded as superior to all the other senses. . . . It is perhaps for this reason that we use the word *see* in a figurative sense, bestowing the character of evidence on all accepted truths." Auguste Schwenger, *Mémoires sur les aveugles, sur la vue et la vision* (Paris: Köenig, 1800), pp. 24–25.

36. "Already beneath their touch, which has become as it were a kind of vision, thoughts were taking shape." Haüy, *Essai*, pp. 17–18.

37. . . . "their skillfully exercised fingers will teach them all that the seeing learn through the eyes." Gleize, *Règlement de vie*, p. 93.

38. . . . "our aim being to place the blind ever in contact with the seeing, we believed that we should choose the method of the latter. Haüy, *Essai*, pp. 72–73.

39. Charles Barbier, *De l'instruction des aveugles* (Paris, 1830).

40. "But, it was said, those are but conventions, and only initiates can

read the pages written according to these two methods." Louis Braille, *Nouveau procédé pour représenter par des points la forme même des lettres* (Paris: Institution Royale, 1839), p. 4.

41. Rodenbach, *Lettre*, p. 24.

42. "With respect to the formation of reason, to the development of intelligence, nothing replaces language; but for social relations, for the necessities of material life, nothing could replace sight." Pierre-Armand Dufau, *Des aveugles*, 2d ed. (Paris: Renouard, 1850), pp. 85–86. Further references to this work signaled by "*D*" in parentheses in the text.

43. "The Arts and Virtues lend him their torch, / To enlighten the Blind man in the depths of his tomb." In Haüy, "Troisième note," p. 10.

44. "On seeing the darkened and monotonous face of the unfortunate blind man, where shines neither the pride of a noble gaze, nor vivacity of mind, nor the affectionate bond of recognition, one would call it the face of a reprobate." Pierre-Nicolas Gerdy, *De la supériorité de la vision sur les autres sensations* (Paris: Coisson, n.d.), p. 27.

45. . . . "an imitation, a representation of the expression that we have seen . . . the speech of the blind is dead and inanimate." Bonald, *Recherches philosophiques sur les premiers objets des connoissances morales* (Paris: Le Clerc, 1818), p. 124.

46. "[The blind] are constantly, in their relations with other men, in the position one occupies with respect to an individual whom one knows only by correspondence: one indeed knows that he exists, but one cannot imagine how."

47. . . . "a multitude of nuances that escape us . . . they study the voice just as we study physiognomy, to discover the qualities of the heart."

48. "One can read on the faces of the blind the feelings that they experience: this portrayal is all the better for the fact that they don't try to hide them, and that they are unaware of the effect of this impression on the seeing." Alexandre Rodenbach, *Les Aveugles et les sourds-muets* (Brussels: J. A. Slingeneyer aîné, 1835), p. 140.

49. "Their manner is not without that timid grace that is the principal charm of adolescence in women; their movements don't have the stiffness that is usually noticed in those of the young [blind] men. In society, sometimes nothing will set apart the young blind girl whose eye has not undergone a disagreeable obliteration at the dazzling and joyous ball, she will be able not to remain always silent and inactive."

50. "Love, for example, which is most often for the seeing a merely

sensuous passion, has in them a more moral character. As they do not catch it by their eyes, they are spared physical seductions. What is it to them if coquettes make eyes, smile gracefully, or have mincing ways? All these agents of women's power are indifferent to them, and no woman strikes them as beautiful if she does not start by being good!" Niboyet, *Des aveugles et de leur éducation*, p. 68.

51. August Zeune, *Belisar oder über Blinde und Blinden-Anstalten*, 7th ed. (Berlin: Blinden-Anstalt, 1846), pp. 39, 41.

52. "Their minds free of that multitude of images whose impressions, in spite of ourselves, never stop running into each other in our brains, everyone knows to what extent the blind enjoy this sweet calm so favorable to study." "Mémoire de M. Haüy sur l'éducation des aveugles," *Séance publique du bureau académique de l'écriture*, November 18, 1784, p. 39.

53. Guillié and Dufau attributed to a sightless childhood both the deprivation and the serious demeanor of their students. For the latter, the blind child is "condamné à un état de calme et d'inaction qui semble en général antipathique à l'enfance" (*D*, p. 2). Guillié argued that children learn most naturally and extensively by visual imitation, so that teachers of the blind must replace this imitation by method and analysis.

54. "It is not so much by the distraction that it causes us, as by the simultaneity of the impressions of which it is the origin, that sight works in us to the detriment of attention. . . . The impressions of hearing and touch, on the contrary, are isolated by their nature. The soul perceives them as it were one by one."

55. "It follows naturally from there that the intelligence of the person born blind, which excels in analysis, remains at an inferior stage with respect to the synthetic operation, which is its inverse."

56. "They can, it is true, devote themselves successfully to the most profound meditations, to philosophy, to mathematics, and make veritable discoveries in the field of metaphysics." Gerdy, *De la supériorité*, p. 25.

57. "Since their intelligence always follows a slow and gradual course, its various acquisitions ought to be more easily linked in a methodical order."

58. "His ideas never present themselves to him in material forms; his thoughts are always distinct, and for him an image cannot take the place of an argument or a sentiment." Rodenbach, *Les Aveugles et les sourds-muets*, p. 137.

59. . . . "they see things in a more abstract way than we."

60. "We know how many errors sight exposes us to."
61. "They feel things as they are."
62. "Finally, I shall say that, being essentially reflective and pragmatic, these beings to whom our visible world is foreign appear destined, if they are not as it were depraved by us, to give far more to reason, and to cross more wisely this rapid span of life, like these grave men whom we sometimes see living in the midst of society's whirlwind as if they did not see it, remaining forever foreign to the crazy passions that stir around them."
63. "This considerable faculty of analysis and decomposition, which is noticed in those born blind, is much more intense while they are in [their] natural state; it can be seen to weaken when, by ideas communicated [to them], they adopt our methods and forms of reasoning."
64. . . . "and spoils, so to speak, what is special about their blind condition."
65. . . . "strong conceptions, dogged labors on the one hand, the easy graces of wit, the vivacity of imagination on the other."
66. "They enter more easily into our ideas, into our social conventions; they are less blind, if I may say so."
67. . . . "this prodigious memory that, in the blind, retains ideas as surely as it receives them easily." "Mémoire de M. Haüy," p. 39.
68. "We carefully avoid, whether in teaching them or in talking with them, having them pass too abruptly from one idea to another, especially when the ideas are disparate and of necessity leave between them too many unoccupied echelons. We try, rather, by proceeding analytically, to attach what is already known to what we want to have known, and, to use the theory developed above, always to attack one vibrating string with another."
69. "Consider indeed whether there is not of necessity in the story of an important event, of a battle, for example, a far smaller sum of partial ideas for a blind person than for a seeing person, and if, consequently, its trace ought not to remain clearer and more precise in the mind."
70. "More concentrated attention causes objects that would leave only imperceptible impressions in us to be engraved very strongly in their minds."
71. "The nature of things demands that he live much more in himself, that he remain in a state of habitual concentration, that his thoughts, his sentiments ordinarily remain veiled for us, and finally that the truly intimate life of his soul be a sort of mystery to be pierced." "Des

235

aveugles-nés, considérations sur l'état physique, moral, et intellec-
tuel, l'éducation et la condition sociale de cette classe d'êtres," *Revue
de Paris*, 1st ser., 31 (1831): 156. See also *D*, p. 15.

72. . . . "a language of his own, a language in which he could cease to
be a pale imitator, and begin to be an original writer."

73. "He would have made for himself, by intuition, vivid images of
everything that must remain forever veiled for him, and in the mysterious voices of his soul would be revealed a whole intimate world
that his imagination really creates in the bosom of that silent solitude—the veritable shadows of hearing—where he finds satisfaction, especially if he is gifted with poetic feeling."

74. "The idea of a kind of absolute superiority in the individual deprived of sight, with respect to the functions of the mind, is moreover not new: I encounter it among the ancients, who often attached
a mysterious and sacred character to blindness, even the gift of divination."

5 • FROM CHATEAUBRIAND TO BALZAC: LITERATURE AND LOSS OF SIGHT

1. "There exist, it seems to me, two altogether distinct literatures, that
whose first source is Homer, that whose origin is Ossian." Madame
de Staël, *Oeuvres complètes* (Paris: Treuttel et Würtz, 1820), 4:24.

2. See A. Tedeschi, *Ossian "L'Homère du Nord" en France* (Milan: Ti-
pographia Sociale, 1911); and P. Van Tieghem, *Ossian en France*, 2
vols. (Paris: Rieder, 1917).

3. "I admit that this idea of Mme. de Staël pleases me greatly. I like to
picture the two blind men: one, on the peak of a mountain in Scot-
land, his head bald, his beard moist, harp in hand, and dictating his
laws, from amid the fog, to all the poetic people of Germania; the
other, seated on the summit of Pindus, surrounded by the Muses
who bear his lyre, raising his crowned head beneath the beautiful sky
of Greece, and governing, with a laurel-adorned scepter, the country
of Tasso and Racine." "A Louis de Fontanes," December 1800, Letter 51, *Correspondance générale*, ed. B. d'Andlau, P. Christovorov,
and P. Riberette (Paris: Gallimard, 1977), 1:115.

4. "These wrinkles, this hair, this eternal night, / See; is this the brow
of a dweller of the heavens? / I am but a mortal, one of the most unfortunate!" André Chénier, *Oeuvres complètes*, ed. G. Walter (Paris:
Bibliothèque de la Pléiade, 1958), p. 43.

5. "Blind man, vagabond, said the insolent troop, / Sing, if your mind is not like your eyes, / Amuse our boredom, you will be giving thanks to the Gods." Ibid., p. 45.

6. Jean Starobinski, "André Chénier and the Allegory of Poetry," in *Images of Romanticism: Verbal and Visual Affinities*, ed. K. Kroeber and W. Walling (New Haven: Yale University Press, 1978), p. 49.

7. Concerning the concept of origin in the eighteenth and nineteenth centuries, see Michel Foucault, *Les Mots et les choses* (Paris: Gallimard, 1966), pp. 339–346.

8. See Chateaubriand's remarks at the beginning of his preface to the first edition of *Atala*, and the study by Michel Butor, "Chateaubriand et l'ancienne Amérique," *Répertoire II* (Paris: Editions de Minuit, 1964), pp. 152–192.

9. "So there it is then, that religion which you praised so highly to me! Perish the oath that takes Atala from me! Perish the God who goes against nature! Man, priest, what have you come to do in these forests?" Hereafter, numbers given in parentheses refer to Chateaubriand's *Oeuvres romanesques et voyages*, ed. M. Regard (Paris: Bibliothèque de la Pléiade, 1969), vol. 1.

10. "I shall like to hear of that great chief who is no more, and whose magnificent cabin I visited."

11. "Nature seemed upside down to me; I could find it in society only in the manner of those objects whose inverted images we see in water."

12. "Chactas, that was his name, resembled the heroes represented by those ancient busts that express repose in genius, and that seem naturally blind."

13. . . . "as Antigone guided the steps of Oedipus on Cithaeron, or as Malvina led Ossian on the rocks of Morven."

14. In his study of the Homeric influence in the writings of Chateaubriand, Charles Hart suggests that "Chactas . . . was perhaps suggested by the Homer of legend" (p. 38). Hart finds evidence of attempts at Homeric effects in *Les Natchez*, but he judges them to be unsuccessful and indicative of Chateaubriand's poor knowledge of Greek literature at this point in his career. See Charles Hart, *Chateaubriand and Homer*, Johns Hopkins Studies in Romance Literatures and Languages 11 (Baltimore: Johns Hopkins University Press, 1928), pp. 26–86.

15. Hart, who applies the aesthetic standards of Homeric epic to Chateaubriand's work, writes that "of the several blots on *Les Natchez* the narration of Chactas is the greatest" (p. 48).

16. "Setting aside for a moment the great principles of Christianity, leaving out the interests of Europe, a philosophic mind could have desired that the peoples of the New World had had the time to develop outside the circle of our institutions. We are reduced everywhere to the worn-out forms of a civilization grown old . . . beginnings of all the customs and all the laws of the Greeks, the Romans and the Hebrews have been found among the Savages of Canada, of New England and of the Floridas. A civilization of a different nature from ours could have *reproduced the men of antiquity, or made unknown enlightenment burst forth from an as yet unknown source*. Who knows if we would not have seen one day approaching our shores some American Columbus coming to discover the Old World?" (Emphasis added.)

17. Jean Pommier, "Chateaubriand en Amérique et le cycle de Chactas," in *Dialogues avec le passé* (Paris: Nizet, 1967), pp. 57–78.

18. Butor, "Chateaubriand et l'ancienne Amérique," p. 181.

19. "Such a Sachem will never be found again. He knows the language of all the forests; he knows all the tombs that serve as limits of peoples, all the rivers that separate nations. Our fathers were more fortunate than we: they have spent their lives with his wisdom; we shall only see him die."

20. . . . "peoples who lend meanings to everything, who hear voices in every murmur, who give hates and loves to plants, desires to the wave, immortal spirits to animals, souls to rocks."

21. Jean-Pierre Richard, *Paysage de Chateaubriand* (Paris: Seuil, 1967), p. 138.

22. "One day the Mississippi, still near its source, becomes tired of being but a clear stream. It asks snows of the mountains, waters of the torrents, rains of the tempests; it oversteps its banks, and devastates its lovely shores. The prideful stream at first applauded its own power, but seeing that everything was becoming deserted along its path, that it was flowing, abandoned in its solitude, that its waters were always troubled, it regretted the humble bed that nature had dug for it, the birds, the flowers, the trees and the streams, once the modest companions of its peaceful flow."

23. "For some years now, back in the bosom of his country, Chactas had been enjoying rest. However, heaven was selling him this favor dearly; the old man had become blind."

24. "The peace of extinguished passions mingled on the brow of Chactas with the serenity noticeable in men who have lost their sight; whether by being deprived of terrestrial light we enter into more in-

timate commerce with that of the heavens, or whether the dark in which the blind live has a calm that extends to the soul, just as night is more silent than day."

25. . . . "always wandering outside the present, it doubles existence, sometimes by the memory of past pains or pleasures, sometimes by the premonition of fear or of hope, that makes it tread upon the future." Pierre-Simon Ballanche, *Du sentiment* (Lyon: Ballanche et Barret, 1801), p. 121. Subsequent page references given in parentheses.

26. "Soon this divine Homer found a continual solitude around him; his eyes, closed to the light of the skies, ceased to see the cheerful finery of nature, the brow of man. . . ."

27. "The English Homer believed that the loss of the exterior organ of sight made the interior organ more sensitive to intellectual light, which is the real light."

28. "Nonetheless, let us admit that there is something painful indeed in the thought of an enforced and continual solitude; but this very state of loss and chagrin, painted in such a sublime manner by Ossian and Milton, this state, I say, is still favorable to the genius, by the intensity and depth that a habitual melancholy makes him acquire."

29. "Then, Evander, I had less-confused notions concerning the highest matters; then I conceived of time being part of eternity, identical to it. . . . Thus my blindness taught me the marvels of the world where we no longer need our senses to know; thus I understood how, for the mind freed from the organs, the past, the present, the future are contemporaneous." Pierre-Simon Ballanche, *Oeuvres* (Paris: Bureau de l'Encyclopédie des connaissances utiles, 1833), 6:220.

30. "Love of knowledge had cast me into a garret where I worked at night, and I spent my days in a neighboring library. . . ." Balzac, *La Comédie humaine*, ed. P.-G. Castex et al. (Paris: Bibliothèque de la Pléiade, 1976–1981). Hereafter, numbers in parentheses refer to volume and pages in this edition.

31. "Locke proved irrefutably that there was no innate principle." Balzac, "Notes philosophiques," folio 63, in *Oeuvres complètes* (Paris: Club de l'Honnête Homme, 1956–1971), 21:526.

32. "A proof of the birth, etc., of the soul is that there are no innate ideas and that they come to us only along with sensations: for the soul without the sensations that strike us would not manifest itself. Prove it— Example of a man blind, deaf, mute, without smell, etc." Ibid., folio 57, p. 524.

33. "Dissertation sur l'homme," ed. H. Gauthier, *L'Année balzacienne*, 1968, pp. 94–95.

34. "Notes philosophiques," folios 25, 24, 26, p. 534.

35. "Dissertation sur l'homme," p. 99.

36. Balzac, *Sténie*, in *Oeuvres complètes*, 21:137.

37. "There, a supernatural light, the fruit of my all-powerful art, can show him to you, in whatever place he may be. —You will enter the pure and empty atmosphere of thought, you will range over the ideal world, this vast reservoir whence come *Nightmares*, the *Shadows* that raise the curtains of the dying, this arsenal of the *Incubi* and the *Magicians*; you will visit the *shadow* no *light* causes, the *shadow* that has no sun! . . . you will see, by a gaze *outside the gazes* of life!" Balzac, *Le Centenaire* (Paris: Pollet, 1822; reprint, Paris: Les Bibliophiles de l'Originale, 1962), 4:46–47.

38. . . . "giving himself over to a perpetual contemplation, possessed by a curious hatred for physical realities and bodies, unaware of his own physical existence; living, so to speak, by only the forces of those internal senses that constitute, according to him, a double being in man, but exhausted by this profound intuition of things."

39. . . . "the furnishings with which chastity enriched their brains."

40. "But to end this unimportant trial in favor of his innocence, it will doubtless suffice him to lead people who are hardly familiar with the operations of human intelligence to the sources of thought."

41. . . . "does not constitute the will that engenders a work of art."

42. "In addition to these two conditions essential to talent, there occurs in poets or in truly philosophical writers an inexplicable, unprecedented moral phenomenon, which science has difficulty accounting for. It is a kind of second sight that permits them to guess the truth in all possible situations; or, better yet, I know not what power that transports them where they have to be. They invent the true, by analogy, or see the object to be described, whether the object come to them or whether they themselves go toward the object."

43. "Do men have the power to bring the universe into their brain, or is their brain a talisman with which they abolish the laws of time and space? Science will hesitate a long time in choosing between these two equally inexplicable mysteries. The fact remains that inspiration unfolds before the poets countless transfigurations that resemble the magic phantasmagorias of our dreams. A dream is perhaps the natural play of this singular power, when it remains unoccupied!"

44. Unpublished communication at "Balzac: l'invention du roman," Centre Culturel International de Cerisy-la-Salle, July 7, 1980.

45. "Louis Lambert was born in 1797 at Montoire, a little town in the Vendômois. . . ."
46. " 'Whenever I wish it,' he said to me . . . 'I can draw a veil over my eyes. Suddenly I go within myself, and there I find a camera obscura where the phenomena of nature are reproduced in purer forms than those under which they first appeared to my external senses.' "
47. . . . . "he in some degree lost consciousness of his physical life . . . he left space behind him, to use his own words."
48. "Already, in spite of myself, I have just reversed the order in which I ought to lay out the history of this man, who transferred all his action to thinking, as others throw all their life into action."
49. "I know how chilling the use of *I* and *me* can be to a narrative; but if we are within our rights to hide, and even must hide, the sources from whence we draw certain novelistic compositions, could it be so for facts likely to interest the sciences?"
50. "Like two lovers, we got into the habit of thinking together, of sharing our reveries. . . . There was no distinction between the things that came from him and those that came from me."
51. "Perhaps the words materialism and spiritualism express the two sides of the same fact."
52. . . . . "the mass of force by which man can reproduce, outside himself, the actions that constitute his external life."
53. . . . . "a look full of some savage contempt, charged with thought, as a Leyden jar is charged with electricity."
54. "At one moment astonishingly clear and piercing, at another possessed of heavenly sweetness, his gaze became dull, colorless, so to speak, in the moments when he was lost in his contemplations. Then his eye resembled a windowpane from which the sun had suddenly vanished after lighting it up."
55. "Specialism consists in seeing the things of the material universe and the things of the spiritual universe in all their original and causative ramifications. The greatest human geniuses are those who started from the darkness of Abstraction to attain to the light of Specialism. (Specialism, *species*, sight, to speculate, to see everything, and all at once; *speculum*, mirror or means of apprehending a thing by seeing the whole of it.) Jesus was a Specialist, he saw each fact in its roots and in its results, in the past that had engendered it, in the present where it appeared, in the future where it would develop; his sight pierced the understanding of others. The perfection of interior sight gives birth to the gift of Specialism."
56. Félix Davin, "Introduction aux *Etudes philosophiques*," in *La Comé-*

241

die humaine, 10:1210; Balzac, "Avant-propos de *La Comédie humaine,*" 1:19.

57. "There can be between people of genius and others the same distance as between the Blind and the Seeing."

58. "I at once took him off to Paris to place him under the care of Monsieur Esquirol. . . . In Paris, the physicians regarded him as incurable."

59. Jean-Claude Fizaine, "Génie et folie dans *Louis Lambert, Gambara, et Massimila Doni,*" *Revue des sciences humaines,* no. 175 (1979): pp. 61–75.

60. "Lambert exerted on my imagination an influence whose effects I still feel today."

61. "I had placed myself, so to speak, in his life and situation. . . ."

62. "Alas! already wrinkled, already white-headed, his eyes already lightless, grown dull like those of a blind person."

63. "I feared to return to that intoxicating atmosphere where ecstasy was contagious."

64. "Know only that already in those days I had broken down the elements of that heterogeneous mass known as the people. . . . I knew already what use this suburb could have."

65. "Observation had become intuitive with me, it pierced the soul without neglecting the body, or rather it grasped external details so thoroughly that it went immediately beyond and through them; it gave me the power of living the life of the individual whom I observed, permitting me to take his place just as the dervish in the *Arabian Nights* took on the body and soul of persons upon whom he pronounced certain words."

66. Beaudelaire, *Curiosités esthétiques, L'Art romantique,* ed. H. Lemaitre (Paris: Garnier, 1962), p. 679.

67. "To leave one's own habits, to become another than one's self through intoxication of the intellectual faculties, and to play this game at will, such was my recreation."

68. Lagarde and Michard, *XIXe siècle. Les grands auteurs français du programme* (Paris: Bordas, 1969), pp. 304–305.

69. André Lorant, "Introduction" to *Facino Cane,* 6:1015. It is generally admitted that the episode of Raphaël's life of study in a garret in *La Peau de chagrin* is, like the beginning of *Facino Cane,* autobiographical. See Pierre Barbéris, *Balzac et le mal du siècle* (Paris: Gallimard, 1970), 1:293–298.

70. Nicole Mozet, "Préface" to *Le Lys dans la vallée* (Paris: Garnier-Flammarion, 1972), pp. 24–25.

71. "When I came nearer, why I don't know, that was it, the wedding party and its music disappeared, my curiosity was roused to the highest degree, for my soul passed into the body of the clarinet player."
72. Sigmund Freud, "The Uncanny," *Standard Edition* (London: Hogarth, 1953–1974), 17:244.
73. Ibid., pp. 219–252. Freud, in this essay, also develops the idea that blindness and eye injuries symbolize castration; what "returns" with the appearance of a blind double is repressed castration anxiety. For a modern interpretation of this connection, according to which the castration complex is in effect a disruption of vision, a "crisis of phenomenality," see Samuel Weber, "The Sideshow; or, Remarks on a Canny Moment," *MLN* 88 (1973): 1110–1122.
74. Balzac often associated Homer with Dante, describing both as visionaries in *Séraphîta* (11:804–805) and stating in the dedication to *Les Parents pauvres* that Dante was the only modern poet comparable to Homer (7:53).
75. . . . "the so well known face of the blind, earnest, attentive, and grave."
76. "As they are naturally not outgoing . . . we find them cold . . . they are usually docile toward their masters." Pierre-Armand Dufau, "Des aveugles-nés," *Revue de Paris*, 1st ser., 31 (1831): 156.
77. "We doubtless had the same thoughts, for I think that blindness makes thought-communications much more rapid, by preventing attention from being dispersed on external objects."
78. "The bitter and sorrowful expression of that magnificent head was magnified by blindness, for the dead eyes were brought to life by thought; a kind of burning glow broke forth from them."
79. "The fire of despair had burned out into ashes, the lava had cooled, but the furrows, the upheavals, a bit of smoke bore witness to the violence of the eruption, the ravages of the fire."
80. . . . "as one fears to see brigands armed with torches and daggers at the mouth of a cavern. . . . There was a lion in that cage of flesh. . . ."
81. "These ideas, awakened by this man's appearance, were as hot in my soul as they were cold upon his face."
82. "And he made a fearsome gesture of extinguished patriotism and distaste for human things."
"At this question he raised his head toward me, as if to contemplate me in a truly tragic movement, and answered me, 'In misfortunes!' "
". . . with disdainful pity, he made a gesture that expressed all the philosophy of despair."

83. . . . . "this old Homer who kept within him an Odyssey condemned to oblivion."

84. "In the midst of my pleasures, as I enjoyed a fortune of six million, I was stricken blind. I do not doubt that this infirmity was the result of my stay in the cell, of my work in the stone, if indeed my ability to see gold did not imply an abuse of the power of sight that predestined me to lose my eyes."

85. "I feel the presence of gold. Blind though I may be, I stop in front of jewelers' shops."

86. "Whether or not the fantasies of a woman can influence her child when she carries it or conceives it, it is certain that my mother had a passion for gold during her pregnancy." The idea was expressed in the sixteenth century by Paracelsus: "Woman's imagination resembles divine power, its external desires imprint themselves on the child." *Oeuvres médicales* (Paris, 1968), p. 222; quoted in François Jacob, *The Logic of Life*, trans. B. E. Spillman (New York: Pantheon, 1973), p. 26.

87. Peter Lock, "Origins, Desire, and Writing: Balzac's Louis Lambert," *Stanford French Review* 1 (1977): 309.

88. "While I was working, and when weariness overcame me, I heard the sound of gold, I saw gold before me, I was dazzled by diamonds! Oh! wait. One night, my blunted steel found wood. I sharpened my bit of sword, and made a hole in this wood. To be able to work, I slid like a serpent on my belly, I went naked to work mole-fashion, my hands in front of me. . . ."

89. "When I remembered the sensations I had felt, when I saw again that immense treasure . . . a sort of madness began to work in me. I had the gold fever."

90. " 'Then I have found a man,' he cried, his face on fire."

91. "Facino Cane died during the winter after a two-month illness. The poor man had taken a chill."

92. "Limiting himself to this rigorous representation, a writer could become a more-or-less faithful painter . . . but, to deserve the praises to which every artist must aspire, shouldn't I study the reasons or reason of these social effects, discover the hidden meaning of this immense assemblage of figures, passions, and events?"

93. Michel Foucault, *The Order of Things* (New York: Vintage, 1973), p. 239.

94. See Balzac's famous paragraph on Cuvier in *La Peau de chagrin* (10:74–76): "Cuvier n'est-il pas le plus grand poète de notre siècle?" Concerning the ideological motives of Balzac's preference for Saint-

Hilaire over Cuvier in the "Avant-propos," see Françoise Gaillard, "La Science: modèle ou vérité?" in *Balzac: l'invention du roman*, ed. C. Duchet and J. Neefs (Paris: Belfond, 1982), pp. 57–83.

95. Foucault, *The Order of Things*, p. 290.

96. Martin Kanes, *Balzac's Comedy of Words* (Princeton: Princeton University Press, 1975), pp. 41, 121–123, 200–210.

97. Concerning the convertibility of visual metaphors into those of semiotic activity, see Jean-Loup Bourget, "Balzac et le déchiffrement des signes," *L'Année balzacienne*, 1977, pp. 73–89.

98. "Oh! she is not in high spirits to you, you don't catch these nuances that are too delicate for eyes occupied by the spectacle of nature. This gaiety betrays itself in the notes of her voice, in intonations that I catch, that I explain."

99. In the *Théorie de la démarche*, Balzac says of the blind man of Puiseaux from Diderot's *Lettre*: "Il avait remplacé le sens de la vue, relativement à l'appréciation des caractères, par des diagnostics pris dans les intonations de la voix" (12:276). And in *Le Lys dans la vallée*, Madame de Mortsauf "reads" voices in the manner of the blind: "Quoique curieuse de savoir la vérité sur mon apparition, elle ne nous regarda ni l'un ni l'autre; mais à la manière dont elle nous écoutant, vous eussiez dit que, semblable aux aveugles, elle savait reconnaître les agitations de l'âme dans les imperceptibles accents de la parole. Et cela était vrai" (9:993).

6 · HUGO: BLIND SEERS, BLIND LOVERS, AND THE VIOLENCE OF HISTORY

1. "It seems that we see a blind god creating suns." Victor Hugo, *Oeuvres complètes*, ed. Jean Massin et al. (Paris: Club français du livre, 1967–1970). Hereafter, references to volumes and pages of this edition are given in parentheses.

2. "The writers and poets of this century have the astonishing advantage of coming from no ancient school, no second hand, no model. They have no ancestors.... The poets of the nineteenth century, the writers of the nineteenth century, are the sons of the French Revolution. This volcano has two craters, 89 and 93.... All contemporary art results directly and without intermediary from this tremendous genesis."

3. "God said *fiat lux* himself the first time; the second time he had it

said. By whom? By 93. Therefore, we men of the nineteenth century, let us take as an honor this insult: 'You are 93.' "

4. "Poets have created a metaphorical moon and scientists an algebraic moon. The real moon is between the two. It was this moon that I had before my eyes."

5. "There it was, magnificent in its existence. There too the great words had just been spoken: *fiat lux*."

6. Cf. these lines from "Le Verso de la page":
"Quiconque t'osera regarder fixement,
Convention, cratère, Etna, gouffre fumant,
Quiconque plongera la fourche dans ta braise,
Quiconque sondera ce puits: Quatrevingt-treize,
Sentira se cabrer et s'enfuir son esprit." (10:265)

7. "I said to the long golden fruit: but you're just a pear!"

8. See Suzanne Nash, *"Les Contemplations" of Victor Hugo: An Allegory of the Creative Process* (Princeton: Princeton University Press, 1976), p. 88.

9. "All words now soar in light."

10. "I said to darkness: 'Be!' / And there was dark."

11. See Victor Brombert, "Hugo's Condemned Man: Laughter of Revolution," *Romanic Review* 70 (1979): 119–132. Brombert writes in particular: "The death wish and the death guilt remain interlocked. They must in fact be re-inserted into the great 19th-century debate on History. . . . But beyond the historic debate on history, the dialogue is primarily one that Hugo carries on, tirelessly, with himself" (p. 132).

12. "My father an old soldier, my mother a woman of Vendée."

13. At one point in *William Shakespeare*, the Revolution even divides into paternal and maternal components: "89 et 93: les hommes du dix-neuvième siècle sortent de là. C'est leur père et leur mère" (12:307).

14. . . . "observe humanity directly; they accept as a guiding light no refracted ray, not even yours."

15. "Everything caves in as soon as you try to see."
"I've often, with perhaps an expert eye, / Delved into this dark problem where the sounding-line gets lost."

16. *L'Homme qui rit*, in *Romans*, ed. Henri Guillemin, vol. 3 (Paris: Seuil "Intégrale," 1963), p. 319.

17. Charles Baudouin, *Psychanalyse de Victor Hugo*, 2d ed. (Paris: Armand Colin, 1972), p. 66. Despite his overly reductive and deterministic theory of the psychoanalysis of literature, Baudouin's in-

sights remain a starting point for any psychocritical reading of Hugo.

18. "At moments when the mind, whose eye alights everywhere, / Seeks to see in the night the bottom of everything, / In these frightful places my gaze got lost."

19. "A convent in France, at high noon of the nineteenth century, is a college of owls facing daylight."

20. "O God! Consider the men of this era, / Blind, drifting far from you beneath so many shadows."

21. "Man passes without seeing, without believing, without understanding, / Without seeking anything in the darkness, and without raising his eyes / Toward the divine guidance that floats in the heavens."

22. "More light would perhaps blind our eyes."

23. "There is, we know, a philosophy that denies the infinite. There is also a philosophy, classed among the pathologies, that denies the sun: this philosophy is called blindness.

To raise a sense that we lack into a source of truth is fine blind man's nerve.

The curious thing is the haughty, condescending, superior airs that this groping philosophy puts on vis-à-vis the philosophy that sees God. It's like hearing a mole cry out, 'I pity them with their sun.' "

24. "Let us say it now: to be blind and be loved, is indeed, upon this earth where nothing is complete, one of the most strangely exquisite forms of happiness."

25. . . . "who is there because you need her and because she cannot get along without you."

26. . . . "that one is the center of these steps . . . if she goes away, it is to come back."

27. "The soul gropingly seeks the soul, and finds it. . . . One is stroked with soul."

28. "Having love is not losing light. . . . There is no blindness where there is certainty. . . . God made palpable, what ravishment!"

29. "Being a genius, it fraternizes with the geniuses. As for its source, it is where theirs is: outside man."

30. "These men who are called revealers fix their gaze on something unknown that is outside man. There is a light up there, they see it. They aim a mirror in that direction. . . . This revealer is a seer."

31. "I read these verses, I experience this form, and what is its first effect? I forget Augustus, I forget even Virgil; . . . I enter into a vision;

the fabulous sky opens above me; I plunge into it, I soar and throw myself into it, I see the incorruptible and inaccessible reaches, the splendid immanence. . . ."

32. The description of the formal properties of language by metaphors of visionary experience is thus common to Balzac and Hugo, but the former's reflections on the subject were primarily epistemological, while the latter's were ethical.

33. "The nudity of a woman transformed into the nudity of a statue silences the flesh and makes the soul sing. As soon as the gaze becomes contemplative, purification begins."

34. Jean Gaudon, *Le Temps de la contemplation* (Paris: Flammarion, 1971), pp. 25–41.

35. "He must have isolated himself from the external world, to enjoy fully this internal life that develops within him like a new being; and only when the physical world has completely disappeared from his eyes can the ideal world be shown to him."

36. See these lines on spiritual vision and blind poets from "Deux voix dans le ciel":

"L'oeil de chair ment. L'esprit, c'est l'unique prunelle.
Les prophètes muraient leur grotte solennelle,
Et dans l'ombre engloutis, vivaient dans la clarté.
L'âme ignore la nuit comme la cécité.
L'âme voit à travers les paupières fermées.
O pures visions des choses innommées!
Majesté du voyant que l'esprit seul conduit,
Qui n'a plus que son âme ouverte dans la nuit!
Milton était aveugle."   (9:588)

37. "Thank you, poet! at the edge of my pious *lares*,
Like a divine guest, you come and reveal yourself;
And the golden halo of your shining verses
Shines around my name like a circle of stars.

Sing! Milton sang; Sing! Homer did sing.
The poet of the senses pierces the sad mist;
The blind man sees in darkness a world of light.
When the eye of the body goes out, the eye of the mind is lit."

38. *Les Contemplations*, ed. Léon Cellier (Paris: Garnier, 1969), pp. 519–520. See also Victor Hugo, *Oeuvres poétiques*, ed. Pierre Albouy vol. 2 (Paris: Gallimard "Pléïade," 1967), p. 1414.

39.   "Since for us, Baour, you've made
The moon into an ice cube, the sun into a crust,
Don't be astonished to hear every day

Your readers (if there are any whom boredom doesn't repel),
    Deciphering your obscure and heavy style,
Cry out: 'It's so clear, indeed, that we can't see a thing!' "
40. "There is indeed, sir, a big cloud on my eyes, an ophthalmia that is blinding me."
41. "Imagine that since around your departure, I've insisted on doing a singular imitation of Homer, Milton, Ossian and all the sublime blind men who have sung. . . . I don't know when all that will go away, but I assure you that I've already had quite my fill of this sample blindness." Other references to eye illnesses are to be found in Hugo's letters of July 21, 1831, May 5, 1832, January 16, 1833, and February 27 and April 2 and 21, 1839. See Gaudon, *Le Temps de la contemplation*, p. 414.
42. "[Sainte-Beuve] looked at my eyes, and told me softly: *'It's the beginning of an amaurosis. The optic nerve is becoming paralyzed. In a few years blindness will be complete.'* A thought suddenly lit up my mind. *'Well,'* I said to him, *'there will at least be that.'* And so there I began hoping that I would perhaps one day be blind like Homer and Milton. Youth never lacks confidence."
43. "To be stricken is to be proven a Titan. It's already something to share with those above the privilege of a thunderbolt. . . . To be crippled like the greats would be quite a temptation."
44. Pierre Albouy, *La Création mythologique chez Victor Hugo* (Paris: José Corti, 1963), pp. 209–262.
45. "Infirmity or deformity inflicted upon these august and beloved thinkers seems a sinister counterweight, a compensation that could hardly be avowed up there, a concession to jealousies of which it seems the creator should be ashamed."
46. "To be, without knowing it, a Titan; is that possible?"
47. "And your fatal hand, o great stonecutter,
In the sinister Trivelino was sketching Robespierre."
48. Here my reading follows that of Brombert: "Hugo clearly had reason to be upset by his own vindication of regicidal 1793. There was moreover another difficulty. It was bad enough that this messianic act had to be violent. In what terms, if this messianic act was to be unique, could one still be a revolutionary half a century after the Revolution?" "Victor Hugo: History and the Other Text," *Nineteenth-Century French Studies* 5 (1976–1977): 29–30.
49. "The fatal winter night . . . had killed the mother and blinded the daughter." *L'Homme qui rit*, in *Romans*, vol. 3. Page numbers given in parentheses for *L'Homme qui rit* refer to this volume.

50. "It was something like a suffering that was calling, but without knowing that it is a suffering and without knowing that it is calling."

51. The memories of the *comprachicos* are not totally lost to Gwynplaine, but merely to his consciousness. After the confession of his kidnappers is read to him, "Il se mit à parler comme on parle dans l'inconscience," and he recalls some of their characteristics (337).

52. "For Dea, the blind girl, perceived the soul."

53. . . . "presence, that profound mystery that makes the invisible world divine, and from which results that other mystery, confidence."

54. "What is it to be ugly? It is to do wrong. Gwynplaine does only good. He is handsome." Cf. this remark of Diderot's in the *Lettre sur les aveugles*: "Les Aveugles ne sont-ils pas bien à plaindre, de n'estimer beau que ce qui est bon!" (p. 4). Hugo also credits Dea with a defamiliarizing and profoundly true definition of a crowd: "Pour elle une foule était un souffle; et au fond ce n'est que cela" (295).

55. "Gwynplaine lived as it were beheaded, having a face that did not belong to him."

56. "While undressing him, he sees him naked. He grumbles, 'Go on! They've left him a man. How dumb! While they were at it, they could have made him a monster all around. He could have earned his living singing for the Pope.' "

57. "The equestrian statue, reserved for kings alone, is an excellent figure of royalty; the horse is the people. Only the horse becomes transfigured slowly. At the beginning it's an ass; at the end it's a lion. Then it throws its rider, and you have 1642 in England and 1789 in France, and sometimes it devours him, and you have in England 1649 and in France 1793.

That the lion should relapse into the donkey is astonishing, but it is so."

58. "It seemed to him that he saw everything—the past, the future, the present—in the thrill of a sudden flash of light."

59. . . . "for the mind freed from the organs, the past, the present, the future are contemporaneous." Pierre-Simon Ballanche, *Oeuvres* (Paris: Bureau de l'Encyclopédie des connaissances utiles, 1833), 6:220.

60. . . . "in this group that was abandoning him [the *comprachicos*], nothing loved him, and he loved nothing."

61. Sigmund Freud, *Standard edition* (London: Hogarth, 1953–1974), 7:182.

62. "There was dream in Dea. She seemed a dream scarcely embodied . . . she was just enough a woman."

63. "Gwynplaine saw descend toward him in brilliant light, *in an arrangement of destiny that resembled a dream placed in perspective*, a white cloud of beauty having the form of a woman." (Emphasis added.)

64. "They held each other tight in a sort of sidereal chiaroscuro full of perfumes, of lights, of music, of luminous architecture, of dreams. . . ."

65. "Above those closed eyelids, where vision has taken the place of sight, a sepulchral disintegration of outlines and appearances dilutes itself into impalpability."

66. . . . "the inexpressible abstraction where thought lives, when unlighted by the sun."

67. "They felt that she loved her monster. Did she know that he was a monster? Yes, since she touched him. No, since she accepted him. All that darkness and all that light mixed together formed in the mind of the spectator a chiaroscuro of infinite perspectives."

68. "They saw that she was blind and felt that she was a seer. She seemed to stand on the threshold of the supernatural. She seemed to be half in our light and half in the other illumination."

69. Léon Cellier, "Chaos vaincu: Victor Hugo et le roman initiatique," in his *Parcours initiatiques* (Neuchâtel: Editions de la Baconnière, 1977), pp. 164–175.

70. "Mysterious music floated out, accompanying this song of the invisible."

71. . . . "the ferocious forces of nature, unreasoning hungers and savage darkness."

72. Cellier, "Chaos vaincu," p. 172.

73. "Dea touched a lamb whom she knew to be a lion."

74. "You strike me as an observer, you fool! Watch out, it's no business of yours. You have one thing to do, to love Dea."

75. "Sometimes his eyes, movingly curious, sought to see into the depth of this obscurity where so many useless efforts were in their death throes, where so much weariness was struggling. . . . He himself was in port, he watched the shipwreck around him."

76. "What comes down on us is an excess of light, which blinds us, an excess of life, which kills us. . . . A world of lava and embers. Devouring prodigy of the depths."

77. "Ironic destiny, the soul, that heavenly thing, he held, he had it in

his hand, it was Dea; sex, that earthly thing, he perceived in the heights of heaven, it was that woman."

78. "Gwynplaine was flattered in his monster's vanity."

79. "See how much I resemble you. Look in me as in a mirror. Your face is my soul."

80. . . . "the dissipation of a reverie . . . leaves no trace."

81. "And his first, tumultous thoughts about that woman reappeared, as if heated by all this somber fire. Forgetfulness is nothing but a palimpsest. Let an accident happen, and all that was erased lives again between the lines of astonished memory." Elsewhere in *L'Homme qui rit* we read: "Nous n'avons souvent dans la mémoire qu'une couche d'oubli très mince, laquelle, dans l'occasion, laisse tout à coup voir ce qui est dessous" (315).

82. . . . "the memories of youth reappear beneath the passions like the palimpsest beneath the erasures; these memories are foundations for logic, and what was a vision in the child's brain becomes a syllogism in the man's."

83. "The first thing I saw was the law, in the form of a gibbet."

84. "Gwynplaine, stricken by a heartrending emotion, felt sobs rising in his throat, causing him, sinister action, to burst out laughing."

85. Albouy, *La Création mythologique chez Hugo*, p. 253.

86. "To be comic on the outside, and tragic on the inside—there is no suffering more humiliating, no anger deeper. That was what Gwynplaine had in him."

87. "That man had written something obscure in his brain, something that now reappeared, and it had been written with such horrible ink that it was now letters of fire, and Gwynplaine saw flaming in the depths of his thought these enigmatic words, now explained: *Fate does not open one door without closing another.*" My thanks to Joan Peterson for bringing to my attention the image of the palimpsest in *L'Homme qui rit.*

88. "With Gwynplaine, it was simple, I was alive. Now Gwynplaine is gone, I'm dying. It's the same thing."

89. "Paradise was here. Up there is only heaven."

90. "He saw Homo by the edge, baying in the darkness, looking at the sea."

Epilogue

1. Balzac, "Lettres sur Paris," in *Oeuvres complètes*, (Paris: Conard, 1938), 39:114–115.

2. " 'I make no objection,' said Don Pic, 'provided that your Caecelia is not blind.'
(She is.)"
Histoire du roi de Bohême et de ses sept châteaux (Paris: Delangle, 1830; reprint, Paris: Plasma, 1979), p. 47. Subsequent page references given in parentheses.

3. "Oh! If I possessed sight, I would pray the Lord to extinguish my eyes in their sockets, so as not to see all other women, so as to have a memory only of you, and to leave a passage to my heart only to those darts that I would have seen come from your eyes."

4. " 'Gervais,' I continued vehemently, grabbing her by the arm, 'what have you done with him?'
She fell. I don't know if she was dead."

5. "Affectation passed off as grace, sentimentality as tenderness, declamation as eloquence, the commonplace as the naïve."

6. After Nodier's death, his editors did him a disservice by extracting the novella from the antinovel and publishing it in the *Contes de la veillée* as "Les Aveugles de Chamouny." A few changes were made in the text: "Je ne sais pas si elle était morte" became "Je ne me suis pas informé de ce qu'elle devint depuis." This version can be found in Nodier's *Contes*, ed. P.-G. Castex (Paris: Garnier, 1961), pp. 465–466, 473–498.

7. "See them, my soul, they are frightful indeed!
Like mannequins, vaguely ridiculous;
Terrible, singular like sleepwalkers;
And casting who knows where their darkened orbs.

Their eyes, from which the divine spark is gone,
As if they looked afar, remain raised up
To the sky; never toward the paving stones
Do they hang dreamily a weighty head.

Thus do they cross the infinite darkness,
Brother of endless silence. O city!
While about us you sing and laugh and squeal

In pleasure's thrall, even atrocity's,
See! I'm dragging too! but yet more numbed than they,
I say: What seek they in the Sky, all these blind men?"
Les Fleurs du mal, ed. A. Adam (Paris: Garnier, 1961), pp. 102–103.

8. ". . . the wickedness that shone in his eyes, / . . . One would have said

253

that his eye was dripped / In gall; his gaze sharpened the winter's chill." Ibid., pp. 97–98.

9. "His inner eye tries to perceive the eternal light that shines for him in the other world." Quoted by Adam in ibid., p. 386.

10. *Madame Bovary*, ed. C. Gothot-Mersch (Paris: Garnier, 1971), p. 273. Subsequent page references given in parentheses.

11. For a summary and bibliography of critics' comments on the blind beggar, see Max Aprile, "L'Aveugle et sa signification dans *Madame Bovary*," *Revue d'histoire littéraire de la France* 76 (1976): 385–392.

12. Murray Sachs, "The Role of the Blind Beggar in *Madame Bovary*," *Symposium* 22 (1968): 72–80.

13. P. M. Wetherill, "*Madame Bovary*'s Blind Man: Symbolism in Flaubert," *Romanic Review* 61 (1970): 35–42.

14. ". . . in place of eyelids, two gaping, blood covered orbs."

15. "The blind man collapsed onto his knees, and, his head tipped back, rolling his eyes and sticking out his tongue, he rubbed his belly with both hands, while shouting out muffled cries like a famished dog." Victor Brombert has interpreted this passage as "a repellent burlesque of all appetite and gratification, and more specifically a hideous mockery of the sex act." *The Novels of Flaubert* (Princeton: Princeton University Press, 1966), p. 75.

16. Concerning the beggar's evolution in the scenarios, see *Madame Bovary, nouvelle version précédée des scénarios inédits*, ed. J. Pommier and G. Leleu (Paris: José Corti, 1949), pp. 96, 106, 110, 113–114, 119, 122–125, 127, 129.

17. "Often the heat of a fine day / Makes a girl dream of love. / To pick up carefully / The ears that the scythe harvests, / My Nanette leans down / Toward the furrow from which they come. / The wind was blowing hard that day, / And the short skirt flew off!"

18. . . . "the blindness of denying one's self the benefits of science."

19. . . . "that the blind shall see and the lame shall walk!"

20. "These unfortunates should be locked up, and forced to do some sort of work."

21. "The first thing to do is to bind together in a network a few tactile and gustatory sensations and to attach to them, like a label, a sound, a word. . . ." *La Symphonie pastorale* (Paris: Gallimard, 1925), p. 33. Subsequent page references given in parentheses.

22. "I've made the plan to write here everything that concerns the formation and development of this pious soul, whom it seems that I have brought out of darkness only for adoration and love."

23. "When I saw Jacques, I suddenly understood that it was not you I

loved; it was he. He had exactly your face; I mean the face that I imagined you had."

24. Germaine Brée, *André Gide l'insaisissable Protée* (Paris: Les Belles Lettres, 1953), p. 247.

25. *Des aveugles* (Paris: Gallimard, 1985).

INDEX

Library of Congress Cataloging-in-Publication Data

Paulson, William R., 1955–
Enlightenment, Romanticism, and the blind in France.

Includes index.
1. French literature—19th century—History and criticism. 2. Blindness in literature. 3. French literature—18th century—History and criticism.
4. Blindness—France—History. 5. Blind—France—History. 6. Blind in
literature. 7. Enlightenment. 8. Romanticism—France. I. Title.
PQ283.P3   1987   840′.9′35208161   87–2274
ISBN 0–691–06710–4 (alk. paper)